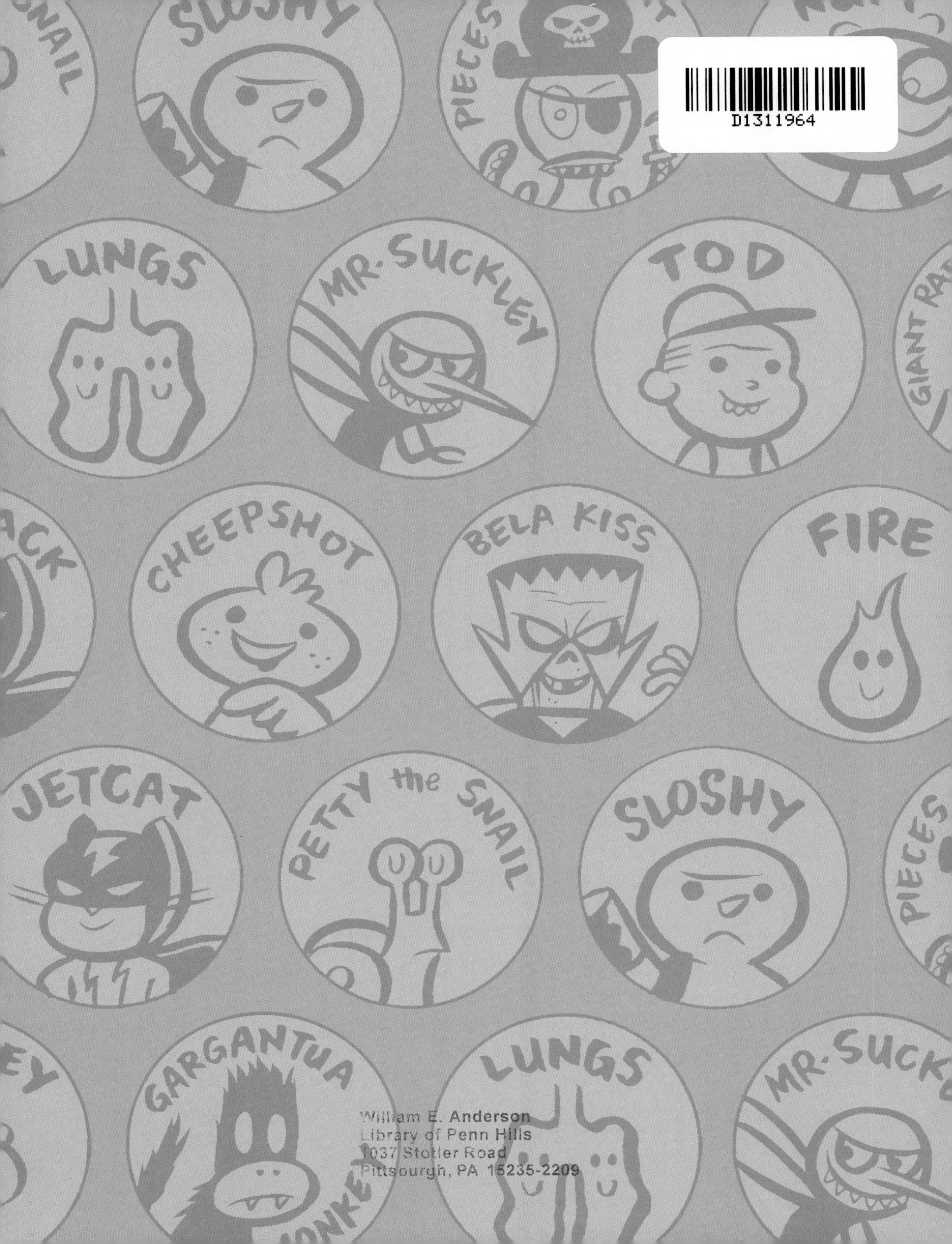
SLOSHY
PIECES
LUNGS
MR. SUCKLEY
TOD
CHEEPSHOT
BELA KISS
FIRE
JETCAT
PETTY the SNAIL
SLOSHY
PIECES
GARGANTUA
LUNGS

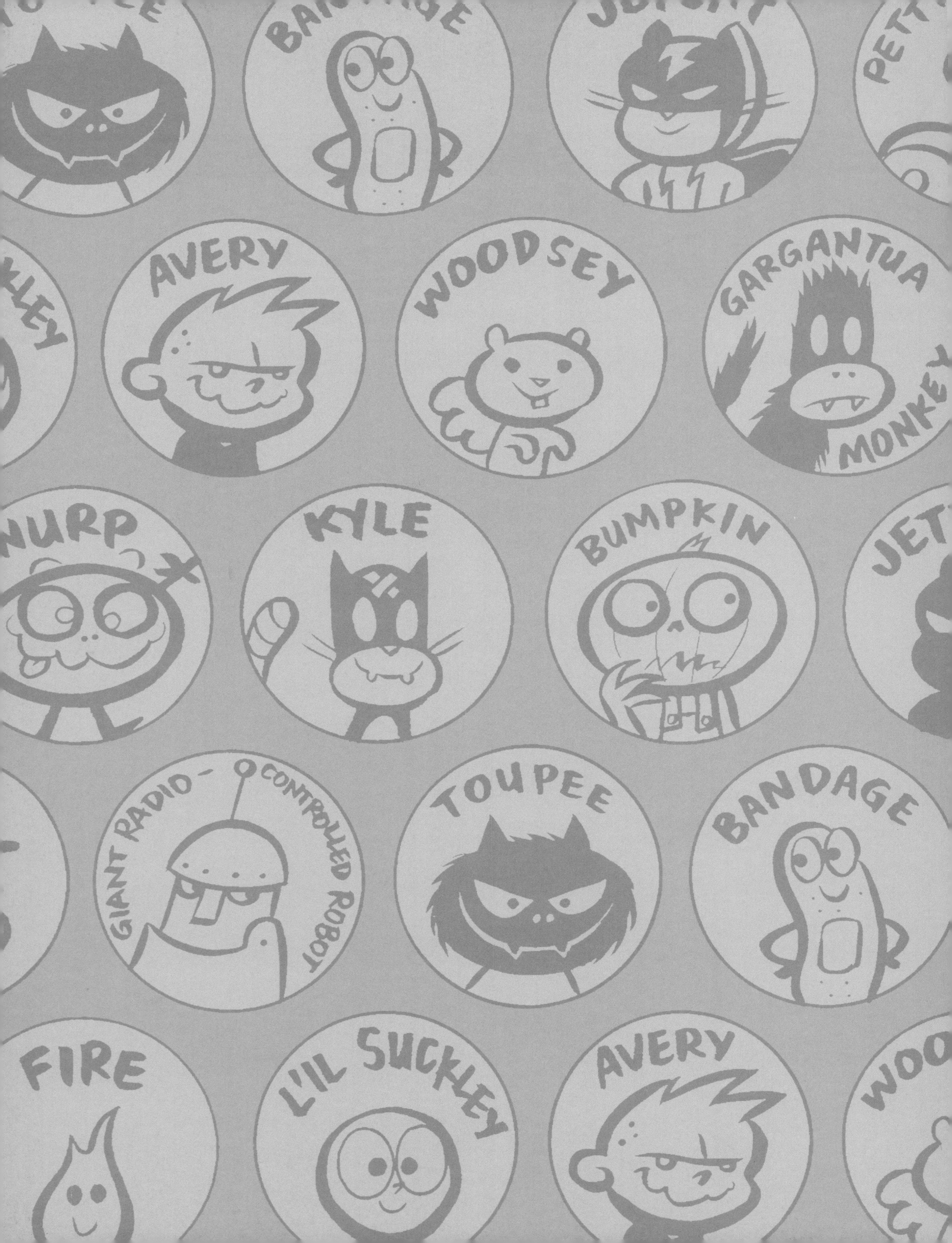

AVERY
WOODSEY
GARGANTUA MONKEY
KYLE
BUMPKIN
GIANT RADIO-CONTROLLED ROBOT
TOUPEE
BANDAGE
FIRE
L'IL SUCKLEY
AVERY

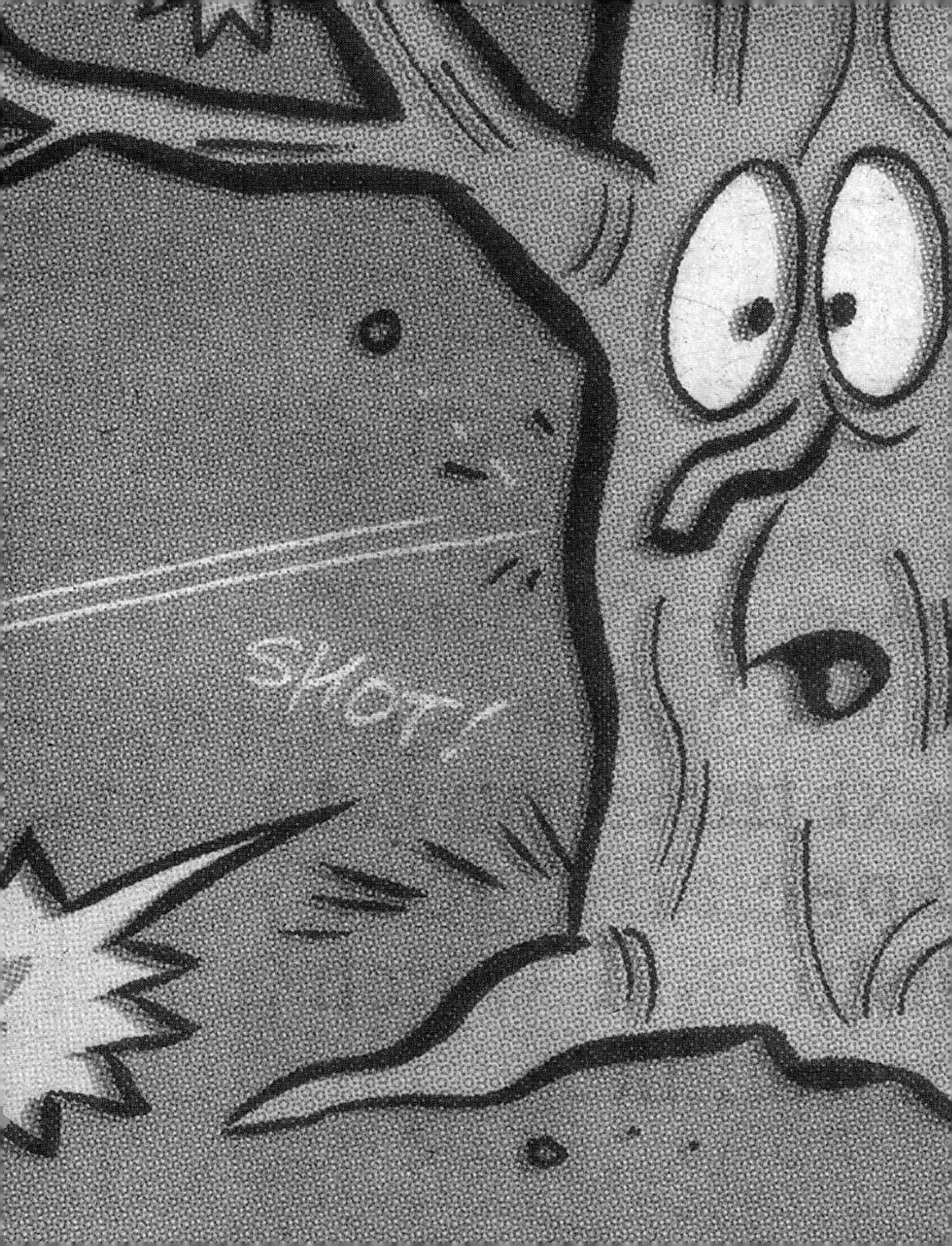
SHOT!

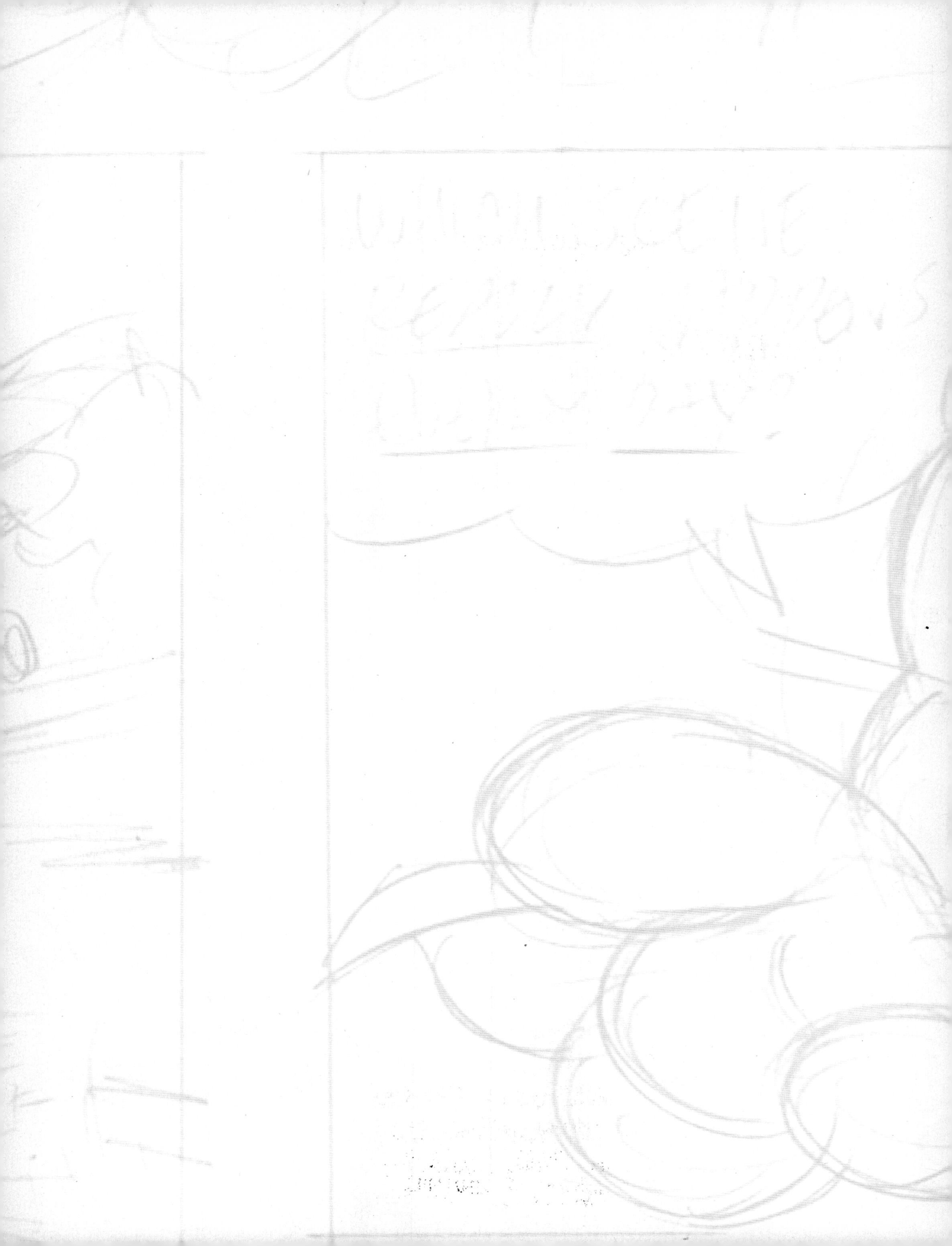

Jay Stephens presents

AdHouse Books
Richmond, VA

Welcome to Oddville
Published by AdHouse Books.

ISBN 1-935233-08-4
ISBN 978-1-935233-08-4
10 9 8 7 6 5 4 3 2 1

Design: Stephens + Pitzer

AdHouse Books
1224 Greycourt Ave.
Richmond, VA 23227-4042
www.adhousebooks.com

First Printing, May 2011

Printed in China

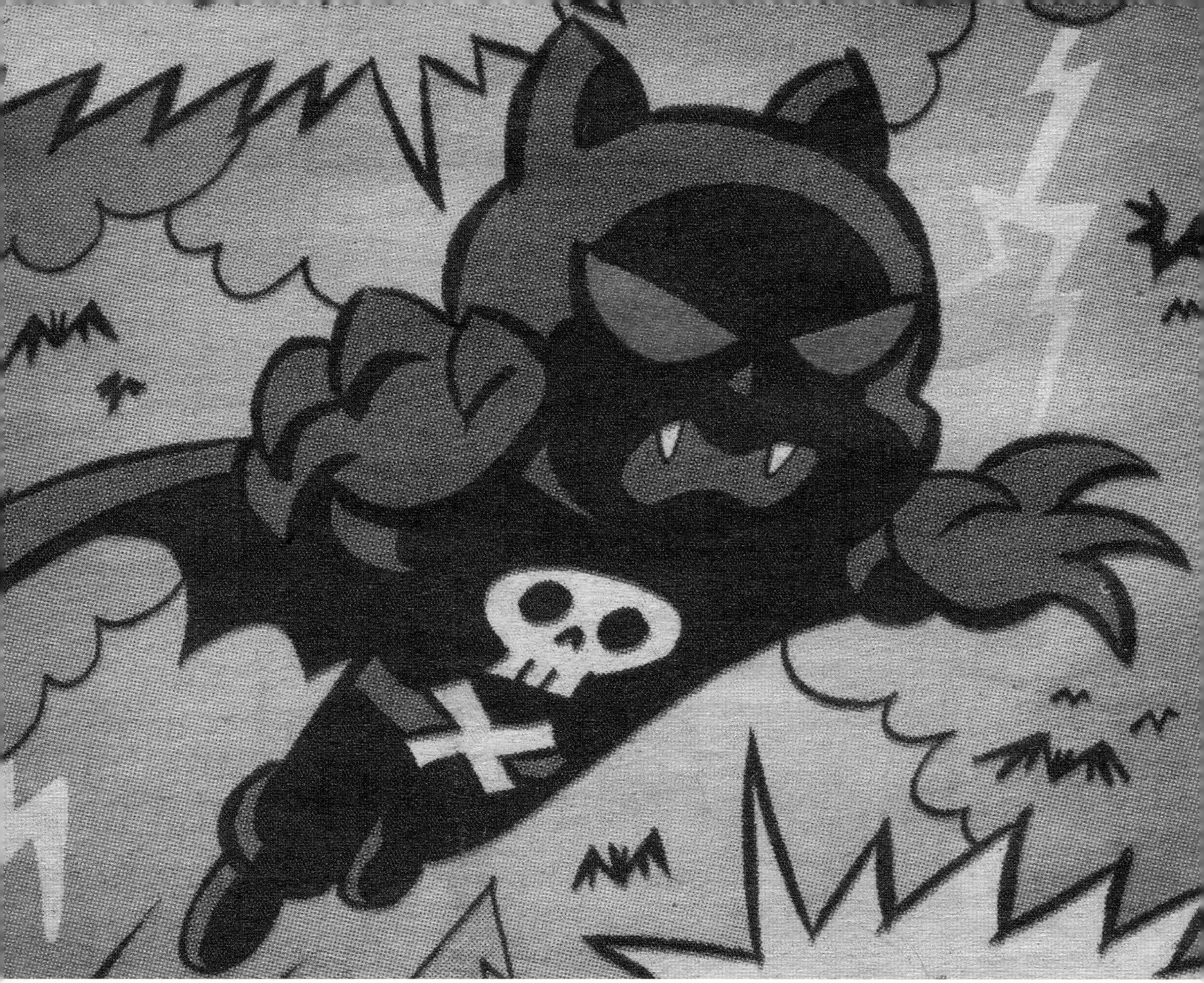

Super thanks to the team at the BRAND NEW PLANET for letting me do whatever I wanted — Susan Grimbly, Kathy Muldoon, and Spencer Wynn.

Shout out to Steven Manale for hooking me up with the TORONTO STAR in the first place, and for challenging me to excell through his strip SUPERSLACKERS.

Thanks to Chris and Macek of CLYDE HENRY for pushing me harder.

Dedicated to Desmond Stephens!

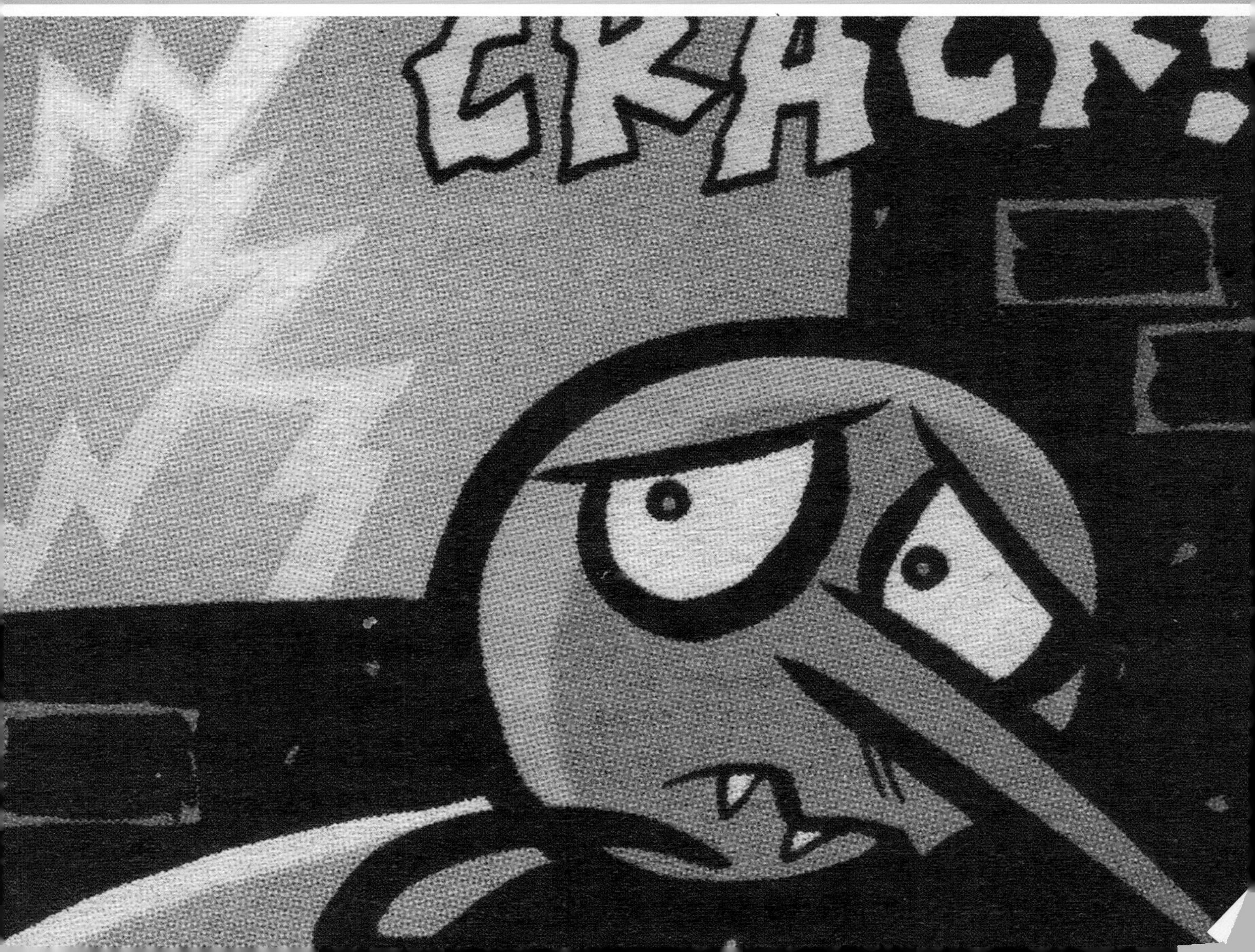
CRACK!

INTRODUCING:

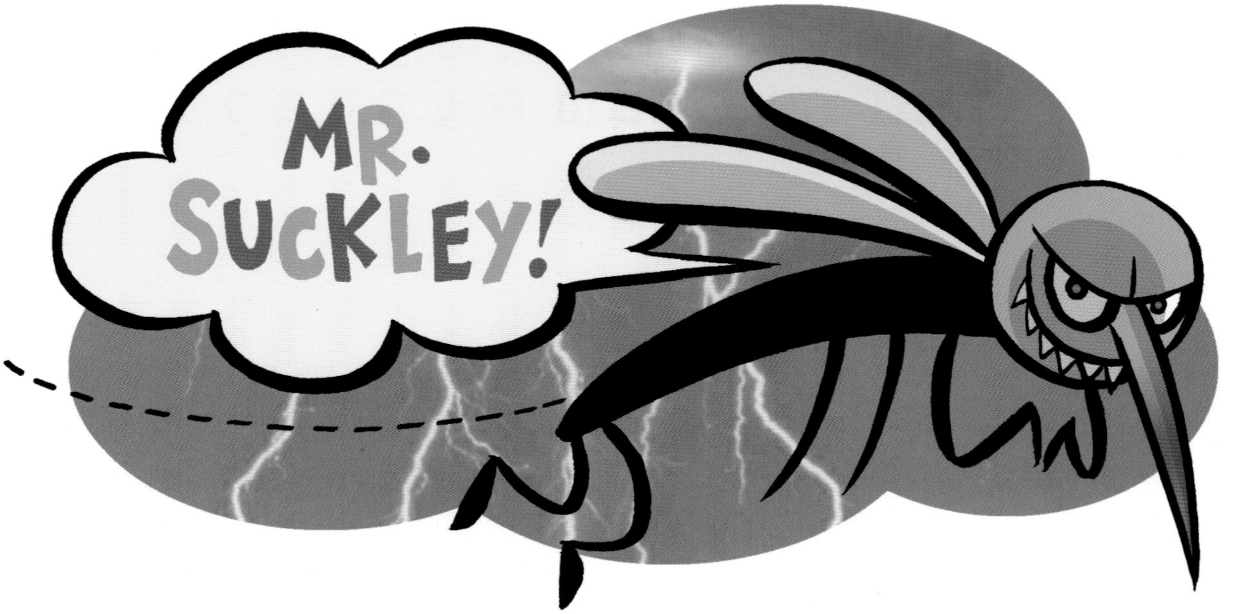

MR. SUCKLEY!

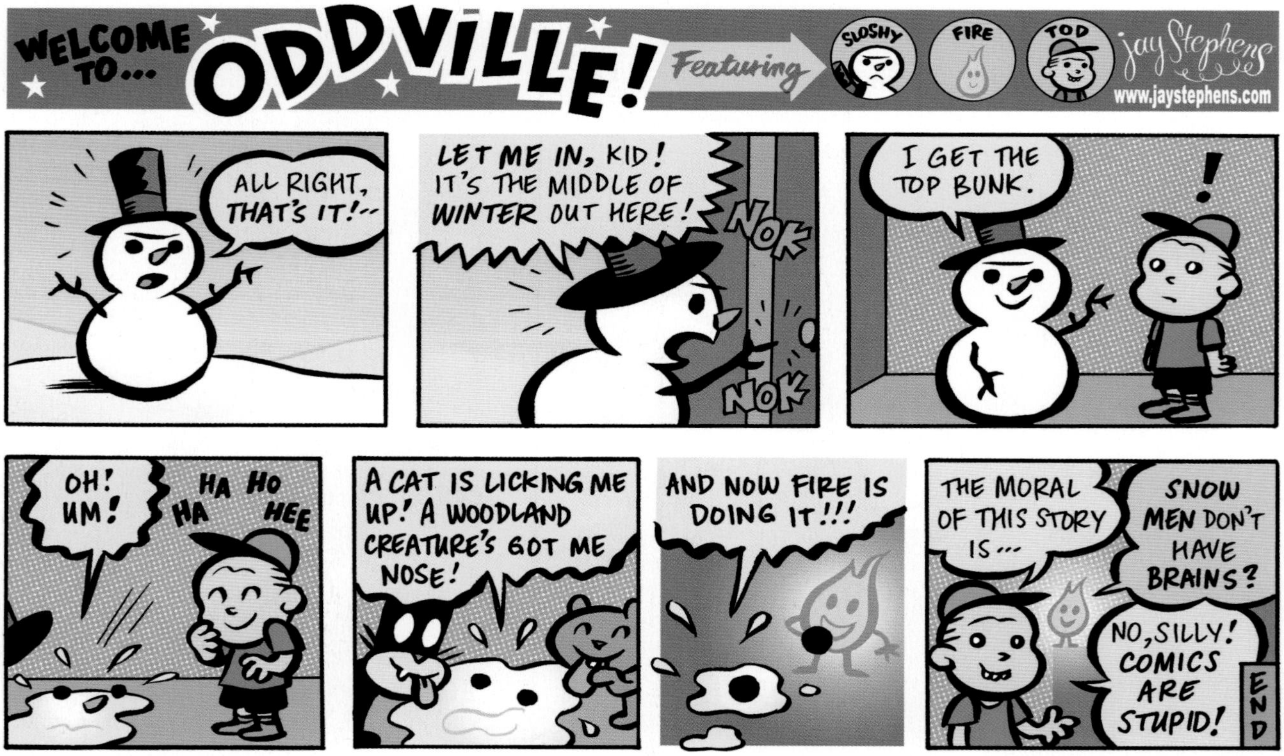

WELCOME TO... ODDVILLE!
Featuring
SLOSHY
FIRE
TOD
jay Stephens
www.jaystephens.com
ALL RIGHT, THAT'S IT!--
LET ME IN, KID! IT'S THE MIDDLE OF WINTER OUT HERE!
NOK
NOK
I GET THE TOP BUNK.
!
OH! UM!
HA HA HO HEE
A CAT IS LICKING ME UP! A WOODLAND CREATURE'S GOT ME NOSE!
AND NOW FIRE IS DOING IT!!!
THE MORAL OF THIS STORY IS...
SNOW MEN DON'T HAVE BRAINS?
NO, SILLY! COMICS ARE STUPID!
END

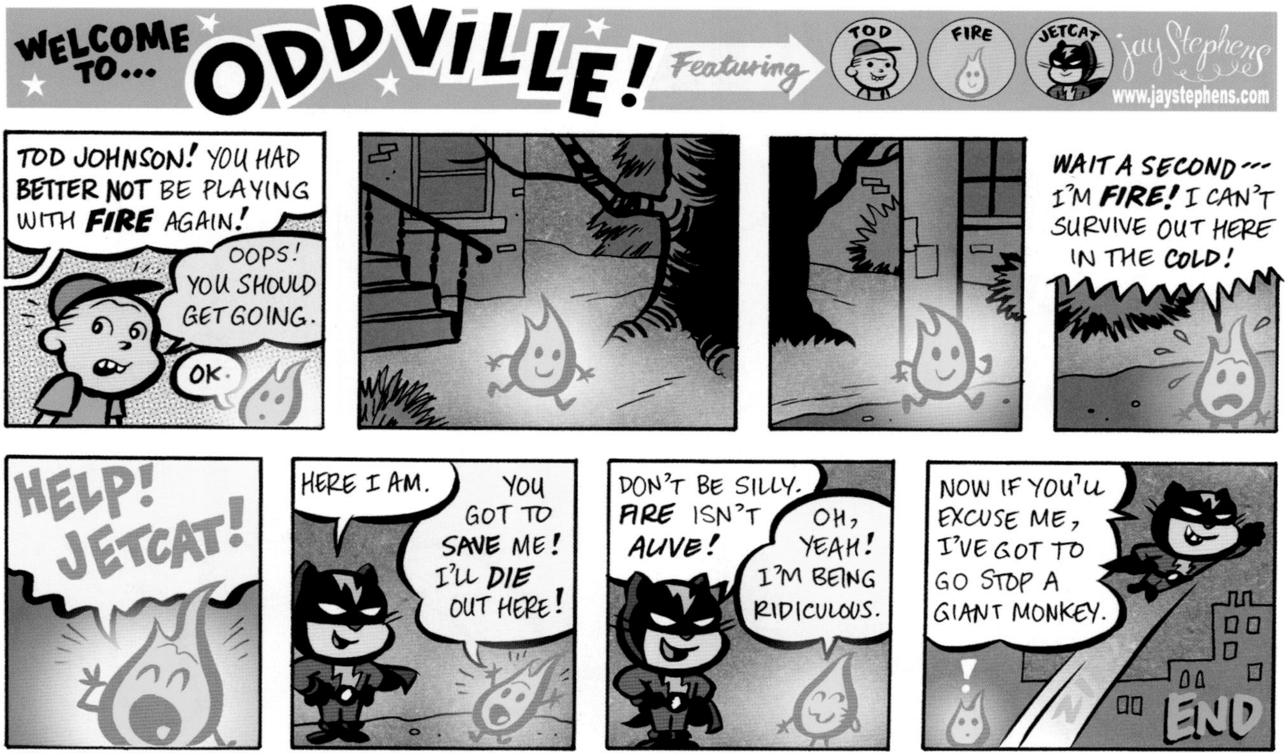
WELCOME TO... ODDVILLE!
Featuring
TOD
FIRE
JETCAT
jay Stephens
www.jaystephens.com
TOD JOHNSON! YOU HAD BETTER NOT BE PLAYING WITH FIRE AGAIN!
OOPS! YOU SHOULD GET GOING.
OK.
WAIT A SECOND--- I'M FIRE! I CAN'T SURVIVE OUT HERE IN THE COLD!
HELP! JETCAT!
HERE I AM.
YOU GOT TO SAVE ME! I'LL DIE OUT HERE!
DON'T BE SILLY. FIRE ISN'T ALIVE!
OH, YEAH! I'M BEING RIDICULOUS.
NOW IF YOU'LL EXCUSE ME, I'VE GOT TO GO STOP A GIANT MONKEY.
!
END

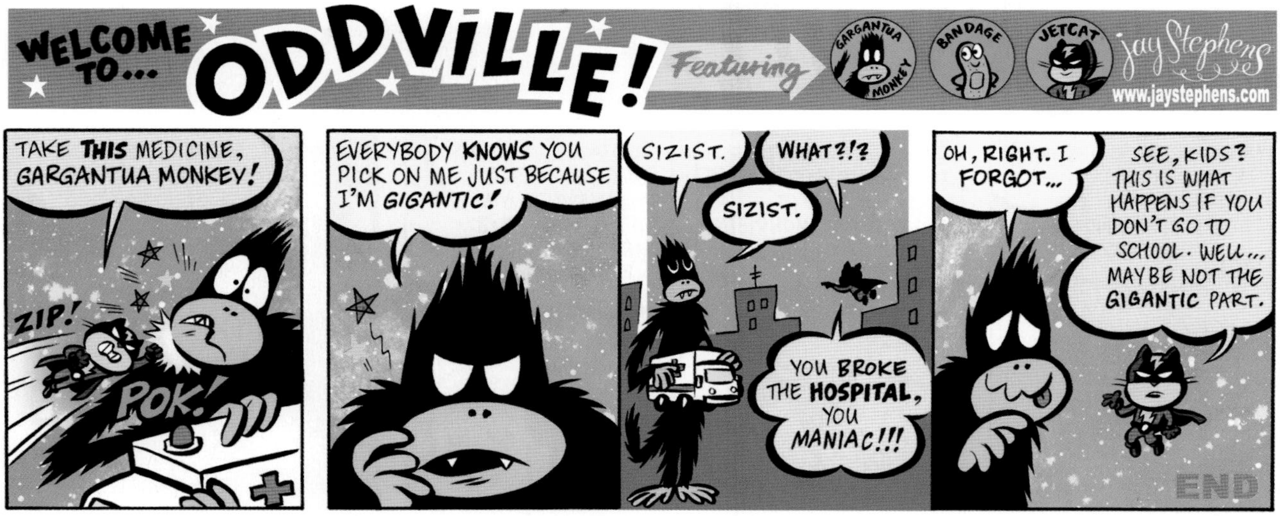
WELCOME TO... ODDVILLE!
Featuring
GARGANTUA MONKEY
BANDAGE
JETCAT
jay Stephens
www.jaystephens.com
TAKE THIS MEDICINE, GARGANTUA MONKEY!
ZIP!
POK!
EVERYBODY KNOWS YOU PICK ON ME JUST BECAUSE I'M GIGANTIC!
SIZIST.
WHAT?!?
SIZIST.
YOU BROKE THE HOSPITAL, YOU MANIAC!!!
OH, RIGHT. I FORGOT...
SEE, KIDS? THIS IS WHAT HAPPENS IF YOU DON'T GO TO SCHOOL. WELL... MAYBE NOT THE GIGANTIC PART.
END

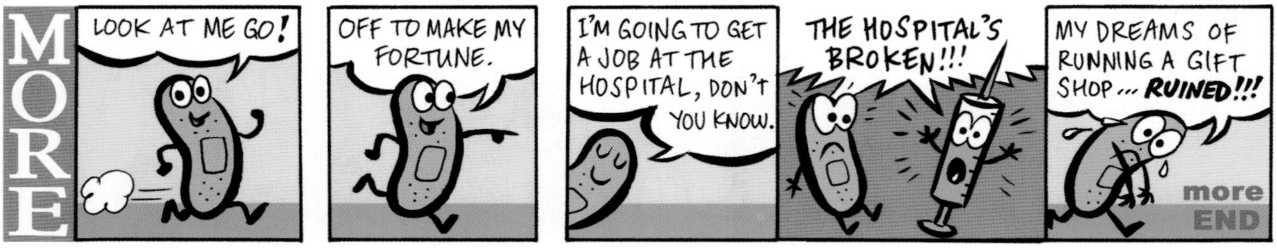
MORE
LOOK AT ME GO!
OFF TO MAKE MY FORTUNE.
I'M GOING TO GET A JOB AT THE HOSPITAL, DON'T YOU KNOW.
THE HOSPITAL'S BROKEN!!!
MY DREAMS OF RUNNING A GIFT SHOP... RUINED!!!
more END

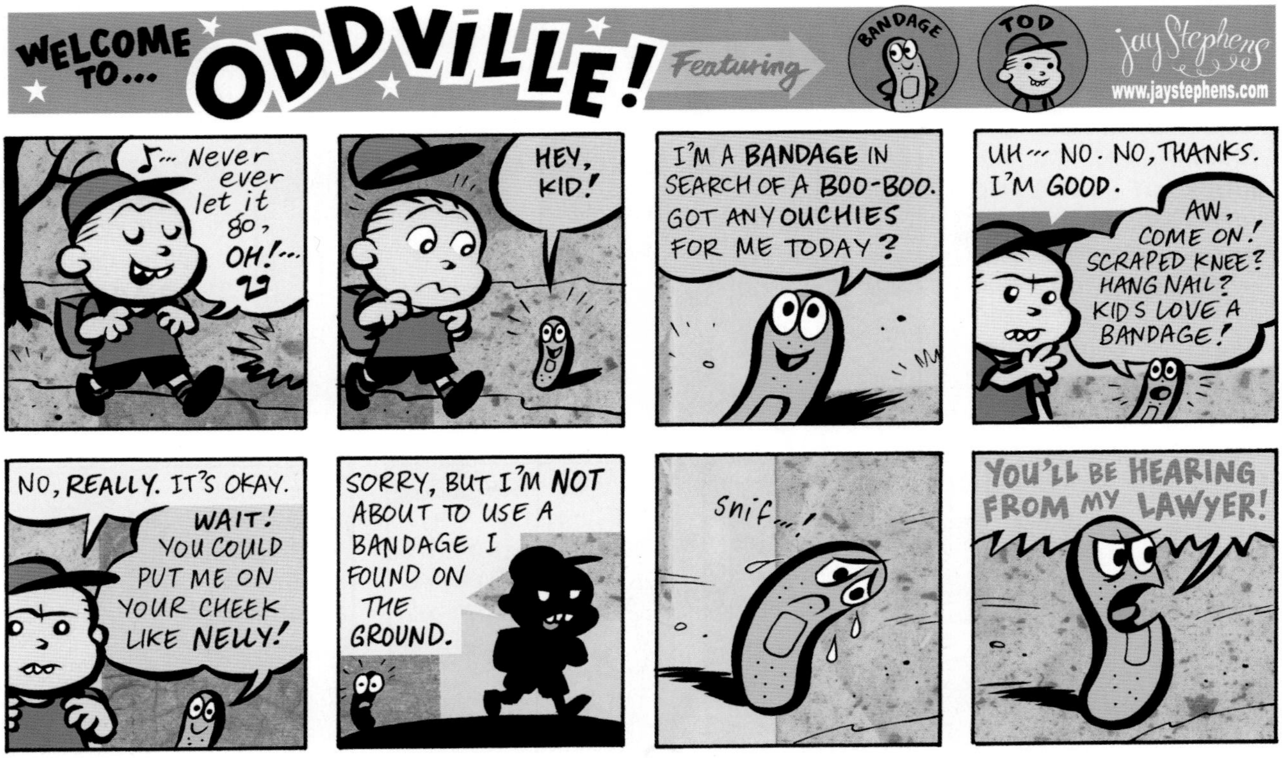
WELCOME TO... ODDVILLE!
Featuring
BANDAGE
TOD
jay Stephens
www.jaystephens.com
Never ever let it go, OH!...
HEY, KID!
I'M A BANDAGE IN SEARCH OF A BOO-BOO. GOT ANY OUCHIES FOR ME TODAY?
UH... NO. NO, THANKS. I'M GOOD.
AW, COME ON! SCRAPED KNEE? HANG NAIL? KIDS LOVE A BANDAGE!
NO, REALLY. IT'S OKAY.
WAIT! YOU COULD PUT ME ON YOUR CHEEK LIKE NELLY!
SORRY, BUT I'M NOT ABOUT TO USE A BANDAGE I FOUND ON THE GROUND.
Snif...!
YOU'LL BE HEARING FROM MY LAWYER!

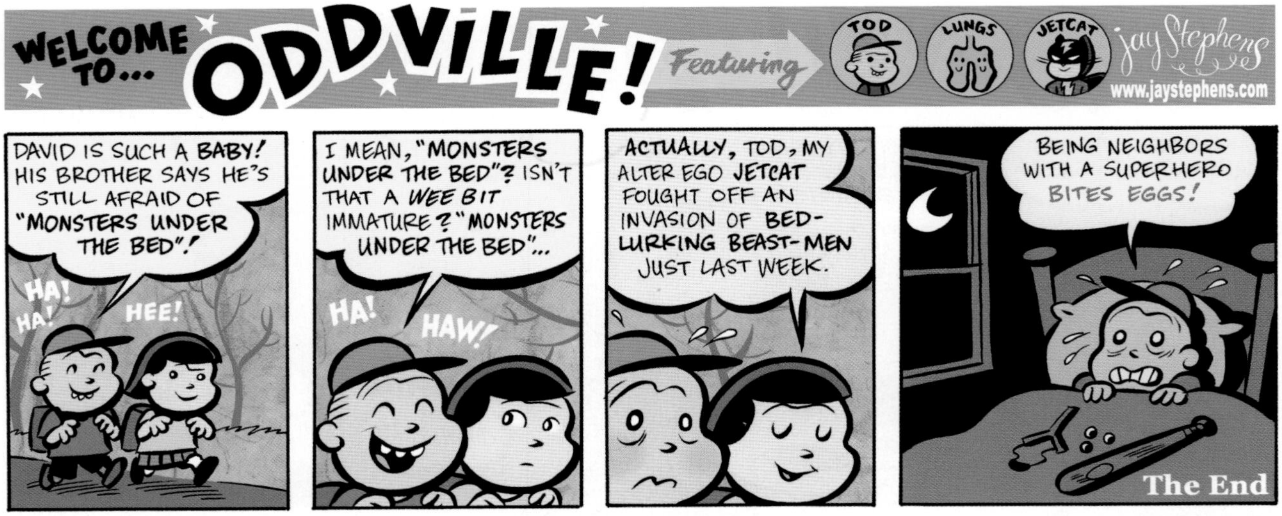
WELCOME TO... ODDVILLE!
Featuring
TOD
LUNGS
JETCAT
jay Stephens
www.jaystephens.com
DAVID IS SUCH A BABY! HIS BROTHER SAYS HE'S STILL AFRAID OF "MONSTERS UNDER THE BED"!
HA! HA!
HEE!
I MEAN, "MONSTERS UNDER THE BED"? ISN'T THAT A WEE BIT IMMATURE? "MONSTERS UNDER THE BED"...
HA!
HAW!
ACTUALLY, TOD, MY ALTER EGO JETCAT FOUGHT OFF AN INVASION OF BED-LURKING BEAST-MEN JUST LAST WEEK.
BEING NEIGHBORS WITH A SUPERHERO BITES EGGS!
The End

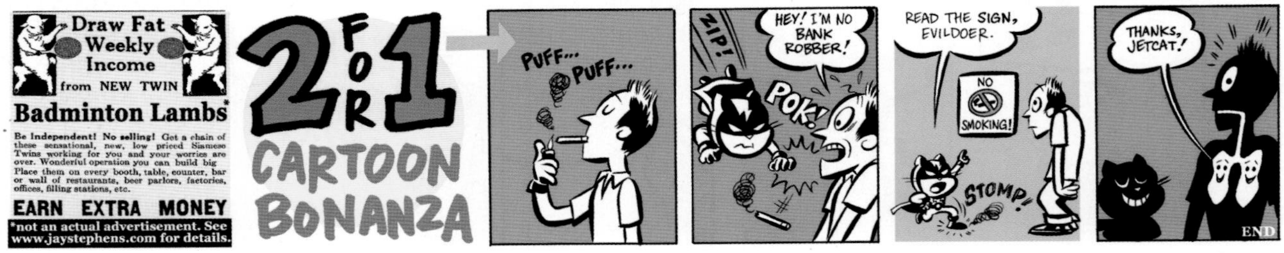
Draw Fat Weekly Income
from NEW TWIN
Badminton Lambs*
Be Independent! No selling! Get a chain of these sensational, new, low priced Siamese Twins working for you and your worries are over. Wonderful operation you can build big Place them on every booth, table, counter, bar or wall of restaurants, beer parlors, factories, offices, filling stations, etc.
EARN EXTRA MONEY
*not an actual advertisement. See www.jaystephens.com for details.
2 FOR 1
CARTOON BONANZA
PUFF... PUFF...
ZIP!
HEY! I'M NO BANK ROBBER!
POK!
READ THE SIGN, EVILDOER.
NO SMOKING!
STOMP!
THANKS, JETCAT!
END

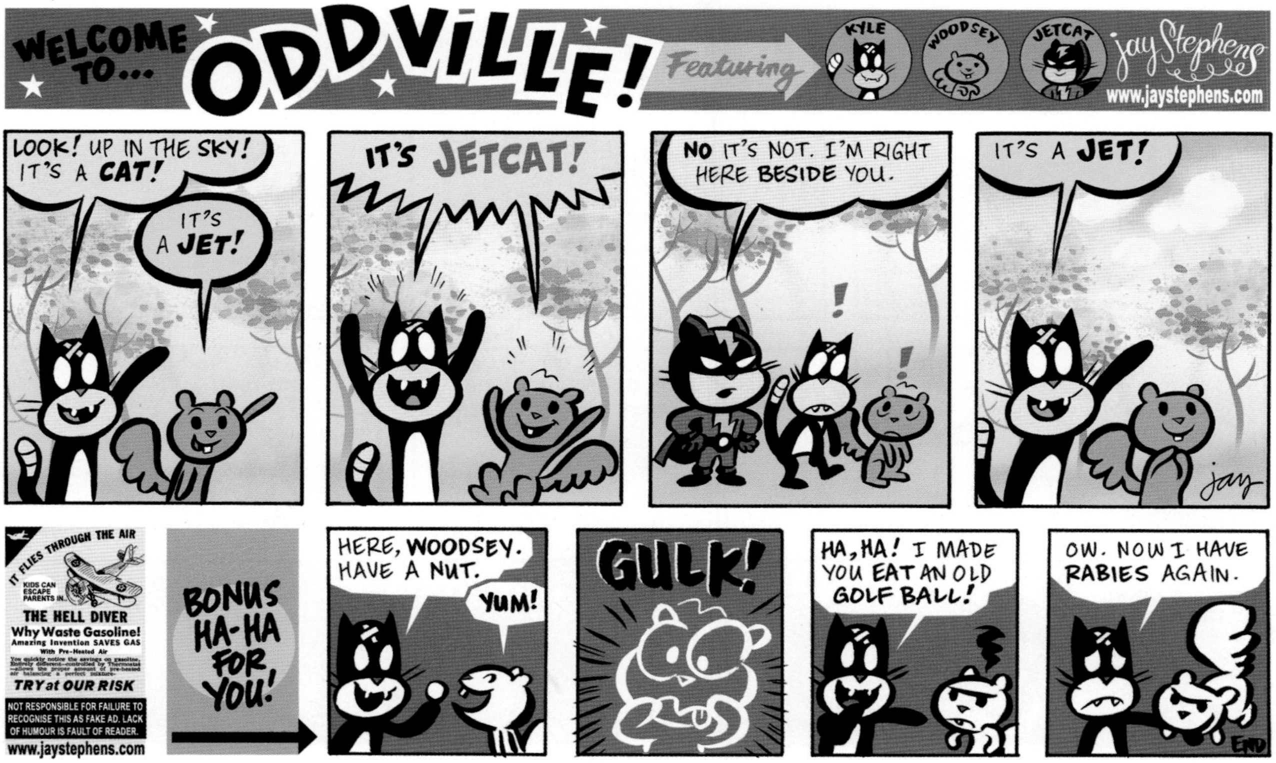
WELCOME TO...
ODDVILLE!
Featuring
KYLE
WOODSEY
JETCAT
jay Stephens
www.jaystephens.com
LOOK! UP IN THE SKY! IT'S A CAT!
IT'S A JET!
IT'S JETCAT!
NO IT'S NOT. I'M RIGHT HERE BESIDE YOU.
IT'S A JET!
jay
IT FLIES THROUGH THE AIR
KIDS CAN ESCAPE PARENTS IN..
THE HELL DIVER
Why Waste Gasoline!
Amazing Invention SAVES GAS
With Pre-Heated Air
TRY at OUR RISK
NOT RESPONSIBLE FOR FAILURE TO RECOGNISE THIS AS FAKE AD. LACK OF HUMOUR IS FAULT OF READER.
www.jaystephens.com
BONUS HA-HA FOR YOU!
HERE, WOODSEY. HAVE A NUT.
YUM!
GULK!
HA, HA! I MADE YOU EAT AN OLD GOLF BALL!
OW. NOW I HAVE RABIES AGAIN.
END

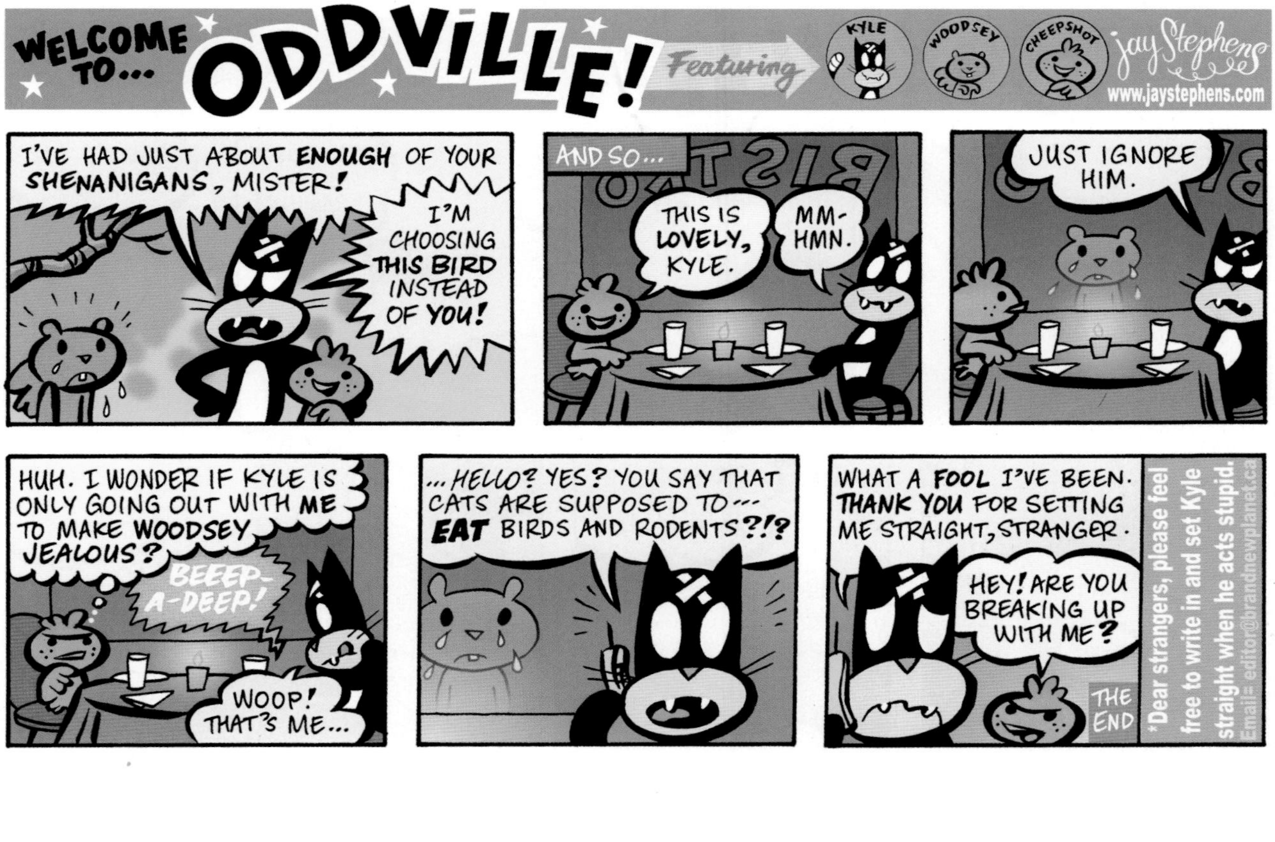
WELCOME TO...
ODDVILLE!
Featuring
KYLE
WOODSEY
CHEEPSHOT
jay Stephens
www.jaystephens.com
I'VE HAD JUST ABOUT ENOUGH OF YOUR SHENANIGANS, MISTER!
I'M CHOOSING THIS BIRD INSTEAD OF YOU!
AND SO...
BISTRO
THIS IS LOVELY, KYLE.
MM-HMN.
JUST IGNORE HIM.
HUH. I WONDER IF KYLE IS ONLY GOING OUT WITH ME TO MAKE WOODSEY JEALOUS?
BEEEP-A-DEEP!
WOOP! THAT'S ME...
...HELLO? YES? YOU SAY THAT CATS ARE SUPPOSED TO--- EAT BIRDS AND RODENTS?!?
WHAT A FOOL I'VE BEEN. THANK YOU FOR SETTING ME STRAIGHT, STRANGER.
HEY! ARE YOU BREAKING UP WITH ME?
THE END
*Dear strangers, please feel free to write in and set Kyle straight when he acts stupid.
Email= editor@brandnewplanet.ca

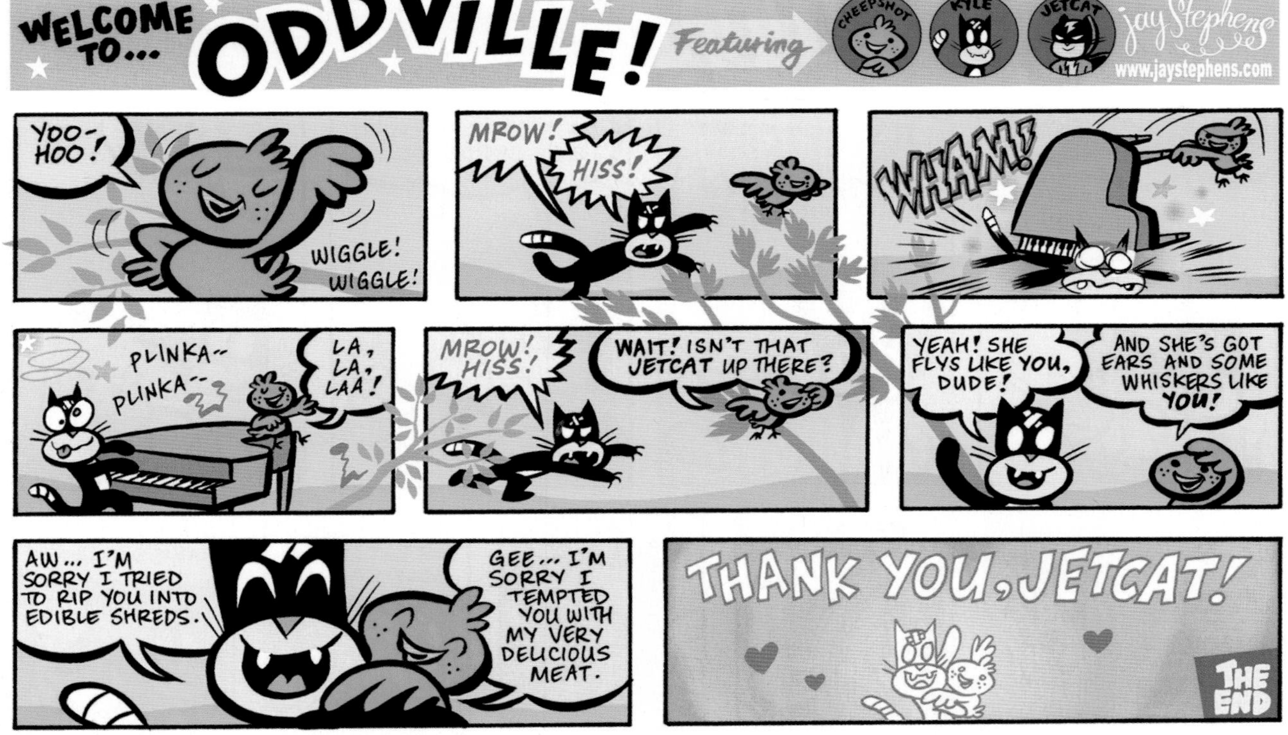
WELCOME TO... ODDVILLE!
Featuring
CHEEPSHOT
KYLE
JETCAT
jay Stephens
www.jaystephens.com
YOO-HOO!
WIGGLE! WIGGLE!
MROW!
HISS!
WHAM!
PLINKA-PLINKA--
LA, LA, LAA!
MROW! HISS!
WAIT! ISN'T THAT JETCAT UP THERE?
YEAH! SHE FLYS LIKE YOU, DUDE!
AND SHE'S GOT EARS AND SOME WHISKERS LIKE YOU!
AW... I'M SORRY I TRIED TO RIP YOU INTO EDIBLE SHREDS.
GEE... I'M SORRY I TEMPTED YOU WITH MY VERY DELICIOUS MEAT.
THANK YOU, JETCAT!
THE END

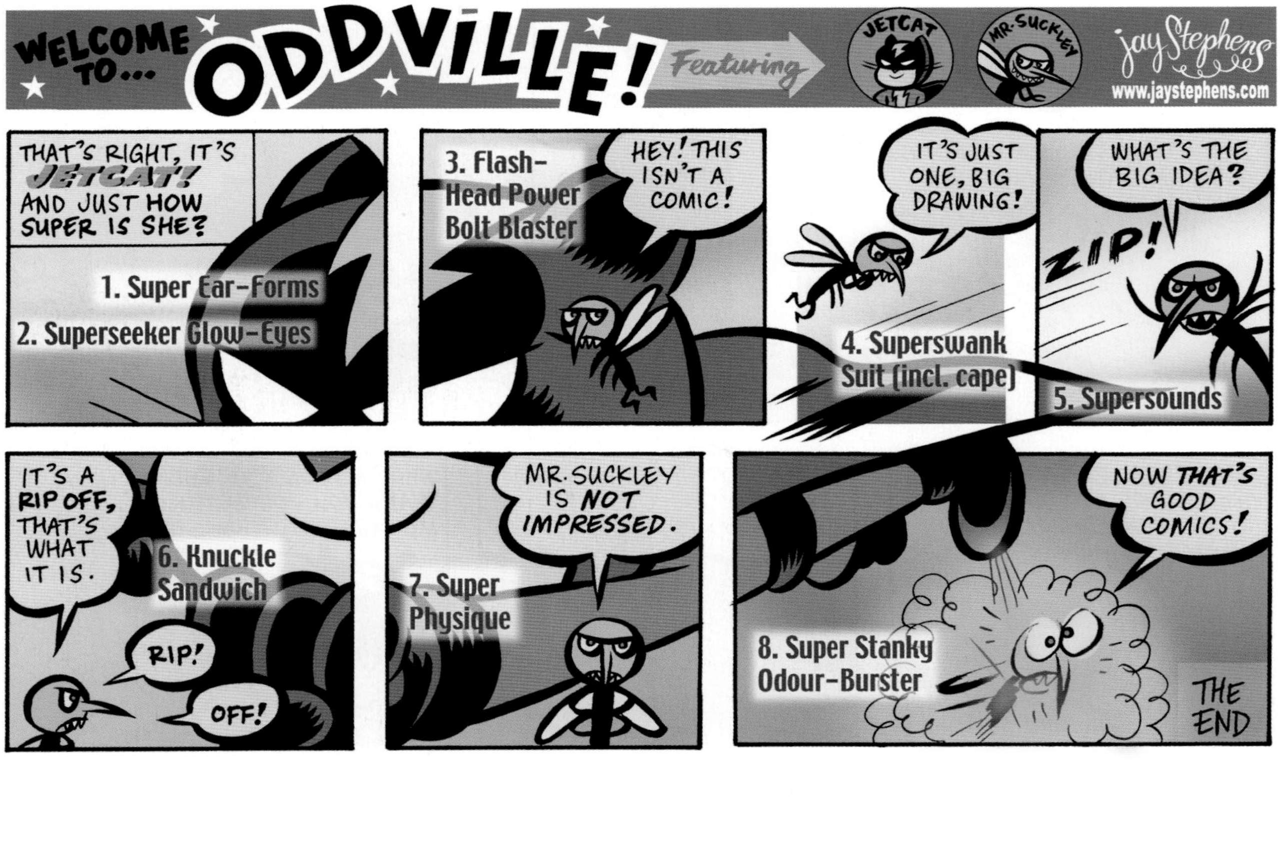
WELCOME TO... ODDVILLE!
Featuring
JETCAT
MR. SUCKLEY
jay Stephens
www.jaystephens.com
THAT'S RIGHT, IT'S JETCAT! AND JUST HOW SUPER IS SHE?
1. Super Ear-Forms
2. Superseeker Glow-Eyes
3. Flash-Head Power Bolt Blaster
HEY! THIS ISN'T A COMIC!
IT'S JUST ONE, BIG DRAWING!
4. Superswank Suit (incl. cape)
WHAT'S THE BIG IDEA?
ZIP!
5. Supersounds
IT'S A RIP OFF, THAT'S WHAT IT IS.
6. Knuckle Sandwich
RIP!
OFF!
MR. SUCKLEY IS NOT IMPRESSED.
7. Super Physique
NOW THAT'S GOOD COMICS!
8. Super Stanky Odour-Burster
THE END

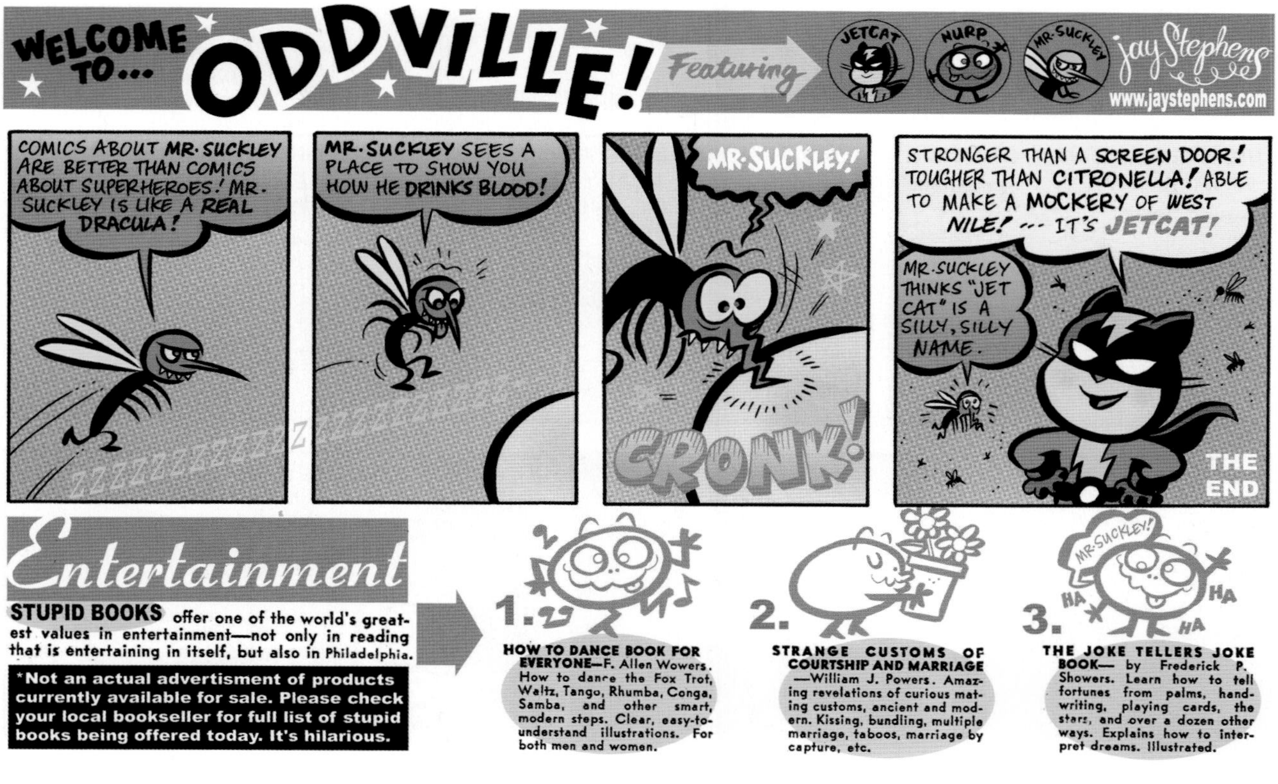
WELCOME TO... ODDVILLE! Featuring
JETCAT
NURP
MR. SUCKLEY
jay Stephens
www.jaystephens.com
COMICS ABOUT MR. SUCKLEY ARE BETTER THAN COMICS ABOUT SUPERHEROES! MR. SUCKLEY IS LIKE A REAL DRACULA!
ZZZZZZZZZZZZZ
MR. SUCKLEY SEES A PLACE TO SHOW YOU HOW HE DRINKS BLOOD!
ZZZZZZZZZZ
MR. SUCKLEY!
CRONK!
STRONGER THAN A SCREEN DOOR! TOUGHER THAN CITRONELLA! ABLE TO MAKE A MOCKERY OF WEST NILE! --- IT'S JETCAT!
MR. SUCKLEY THINKS "JET CAT" IS A SILLY, SILLY NAME.
THE END
Entertainment
STUPID BOOKS offer one of the world's greatest values in entertainment—not only in reading that is entertaining in itself, but also in Philadelphia.
*Not an actual advertisment of products currently available for sale. Please check your local bookseller for full list of stupid books being offered today. It's hilarious.
1. HOW TO DANCE BOOK FOR EVERYONE—F. Allen Wowers. How to dance the Fox Trot, Waltz, Tango, Rhumba, Conga, Samba, and other smart, modern steps. Clear, easy-to-understand illustrations. For both men and women.
2. STRANGE CUSTOMS OF COURTSHIP AND MARRIAGE —William J. Powers. Amazing revelations of curious mating customs, ancient and modern. Kissing, bundling, multiple marriage, taboos, marriage by capture, etc.
MR. SUCKLEY!
HA HA HA
3. THE JOKE TELLERS JOKE BOOK— by Frederick P. Showers. Learn how to tell fortunes from palms, handwriting, playing cards, the stars, and over a dozen other ways. Explains how to interpret dreams. Illustrated.

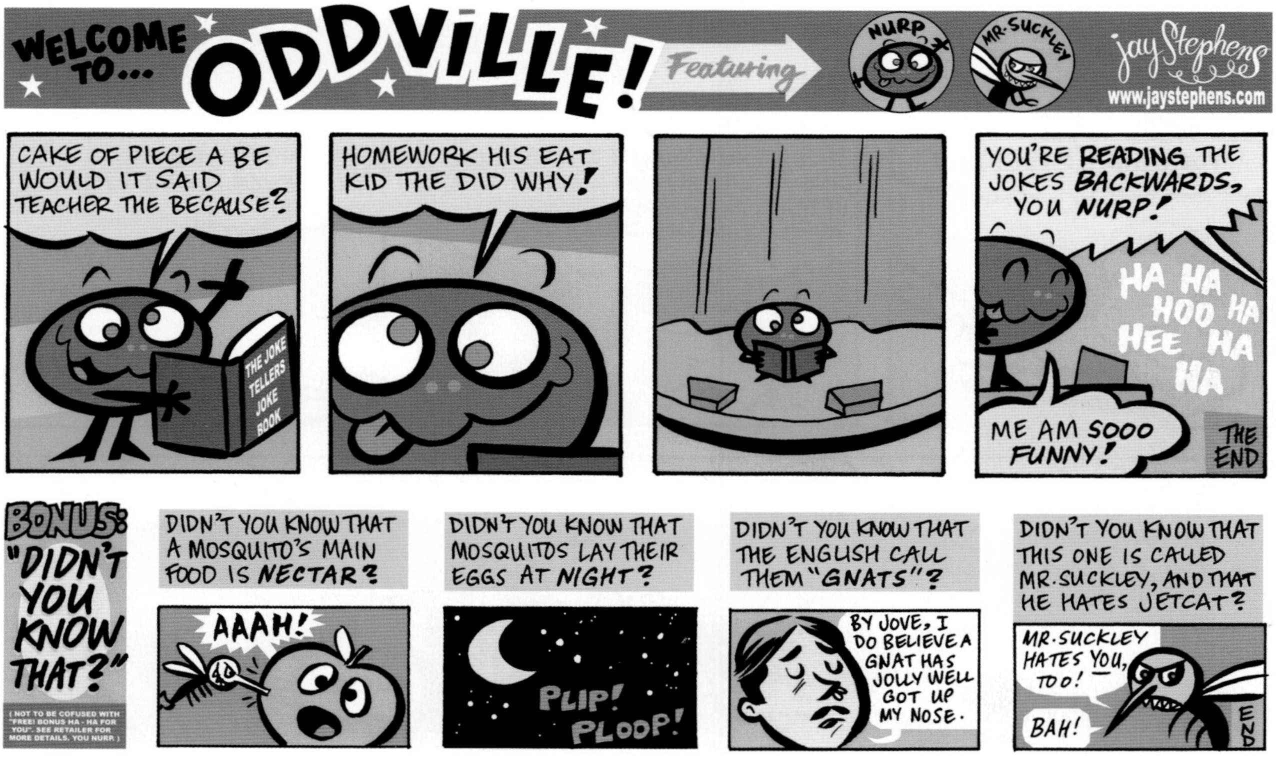
WELCOME TO... ODDVILLE! Featuring
NURP
MR. SUCKLEY
jay Stephens
www.jaystephens.com
CAKE OF PIECE A BE WOULD IT SAID TEACHER THE BECAUSE?
THE JOKE TELLERS JOKE BOOK
HOMEWORK HIS EAT KID THE DID WHY!
YOU'RE READING THE JOKES BACKWARDS, YOU NURP!
HA HA HOO HA HEE HA HA
ME AM SOOO FUNNY!
THE END
BONUS: "DIDN'T YOU KNOW THAT?"
(NOT TO BE COFUSED WITH "FREE! BONUS HA - HA FOR YOU". SEE RETAILER FOR MORE DETAILS. YOU NURP.)
DIDN'T YOU KNOW THAT A MOSQUITO'S MAIN FOOD IS NECTAR?
AAAH!
DIDN'T YOU KNOW THAT MOSQUITOS LAY THEIR EGGS AT NIGHT?
PLIP! PLOOP!
DIDN'T YOU KNOW THAT THE ENGLISH CALL THEM "GNATS"?
BY JOVE, I DO BELIEVE A GNAT HAS JOLLY WELL GOT UP MY NOSE.
DIDN'T YOU KNOW THAT THIS ONE IS CALLED MR. SUCKLEY, AND THAT HE HATES JETCAT?
MR. SUCKLEY HATES YOU, TOO!
BAH!
END

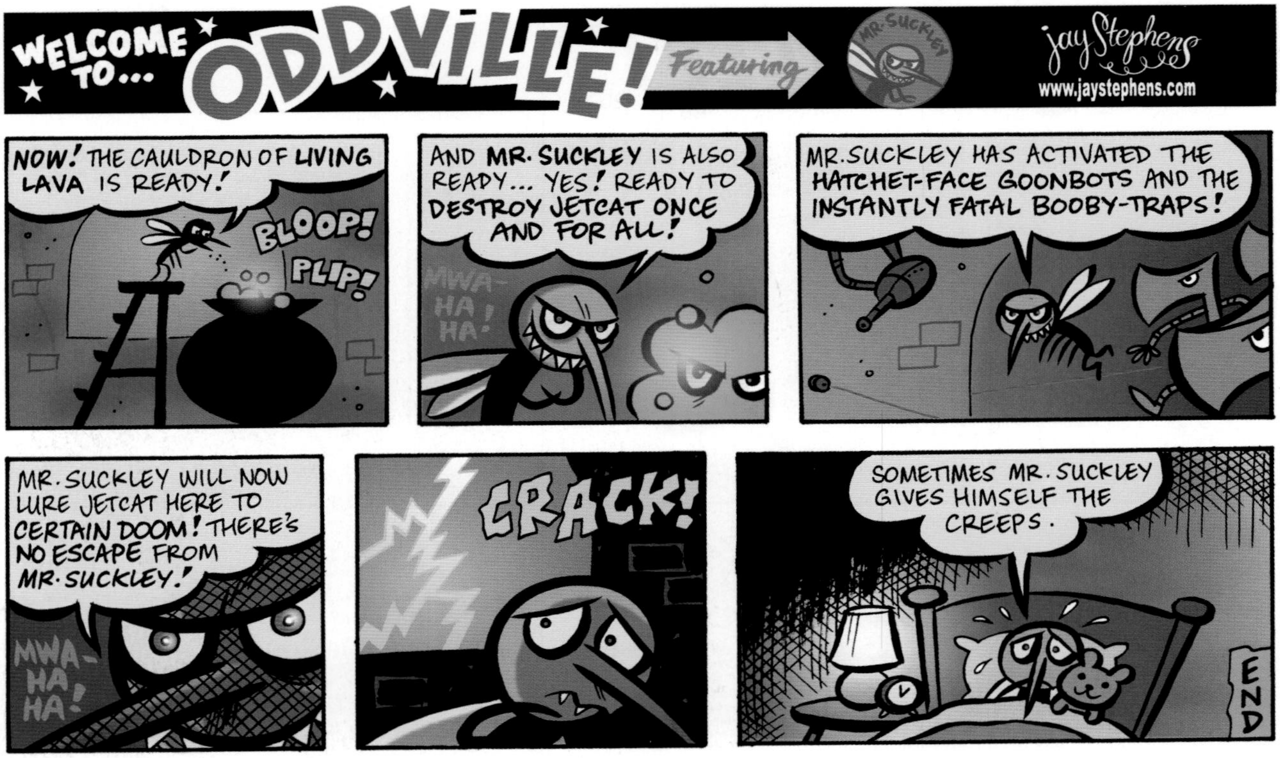
WELCOME TO... ODDVILLE!
Featuring
MR. SUCKLEY
jay Stephens
www.jaystephens.com
NOW! THE CAULDRON OF LIVING LAVA IS READY!
BLOOP!
PLIP!
AND MR. SUCKLEY IS ALSO READY... YES! READY TO DESTROY JETCAT ONCE AND FOR ALL!
MWA-HA! HA!
MR. SUCKLEY HAS ACTIVATED THE HATCHET-FACE GOONBOTS AND THE INSTANTLY FATAL BOOBY-TRAPS!
MR. SUCKLEY WILL NOW LURE JETCAT HERE TO CERTAIN DOOM! THERE'S NO ESCAPE FROM MR. SUCKLEY!
MWA-HA-HA!
CRACK!
SOMETIMES MR. SUCKLEY GIVES HIMSELF THE CREEPS.
END

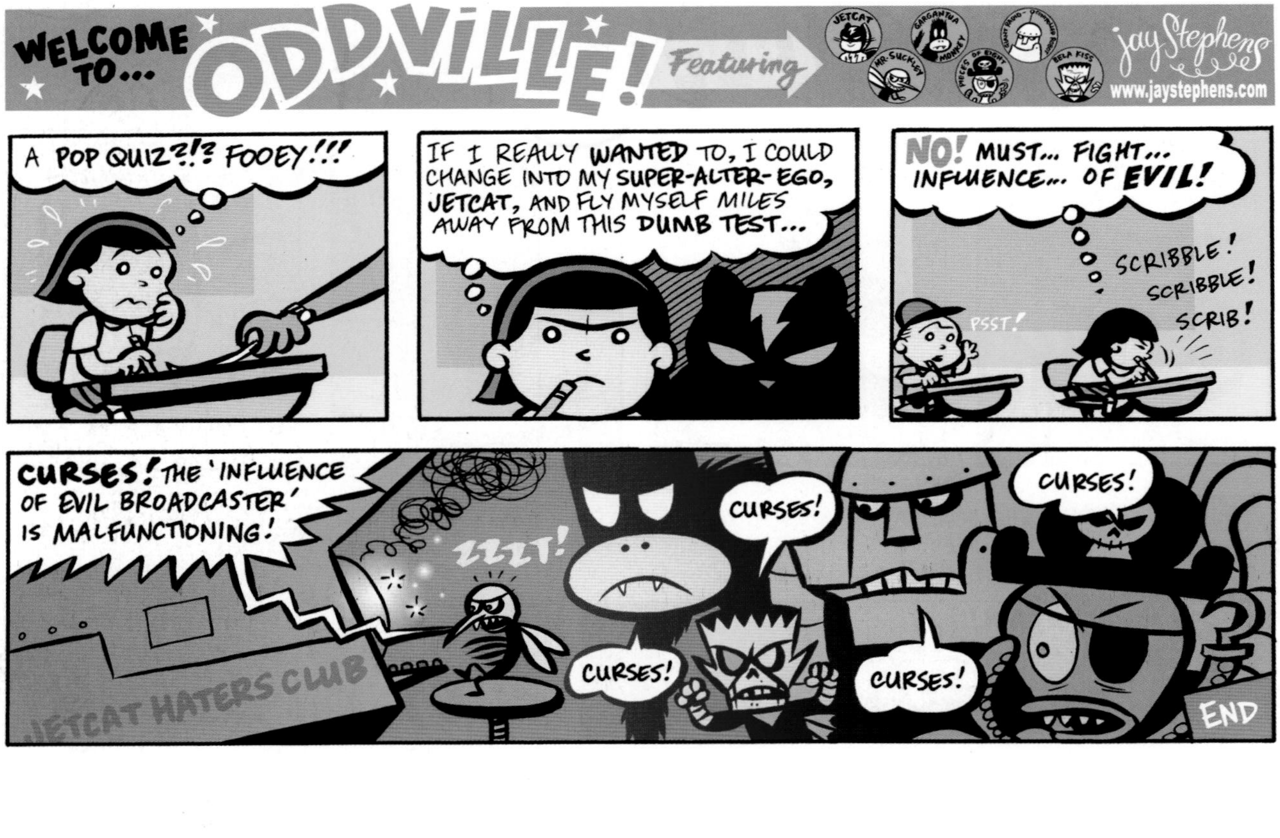
WELCOME TO... ODDVILLE!
Featuring
JETCAT
GARGANTUA MONKEY
MR. SUCKLEY
BELA FISS
jay Stephens
www.jaystephens.com
A POP QUIZ?!? FOOEY!!!
IF I REALLY WANTED TO, I COULD CHANGE INTO MY SUPER-ALTER-EGO, JETCAT, AND FLY MYSELF MILES AWAY FROM THIS DUMB TEST...
NO! MUST... FIGHT... INFLUENCE... OF EVIL!
PSST!
SCRIBBLE!
SCRIBBLE!
SCRIB!
CURSES! THE 'INFLUENCE OF EVIL BROADCASTER' IS MALFUNCTIONING!
ZZZT!
CURSES!
CURSES!
CURSES!
CURSES!
JETCAT HATERS CLUB
END

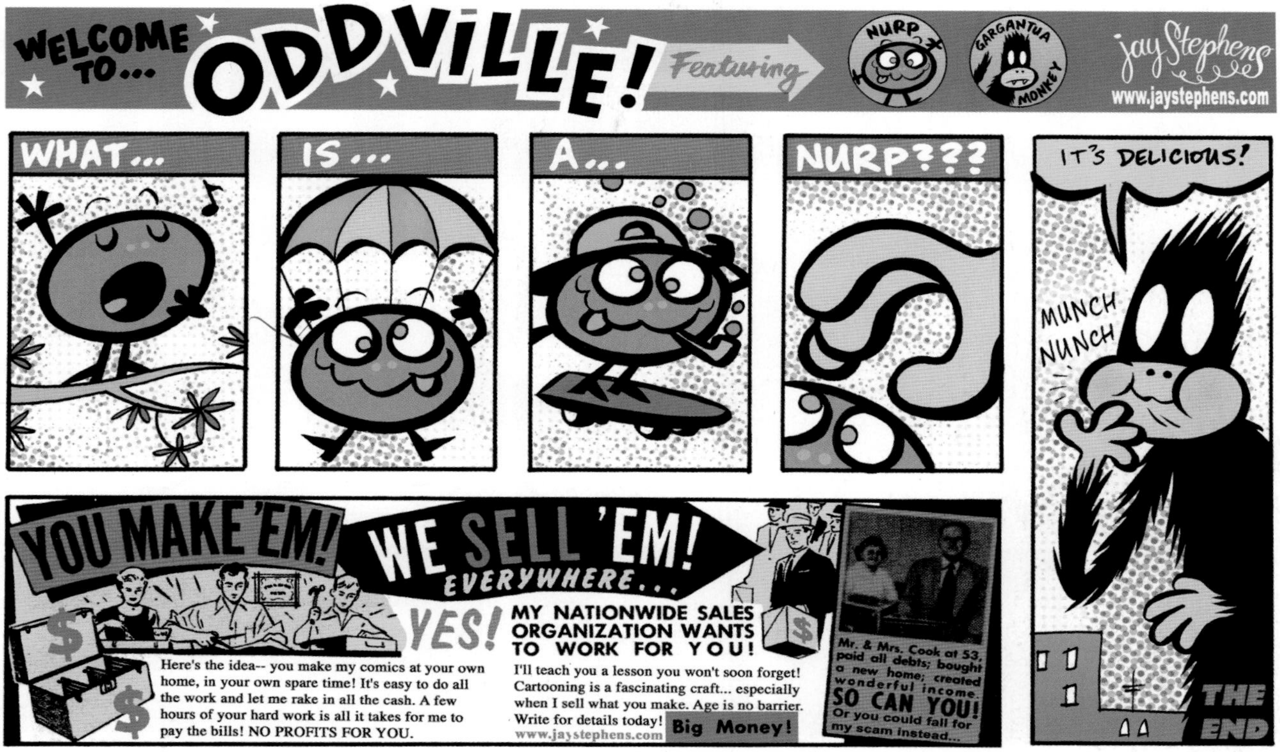
WELCOME TO... ODDVILLE!
Featuring
NURP
GARGANTUA MONKEY
jay Stephens
www.jaystephens.com
WHAT...
IS...
A...
NURP???
IT'S DELICIOUS!
MUNCH NUNCH
YOU MAKE 'EM! WE SELL 'EM! EVERYWHERE...
YES!
MY NATIONWIDE SALES ORGANIZATION WANTS TO WORK FOR YOU!
Here's the idea-- you make my comics at your own home, in your own spare time! It's easy to do all the work and let me rake in all the cash. A few hours of your hard work is all it takes for me to pay the bills! NO PROFITS FOR YOU.
I'll teach you a lesson you won't soon forget! Cartooning is a fascinating craft... especially when I sell what you make. Age is no barrier. Write for details today!
www.jaystephens.com
Big Money!
Mr. & Mrs. Cook at 53, paid all debts; bought a new home; created wonderful income.
SO CAN YOU!
Or you could fall for my scam instead...
THE END

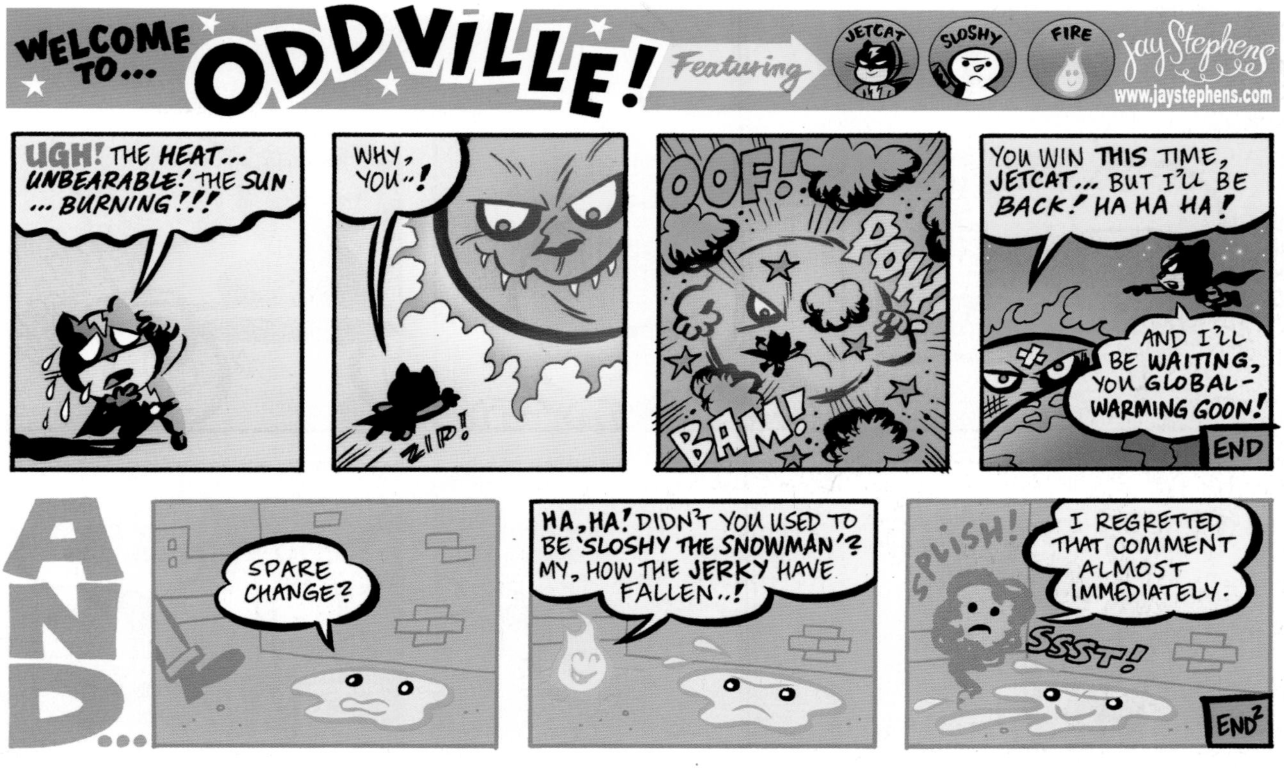
WELCOME TO... ODDVILLE!
Featuring
JETCAT
SLOSHY
FIRE
jay Stephens
www.jaystephens.com
UGH! THE HEAT... UNBEARABLE! THE SUN ... BURNING!!!
WHY, YOU..!
ZIP!
OOF!
POW!
BAM!
YOU WIN THIS TIME, JETCAT... BUT I'LL BE BACK! HA HA HA!
AND I'LL BE WAITING, YOU GLOBAL-WARMING GOON!
END
AND...
SPARE CHANGE?
HA, HA! DIDN'T YOU USED TO BE 'SLOSHY THE SNOWMAN'? MY, HOW THE JERKY HAVE FALLEN..!
SPLISH!
I REGRETTED THAT COMMENT ALMOST IMMEDIATELY.
SSSST!
END²

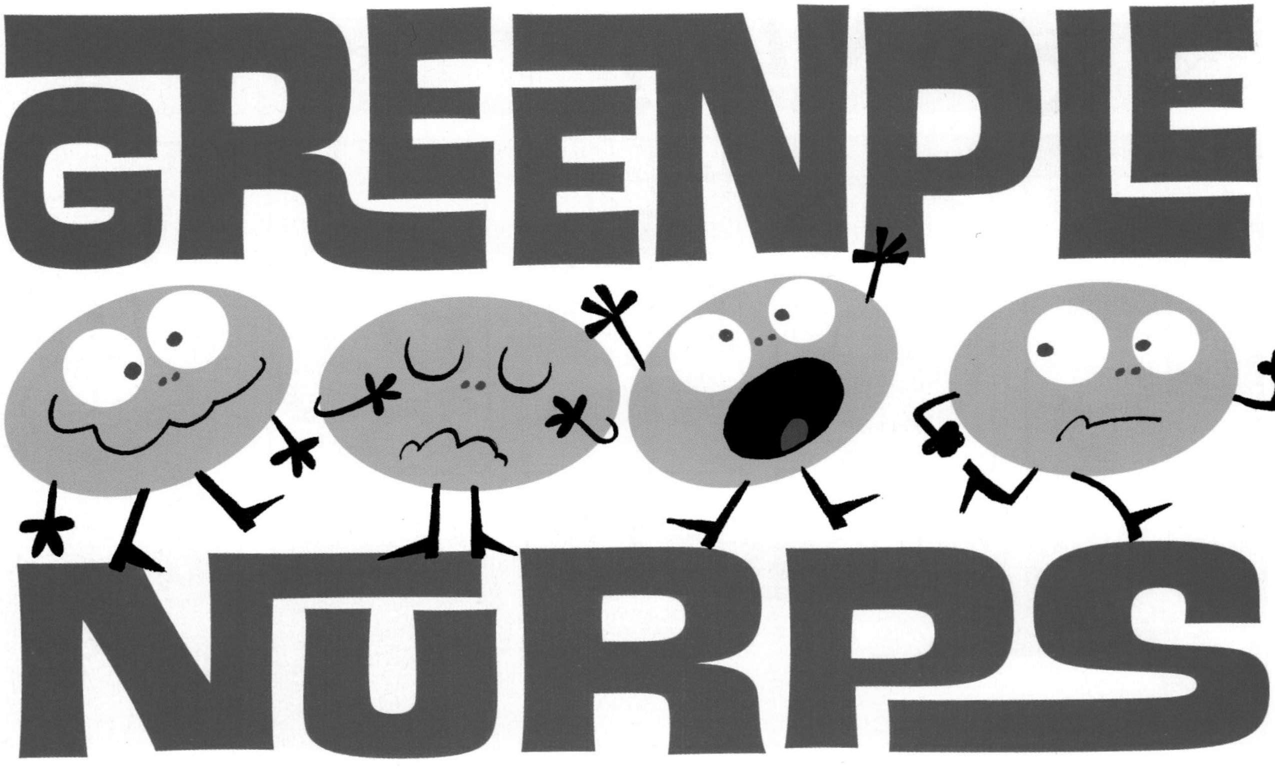
GREENPLE
NURPS

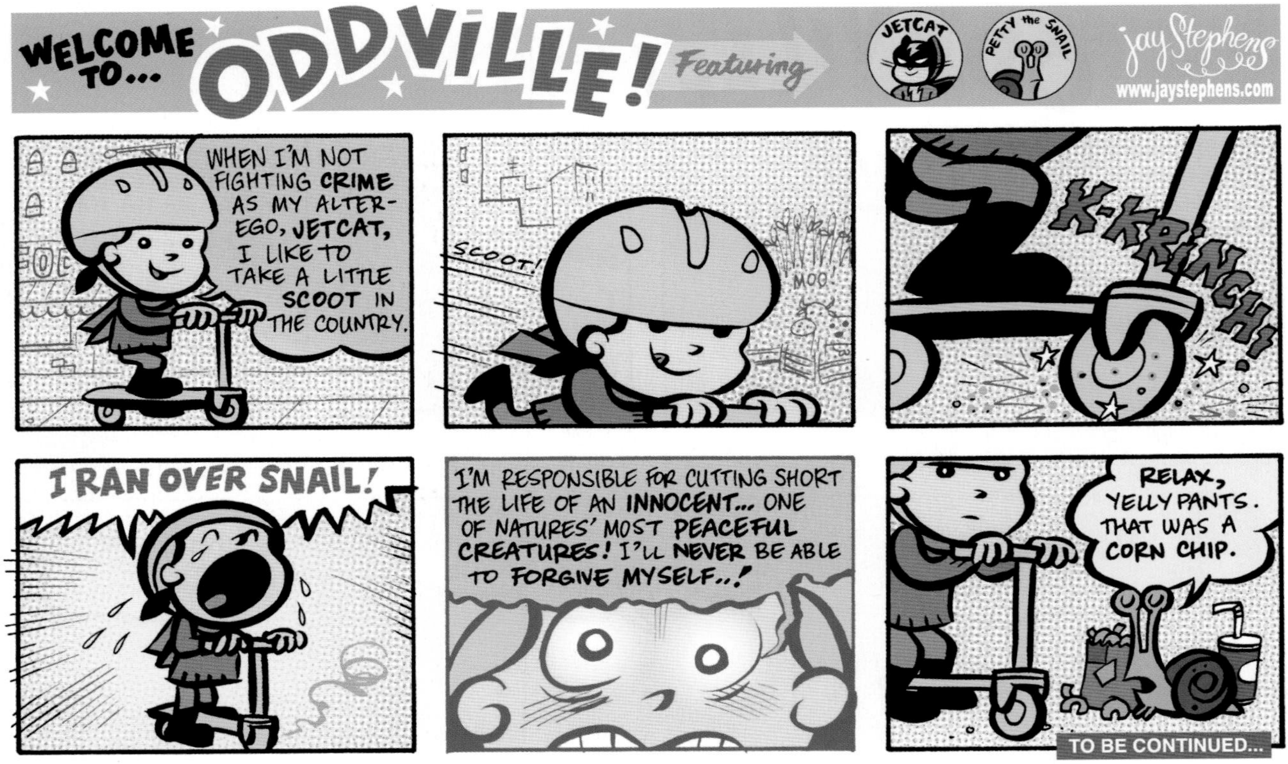
WELCOME TO... ODDVILLE!
Featuring
JETCAT
PETTY the SNAIL
jay Stephens
www.jaystephens.com
WHEN I'M NOT FIGHTING CRIME AS MY ALTER-EGO, JETCAT, I LIKE TO TAKE A LITTLE SCOOT IN THE COUNTRY.
SCOOT!
MOO!
K-KRINCH!
I RAN OVER SNAIL!
I'M RESPONSIBLE FOR CUTTING SHORT THE LIFE OF AN INNOCENT... ONE OF NATURES' MOST PEACEFUL CREATURES! I'LL NEVER BE ABLE TO FORGIVE MYSELF...!
RELAX, YELLY PANTS. THAT WAS A CORN CHIP.
TO BE CONTINUED...

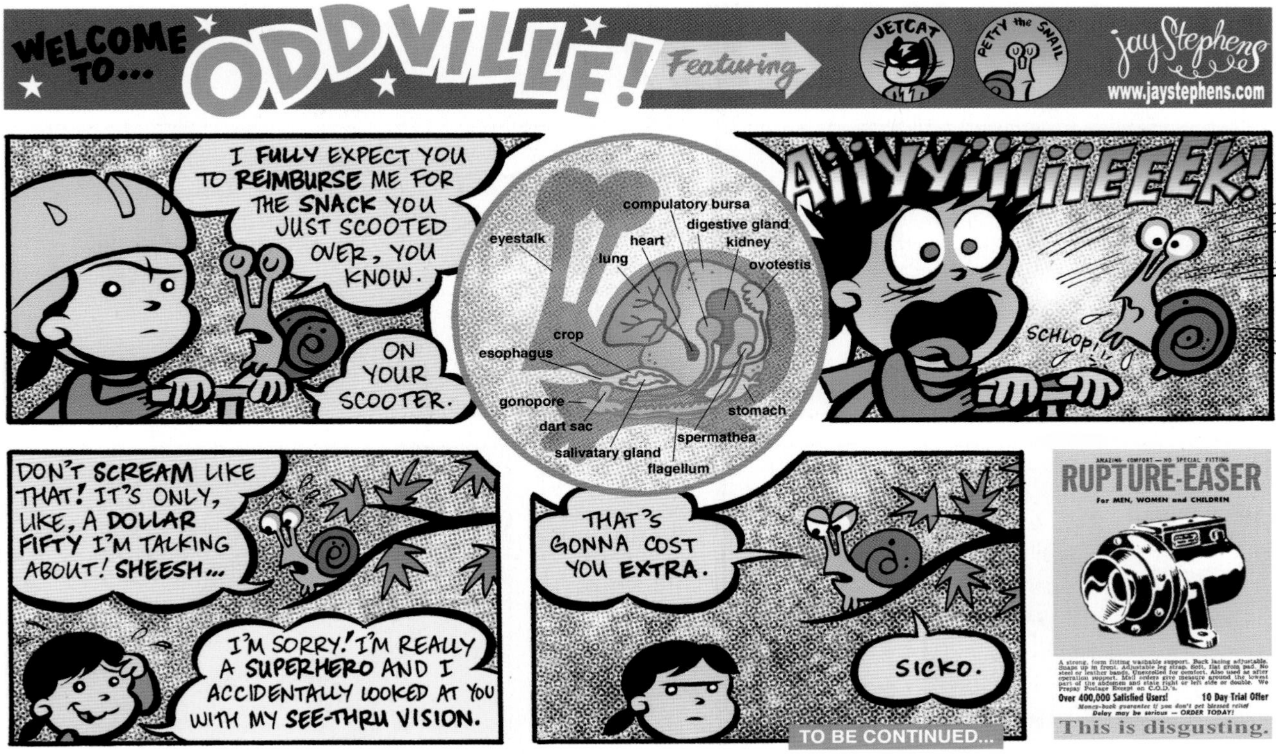
WELCOME TO... ODDVILLE! Featuring
JETCAT
PETTY the SNAIL
jay Stephens
www.jaystephens.com
I FULLY EXPECT YOU TO REIMBURSE ME FOR THE SNACK YOU JUST SCOOTED OVER, YOU KNOW.
ON YOUR SCOOTER.
eyestalk
lung
heart
compulatory bursa
digestive gland
kidney
ovotestis
crop
esophagus
gonopore
dart sac
salivatary gland
flagellum
spermathea
stomach
AIIYYIIIIIIEEEK!
SCHLOP!
DON'T SCREAM LIKE THAT! IT'S ONLY, LIKE, A DOLLAR FIFTY I'M TALKING ABOUT! SHEESH...
I'M SORRY! I'M REALLY A SUPERHERO AND I ACCIDENTALLY LOOKED AT YOU WITH MY SEE-THRU VISION.
THAT'S GONNA COST YOU EXTRA.
SICKO.
TO BE CONTINUED...
AMAZING COMFORT — NO SPECIAL FITTING
RUPTURE-EASER
For MEN, WOMEN and CHILDREN
Over 400,000 Satisfied Users!
10 Day Trial Offer
This is disgusting.

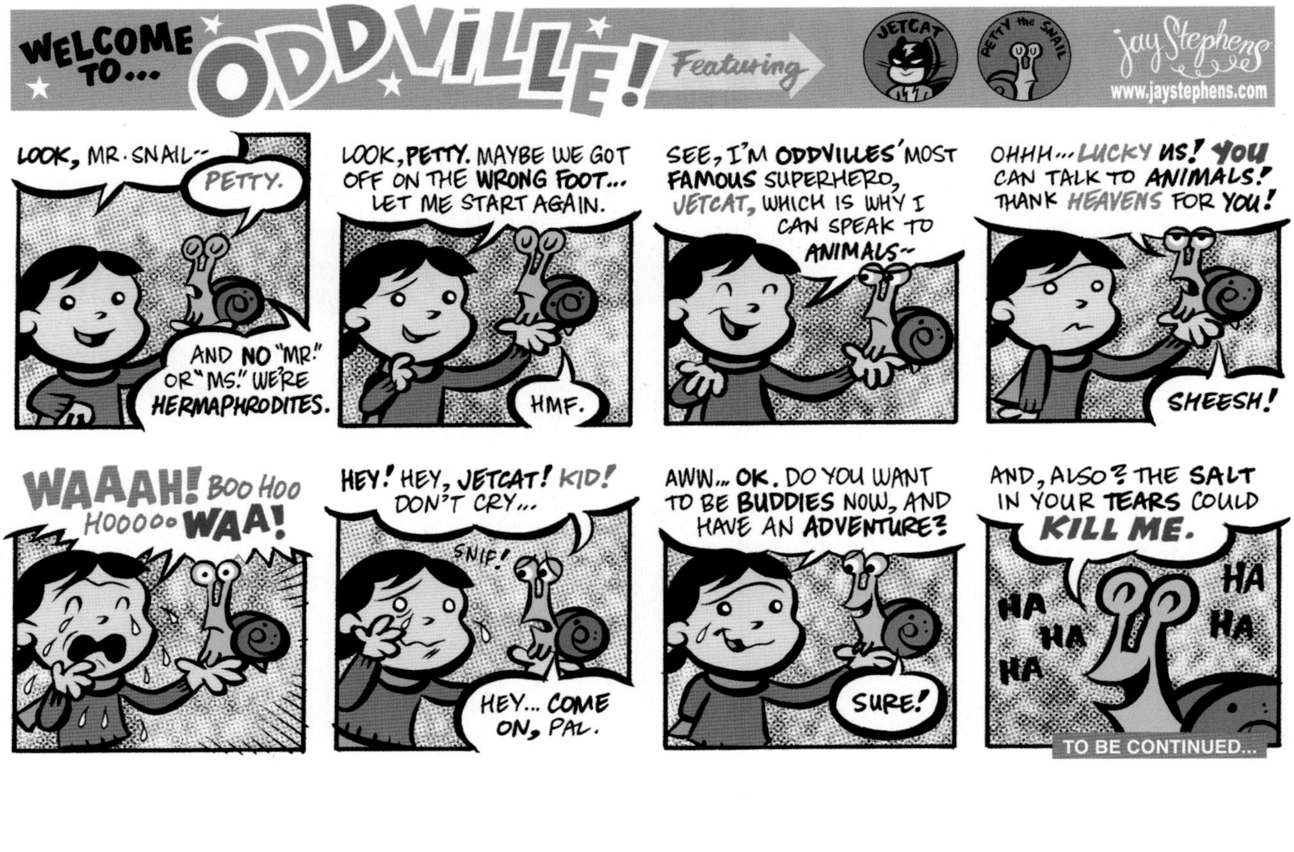
WELCOME TO... ODDVILLE! Featuring
JETCAT
PETTY the SNAIL
jay Stephens
www.jaystephens.com
LOOK, MR. SNAIL--
PETTY.
AND NO "MR." OR "MS." WE'RE HERMAPHRODITES.
LOOK, PETTY. MAYBE WE GOT OFF ON THE WRONG FOOT... LET ME START AGAIN.
HMF.
SEE, I'M ODDVILLES' MOST FAMOUS SUPERHERO, JETCAT, WHICH IS WHY I CAN SPEAK TO ANIMALS--
OHHH... LUCKY US! YOU CAN TALK TO ANIMALS! THANK HEAVENS FOR YOU!
SHEESH!
WAAAH! BOO HOO HOOOOO WAA!
HEY! HEY, JETCAT! KID! DON'T CRY...
SNIF!
HEY... COME ON, PAL.
AWW... OK. DO YOU WANT TO BE BUDDIES NOW, AND HAVE AN ADVENTURE?
SURE!
AND, ALSO? THE SALT IN YOUR TEARS COULD KILL ME.
HA HA HA HA HA
TO BE CONTINUED...

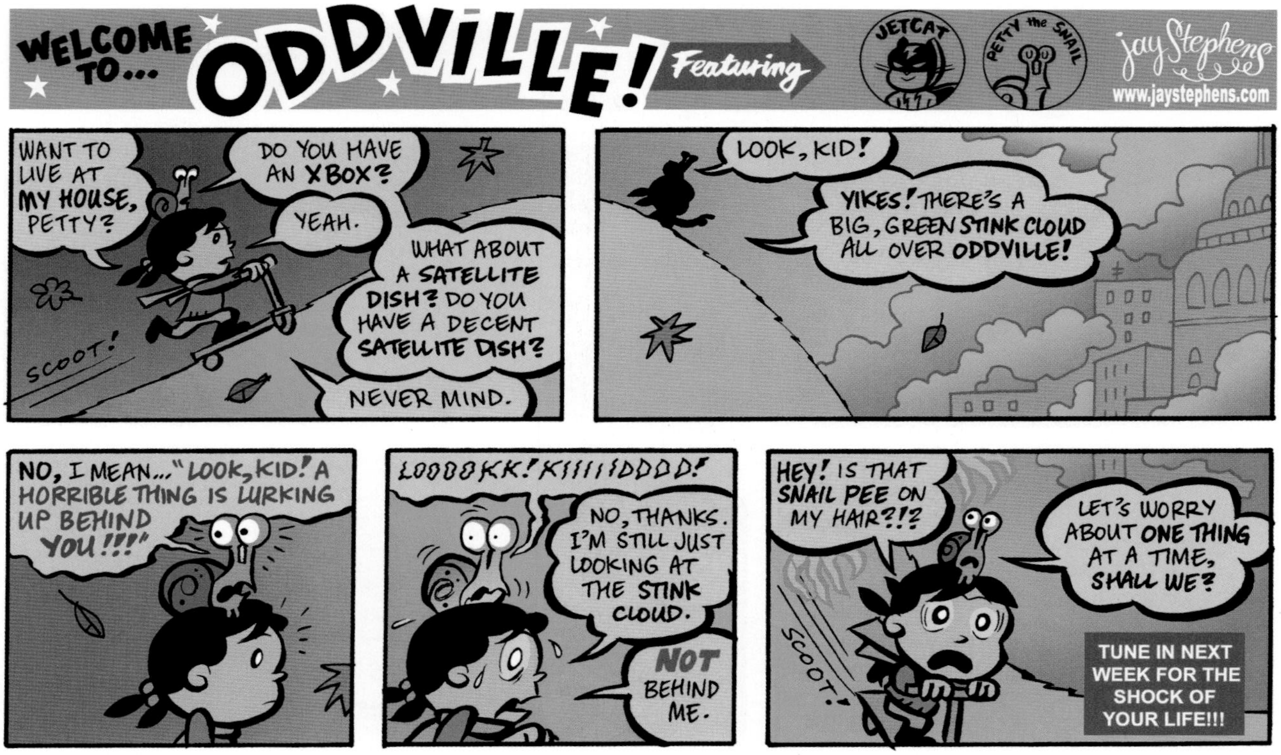
WELCOME TO... ODDVILLE!
Featuring
JETCAT
PETTY the SNAIL
jay Stephens
www.jaystephens.com
WANT TO LIVE AT MY HOUSE, PETTY?
DO YOU HAVE AN XBOX?
YEAH.
WHAT ABOUT A SATELLITE DISH? DO YOU HAVE A DECENT SATELLITE DISH?
NEVER MIND.
SCOOT!
LOOK, KID!
YIKES! THERE'S A BIG, GREEN STINK CLOUD ALL OVER ODDVILLE!
NO, I MEAN..."LOOK, KID! A HORRIBLE THING IS LURKING UP BEHIND YOU!!!"
LOOOOKK! KIIIIIDDDD!
NO, THANKS. I'M STILL JUST LOOKING AT THE STINK CLOUD.
NOT BEHIND ME.
HEY! IS THAT SNAIL PEE ON MY HAIR?!?
LET'S WORRY ABOUT ONE THING AT A TIME, SHALL WE?
SCOOT!
TUNE IN NEXT WEEK FOR THE SHOCK OF YOUR LIFE!!!

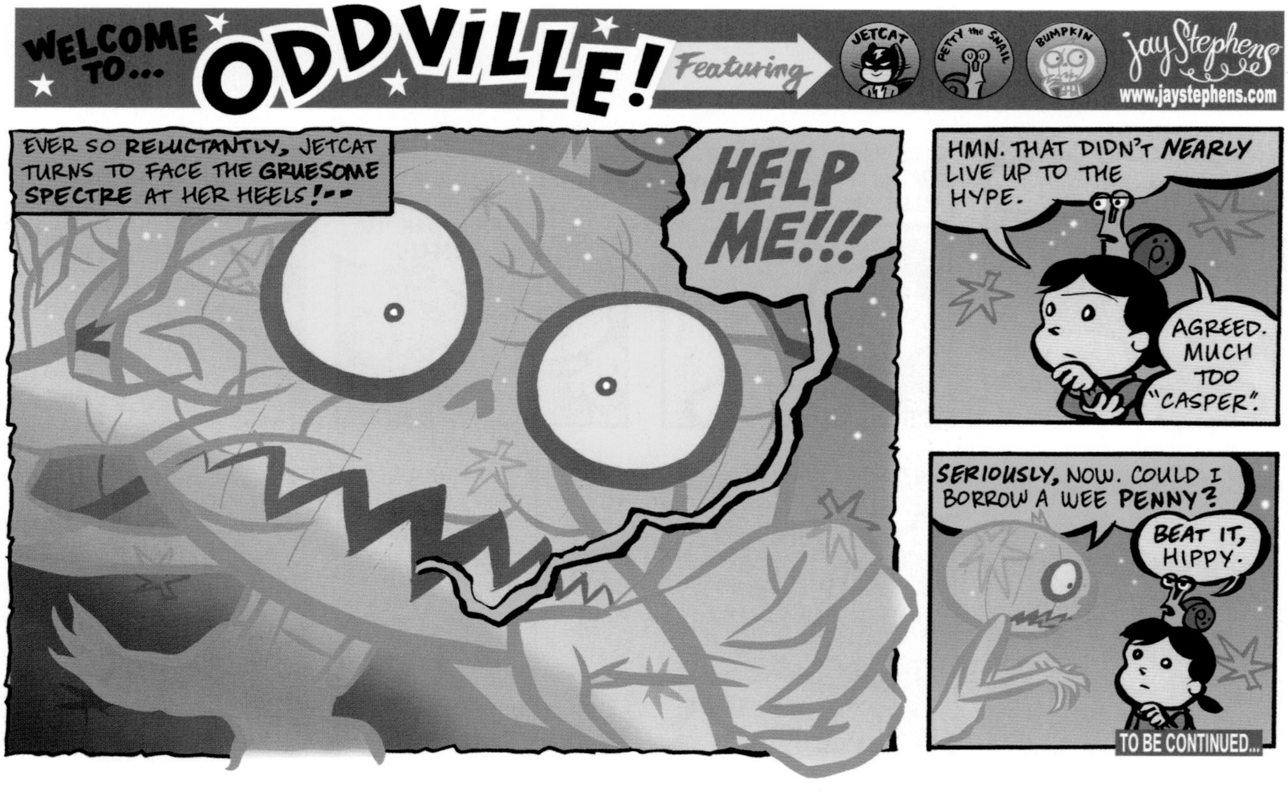
WELCOME TO... ODDVILLE!
Featuring
JETCAT
PETTY the SNAIL
BUMPKIN
jay Stephens
www.jaystephens.com
EVER SO RELUCTANTLY, JETCAT TURNS TO FACE THE GRUESOME SPECTRE AT HER HEELS!..
HELP ME!!!
HMN. THAT DIDN'T NEARLY LIVE UP TO THE HYPE.
AGREED. MUCH TOO "CASPER".
SERIOUSLY, NOW. COULD I BORROW A WEE PENNY?
BEAT IT, HIPPY.
TO BE CONTINUED...

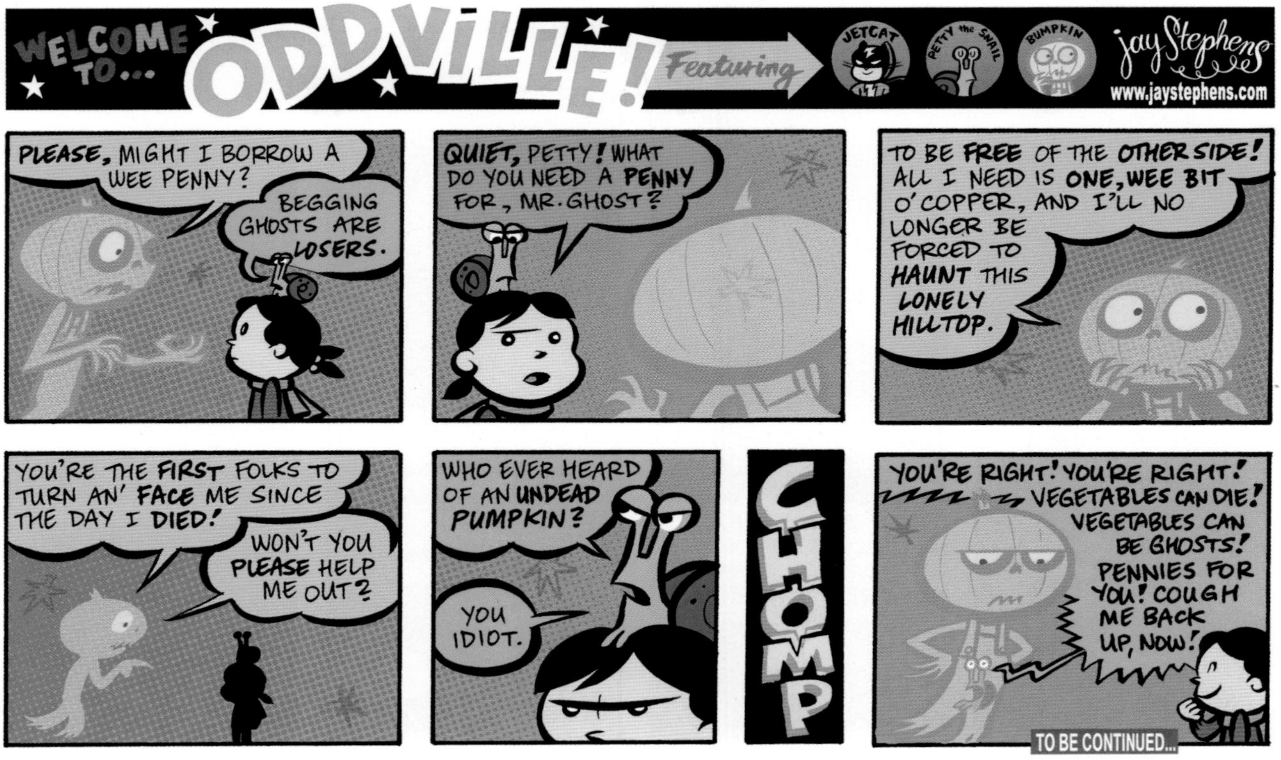
WELCOME TO... ODDVILLE!
Featuring
JETCAT
PETTY the SNAIL
BUMPKIN
jay Stephens
www.jaystephens.com
PLEASE, MIGHT I BORROW A WEE PENNY?
BEGGING GHOSTS ARE LOSERS.
QUIET, PETTY! WHAT DO YOU NEED A PENNY FOR, MR. GHOST?
TO BE FREE OF THE OTHER SIDE! ALL I NEED IS ONE, WEE BIT O' COPPER, AND I'LL NO LONGER BE FORCED TO HAUNT THIS LONELY HILLTOP.
YOU'RE THE FIRST FOLKS TO TURN AN' FACE ME SINCE THE DAY I DIED!
WON'T YOU PLEASE HELP ME OUT?
WHO EVER HEARD OF AN UNDEAD PUMPKIN?
YOU IDIOT.
CHOMP
YOU'RE RIGHT! YOU'RE RIGHT! VEGETABLES CAN DIE! VEGETABLES CAN BE GHOSTS! PENNIES FOR YOU! COUGH ME BACK UP, NOW!
TO BE CONTINUED...

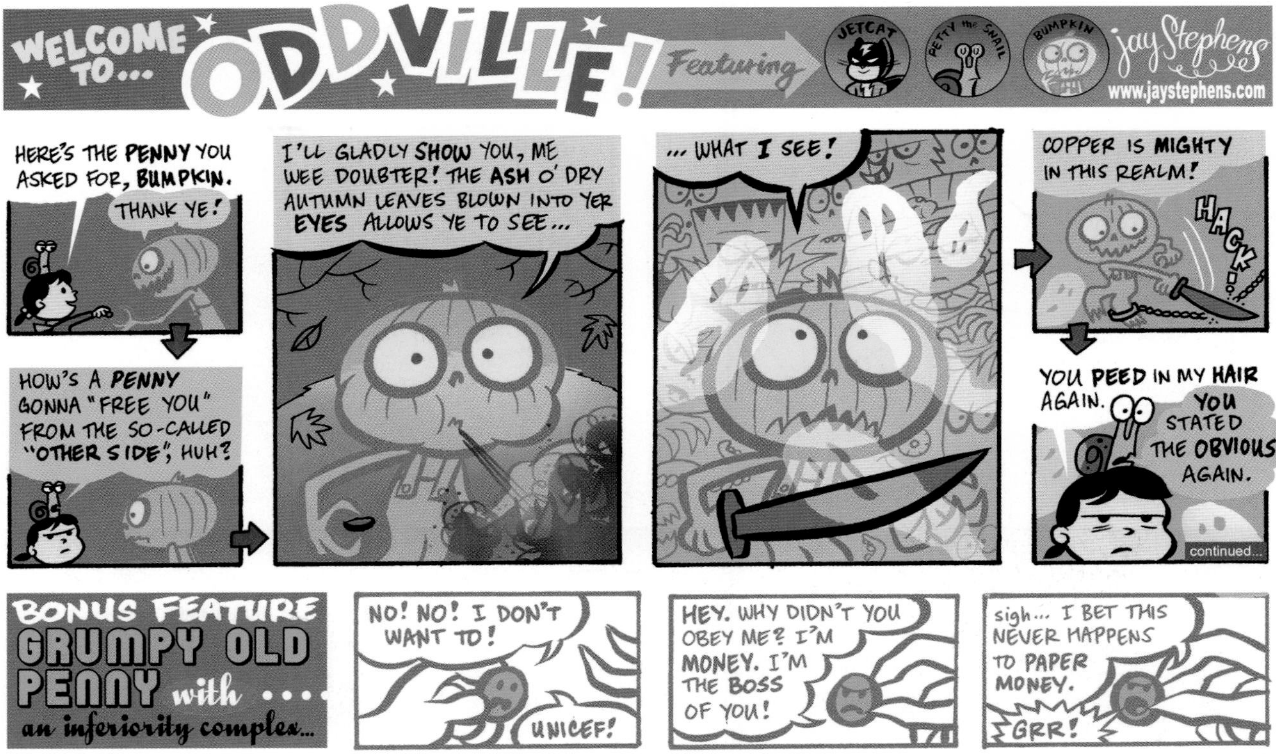
WELCOME TO... ODDVILLE!
Featuring
JETCAT
PETTY the SNAIL
BUMPKIN
jay Stephens
www.jaystephens.com
HERE'S THE PENNY YOU ASKED FOR, BUMPKIN.
THANK YE!
HOW'S A PENNY GONNA "FREE YOU" FROM THE SO-CALLED "OTHER SIDE", HUH?
I'LL GLADLY SHOW YOU, ME WEE DOUBTER! THE ASH O' DRY AUTUMN LEAVES BLOWN INTO YER EYES ALLOWS YE TO SEE...
... WHAT I SEE!
COPPER IS MIGHTY IN THIS REALM!
HACK!
YOU PEED IN MY HAIR AGAIN.
YOU STATED THE OBVIOUS. AGAIN.
continued...
BONUS FEATURE
GRUMPY OLD PENNY with .... an inferiority complex...
NO! NO! I DON'T WANT TO!
UNICEF!
HEY. WHY DIDN'T YOU OBEY ME? I'M MONEY. I'M THE BOSS OF YOU!
sigh... I BET THIS NEVER HAPPENS TO PAPER MONEY.
GRR!

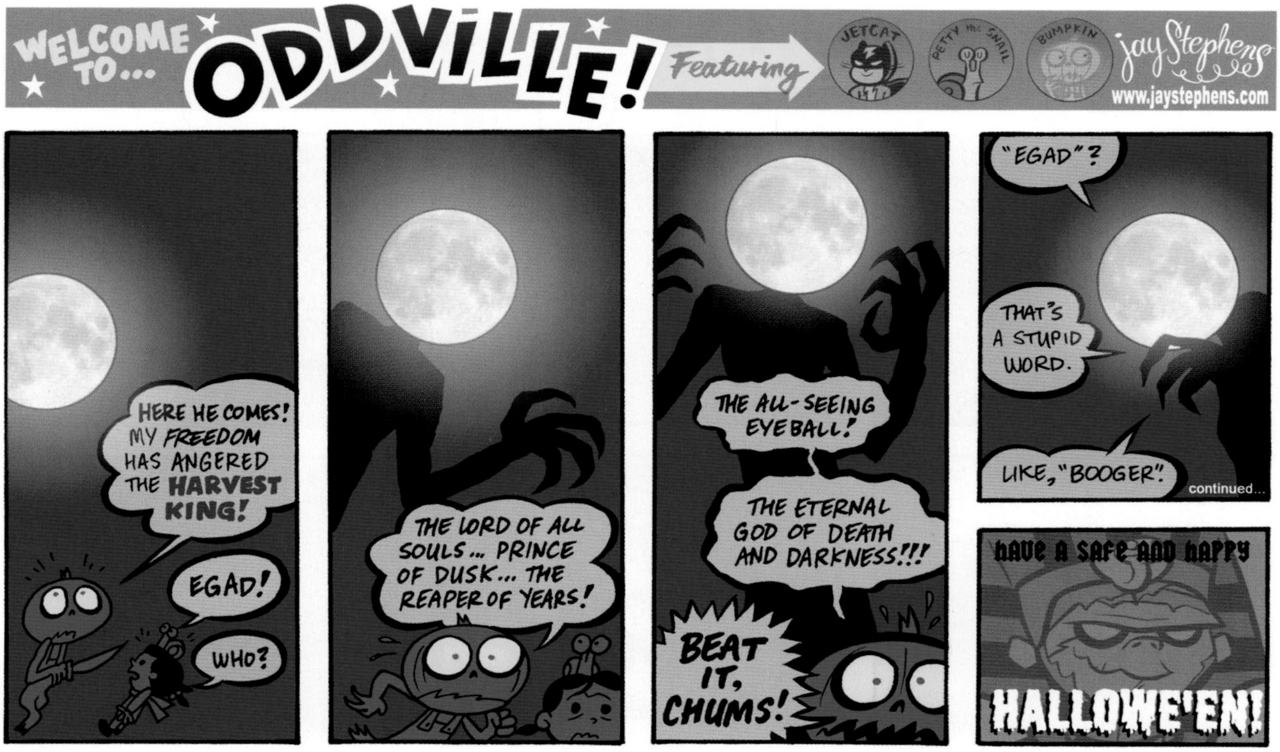
WELCOME TO... ODDVILLE!
Featuring
JETCAT
PETTY the SNAIL
BUMPKIN
jay Stephens
www.jaystephens.com
HERE HE COMES! MY FREEDOM HAS ANGERED THE HARVEST KING!
EGAD!
WHO?
THE LORD OF ALL SOULS... PRINCE OF DUSK... THE REAPER OF YEARS!
THE ALL-SEEING EYEBALL!
THE ETERNAL GOD OF DEATH AND DARKNESS!!!
BEAT IT, CHUMS!
"EGAD"?
THAT'S A STUPID WORD.
LIKE, "BOOGER".
continued...
HAVE A SAFE AND HAPPY
HALLOWE'EN!

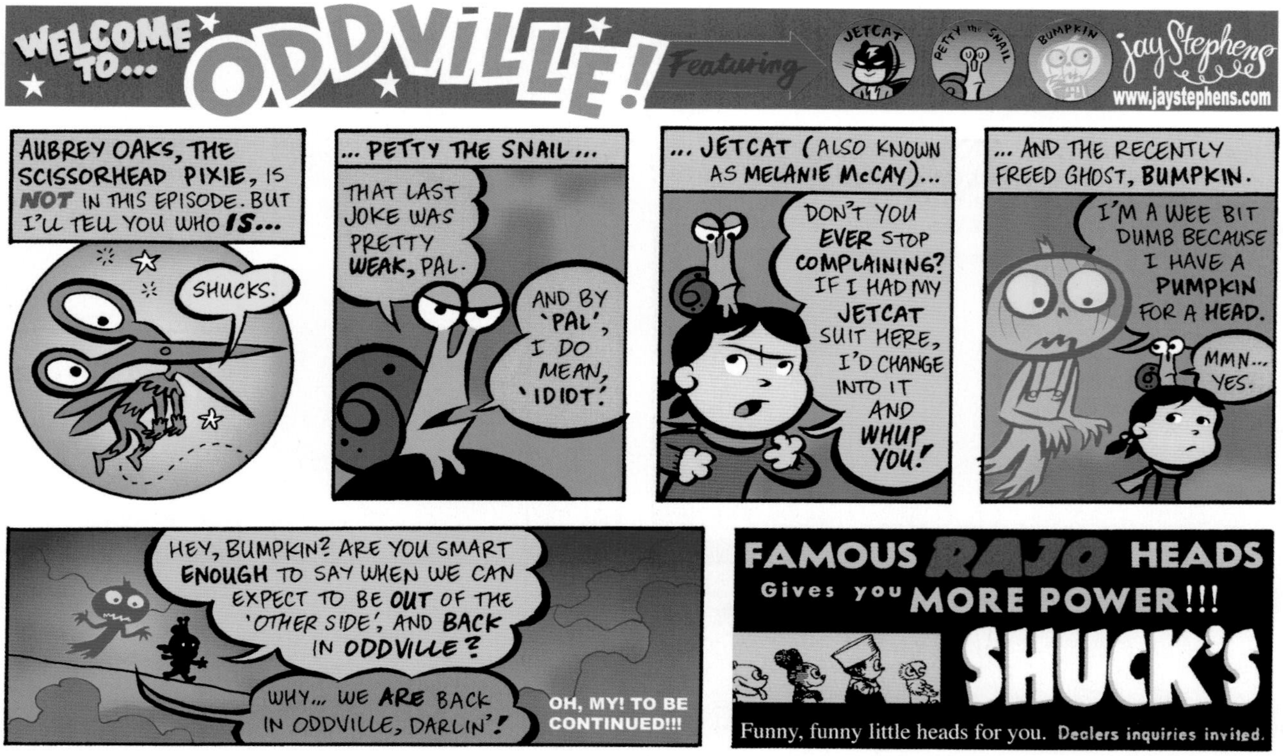
WELCOME TO... ODDVILLE!
Featuring
JETCAT
PETTY the SNAIL
BUMPKIN
jay Stephens
www.jaystephens.com
AUBREY OAKS, THE SCISSORHEAD PIXIE, IS NOT IN THIS EPISODE. BUT I'LL TELL YOU WHO IS...
SHUCKS.
... PETTY THE SNAIL...
THAT LAST JOKE WAS PRETTY WEAK, PAL.
AND BY 'PAL', I DO MEAN, 'IDIOT'.
... JETCAT (ALSO KNOWN AS MELANIE McCAY)...
DON'T YOU EVER STOP COMPLAINING? IF I HAD MY JETCAT SUIT HERE, I'D CHANGE INTO IT AND WHUP YOU!
... AND THE RECENTLY FREED GHOST, BUMPKIN.
I'M A WEE BIT DUMB BECAUSE I HAVE A PUMPKIN FOR A HEAD.
MMN... YES.
HEY, BUMPKIN? ARE YOU SMART ENOUGH TO SAY WHEN WE CAN EXPECT TO BE OUT OF THE 'OTHER SIDE', AND BACK IN ODDVILLE?
WHY... WE ARE BACK IN ODDVILLE, DARLIN'!
OH, MY! TO BE CONTINUED!!!
FAMOUS RAJO HEADS
Gives you MORE POWER!!!
SHUCK'S
Funny, funny little heads for you. Dealers inquiries invited.

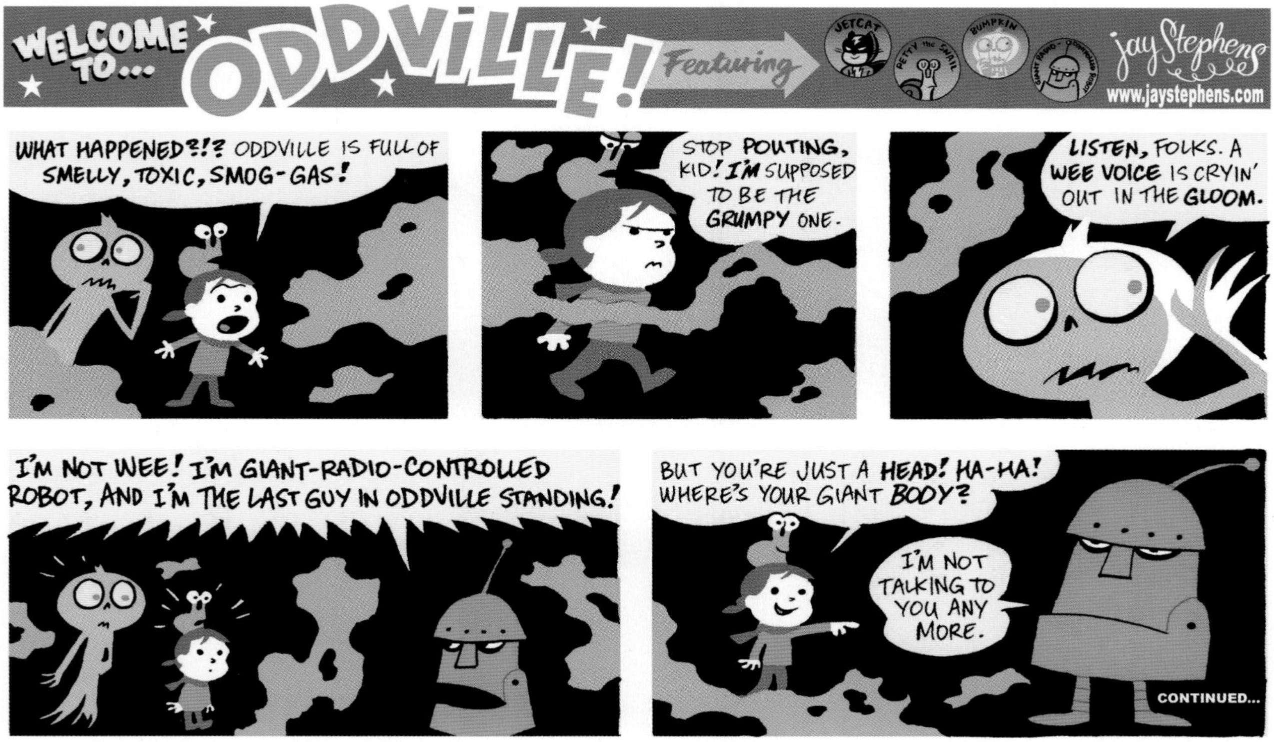
WELCOME TO... ODDVILLE!
Featuring
JETCAT
PETTY the SNAIL
BUMPKIN
jay Stephens
www.jaystephens.com
WHAT HAPPENED?!? ODDVILLE IS FULL OF SMELLY, TOXIC, SMOG-GAS!
STOP POUTING, KID! I'M SUPPOSED TO BE THE GRUMPY ONE.
LISTEN, FOLKS. A WEE VOICE IS CRYIN' OUT IN THE GLOOM.
I'M NOT WEE! I'M GIANT-RADIO-CONTROLLED ROBOT, AND I'M THE LAST GUY IN ODDVILLE STANDING!
BUT YOU'RE JUST A HEAD! HA-HA! WHERE'S YOUR GIANT BODY?
I'M NOT TALKING TO YOU ANY MORE.
CONTINUED...

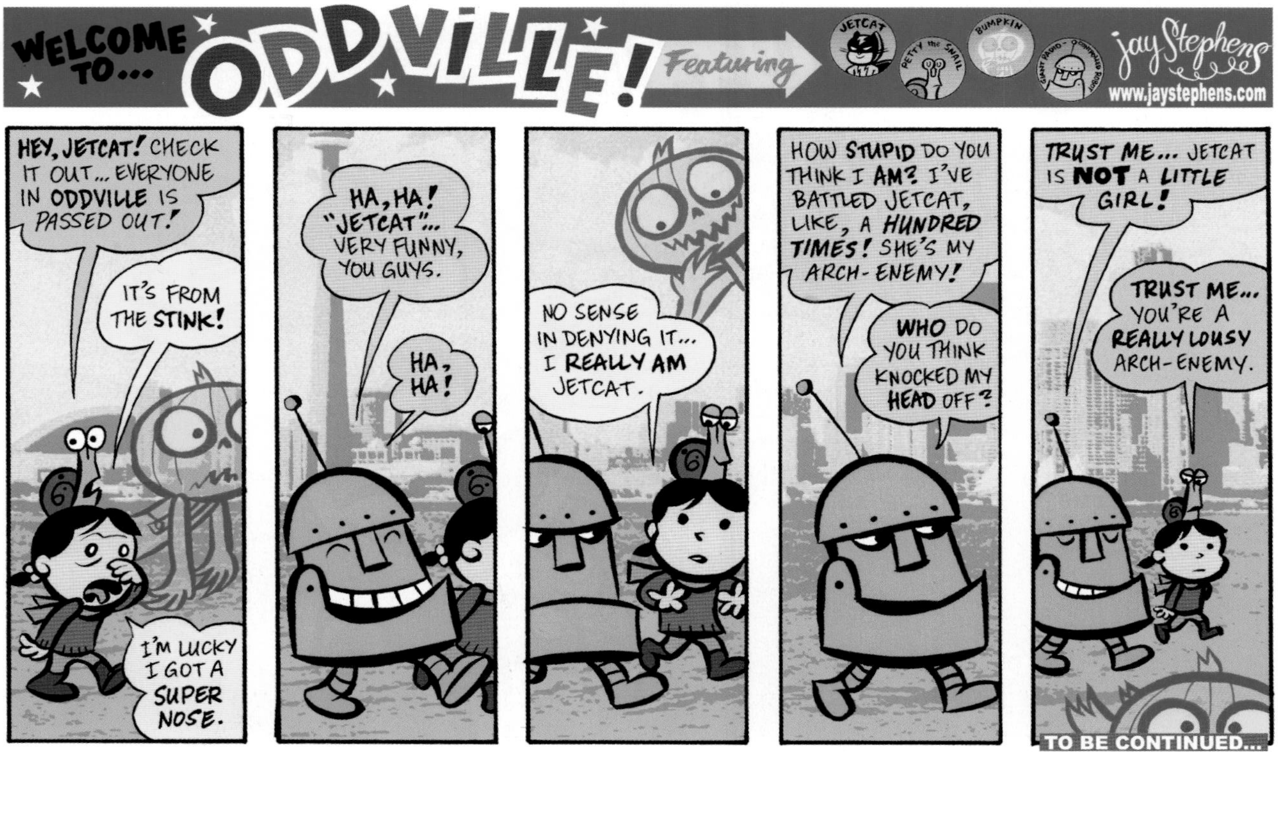
WELCOME TO... ODDVILLE!
Featuring
JETCAT
PETTY the SNAIL
BUMPKIN
jay Stephens
www.jaystephens.com
HEY, JETCAT! CHECK IT OUT... EVERYONE IN ODDVILLE IS PASSED OUT!
IT'S FROM THE STINK!
I'M LUCKY I GOT A SUPER NOSE.
HA, HA! "JETCAT"... VERY FUNNY, YOU GUYS.
HA, HA!
NO SENSE IN DENYING IT... I REALLY AM JETCAT.
HOW STUPID DO YOU THINK I AM? I'VE BATTLED JETCAT, LIKE, A HUNDRED TIMES! SHE'S MY ARCH-ENEMY!
WHO DO YOU THINK KNOCKED MY HEAD OFF?
TRUST ME... JETCAT IS NOT A LITTLE GIRL!
TRUST ME... YOU'RE A REALLY LOUSY ARCH-ENEMY.
TO BE CONTINUED...

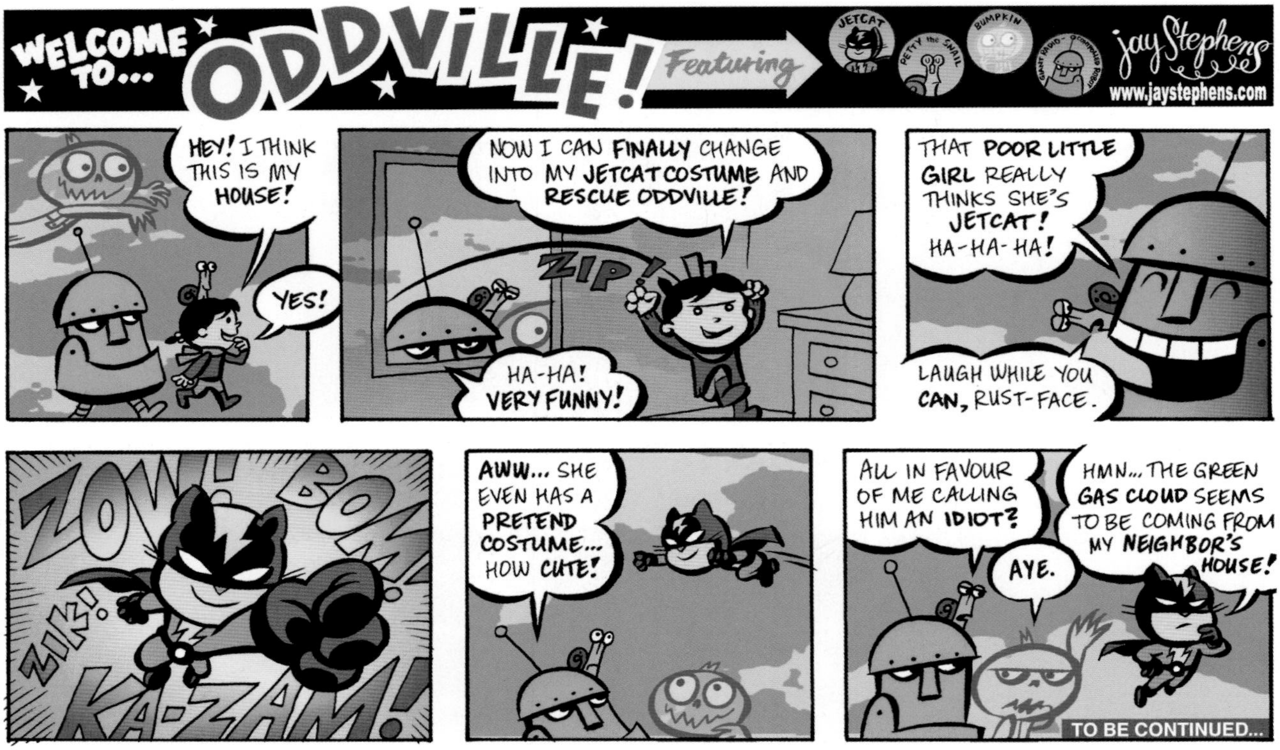
WELCOME TO... ODDVILLE!
Featuring
JETCAT
PETTY the SNAIL
BUMPKIN
jay Stephens
www.jaystephens.com
HEY! I THINK THIS IS MY HOUSE!
YES!
NOW I CAN FINALLY CHANGE INTO MY JETCAT COSTUME AND RESCUE ODDVILLE!
ZIP!
HA-HA! VERY FUNNY!
THAT POOR LITTLE GIRL REALLY THINKS SHE'S JETCAT! HA-HA-HA!
LAUGH WHILE YOU CAN, RUST-FACE.
ZOW! BOM! ZIK! KA-ZAM!
AWW... SHE EVEN HAS A PRETEND COSTUME... HOW CUTE!
ALL IN FAVOUR OF ME CALLING HIM AN IDIOT?
AYE.
HMN... THE GREEN GAS CLOUD SEEMS TO BE COMING FROM MY NEIGHBOR'S HOUSE!
TO BE CONTINUED...

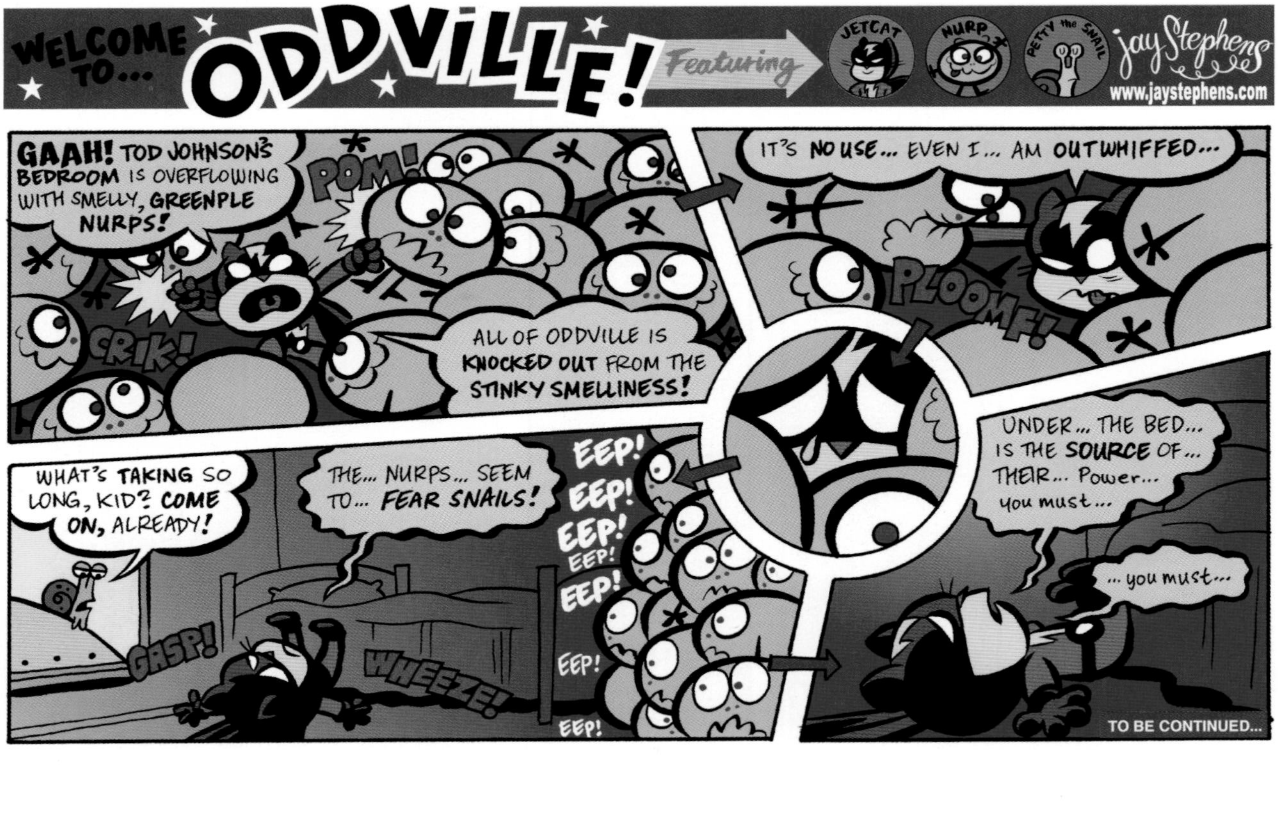
WELCOME TO... ODDVILLE!
Featuring
JETCAT
NURP
PETTY the SNAIL
jay Stephens
www.jaystephens.com
GAAH! TOD JOHNSON'S BEDROOM IS OVERFLOWING WITH SMELLY, GREENPLE NURPS!
POM!
CRIK!
ALL OF ODDVILLE IS KNOCKED OUT FROM THE STINKY SMELLINESS!
IT'S NO USE... EVEN I... AM OUTWHIFFED...
PLOOMF!
UNDER... THE BED... IS THE SOURCE OF... THEIR... Power... you must...
... you must...
WHAT'S TAKING SO LONG, KID? COME ON, ALREADY!
THE... NURPS... SEEM TO... FEAR SNAILS!
EEP! EEP! EEP! EEP! EEP! EEP! EEP!
GASP!
WHEEZE!
TO BE CONTINUED...

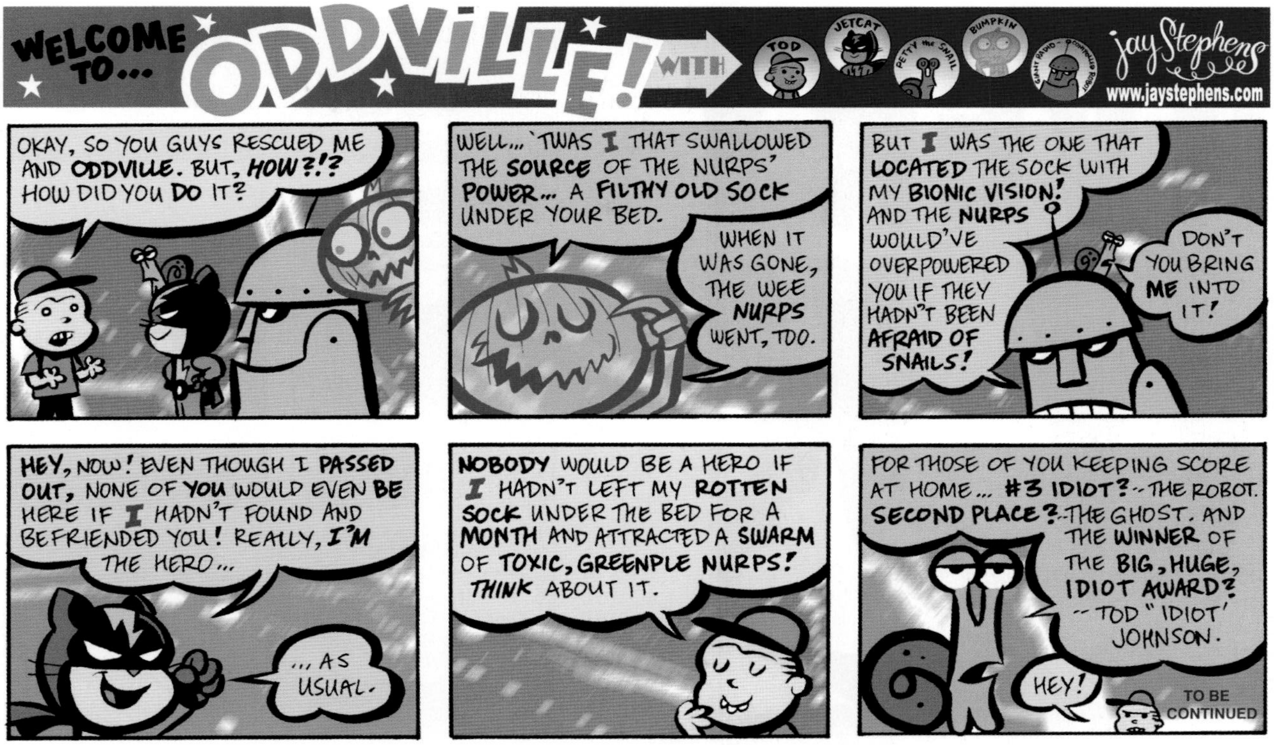
WELCOME TO... ODDVILLE! WITH
TOD
JETCAT
PETTY the SNAIL
BUMPKIN
jay Stephens
www.jaystephens.com
OKAY, SO YOU GUYS RESCUED ME AND ODDVILLE. BUT, HOW?!? HOW DID YOU DO IT?
WELL... 'TWAS I THAT SWALLOWED THE SOURCE OF THE NURPS' POWER... A FILTHY OLD SOCK UNDER YOUR BED.
WHEN IT WAS GONE, THE WEE NURPS WENT, TOO.
BUT I WAS THE ONE THAT LOCATED THE SOCK WITH MY BIONIC VISION! AND THE NURPS WOULD'VE OVERPOWERED YOU IF THEY HADN'T BEEN AFRAID OF SNAILS!
DON'T YOU BRING ME INTO IT!
HEY, NOW! EVEN THOUGH I PASSED OUT, NONE OF YOU WOULD EVEN BE HERE IF I HADN'T FOUND AND BEFRIENDED YOU! REALLY, I'M THE HERO...
...AS USUAL.
NOBODY WOULD BE A HERO IF I HADN'T LEFT MY ROTTEN SOCK UNDER THE BED FOR A MONTH AND ATTRACTED A SWARM OF TOXIC, GREENPLE NURPS! THINK ABOUT IT.
FOR THOSE OF YOU KEEPING SCORE AT HOME... #3 IDIOT?-- THE ROBOT. SECOND PLACE?-- THE GHOST. AND THE WINNER OF THE BIG, HUGE, IDIOT AWARD? -- TOD "IDIOT" JOHNSON.
HEY!
TO BE CONTINUED

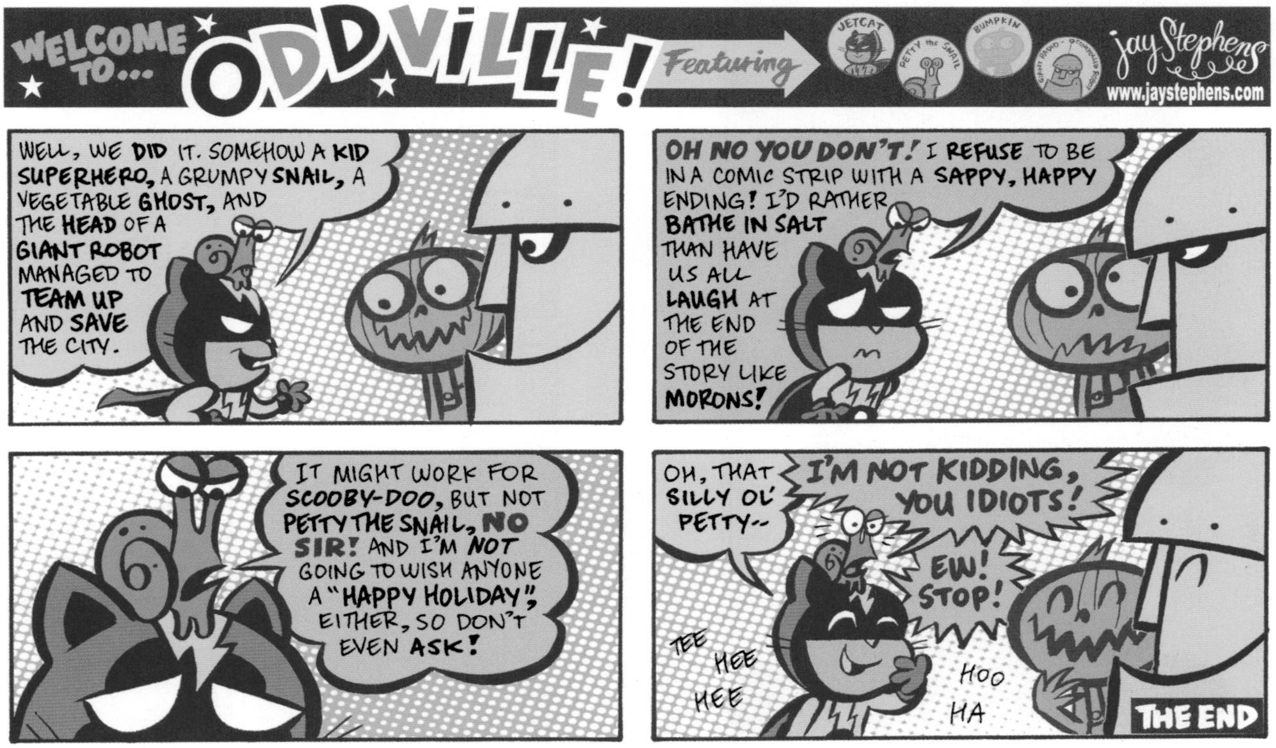
WELCOME TO... ODDVILLE! Featuring
JETCAT
PETTY the SNAIL
BUMPKIN
jay Stephens
www.jaystephens.com
WELL, WE DID IT. SOMEHOW A KID SUPERHERO, A GRUMPY SNAIL, A VEGETABLE GHOST, AND THE HEAD OF A GIANT ROBOT MANAGED TO TEAM UP AND SAVE THE CITY.
OH NO YOU DON'T! I REFUSE TO BE IN A COMIC STRIP WITH A SAPPY, HAPPY ENDING! I'D RATHER BATHE IN SALT THAN HAVE US ALL LAUGH AT THE END OF THE STORY LIKE MORONS!
IT MIGHT WORK FOR SCOOBY-DOO, BUT NOT PETTY THE SNAIL, NO SIR! AND I'M NOT GOING TO WISH ANYONE A "HAPPY HOLIDAY", EITHER, SO DON'T EVEN ASK!
OH, THAT SILLY OL' PETTY--
I'M NOT KIDDING, YOU IDIOTS!
EW! STOP!
TEE HEE HEE
HOO HA
THE END

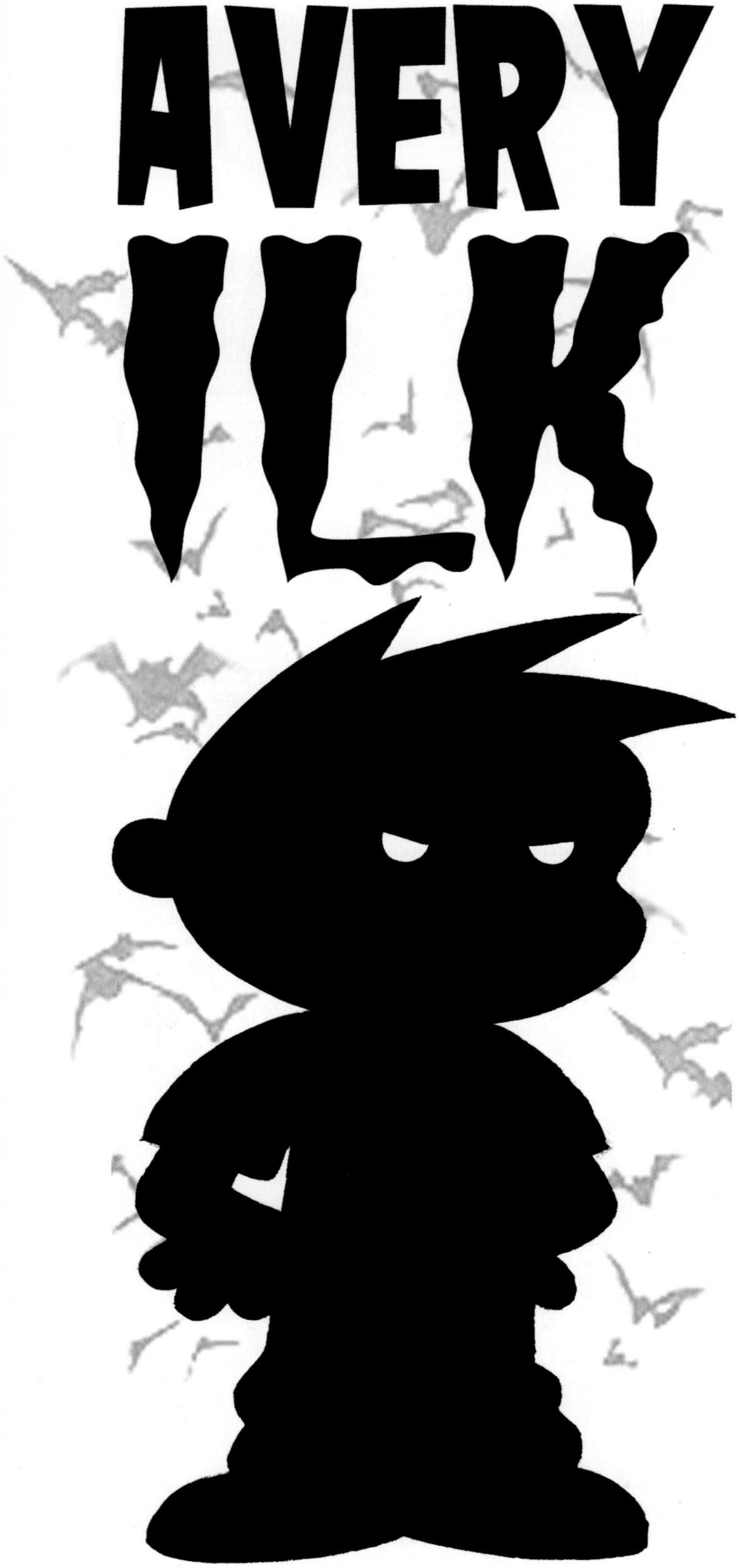
AVERY
ILK

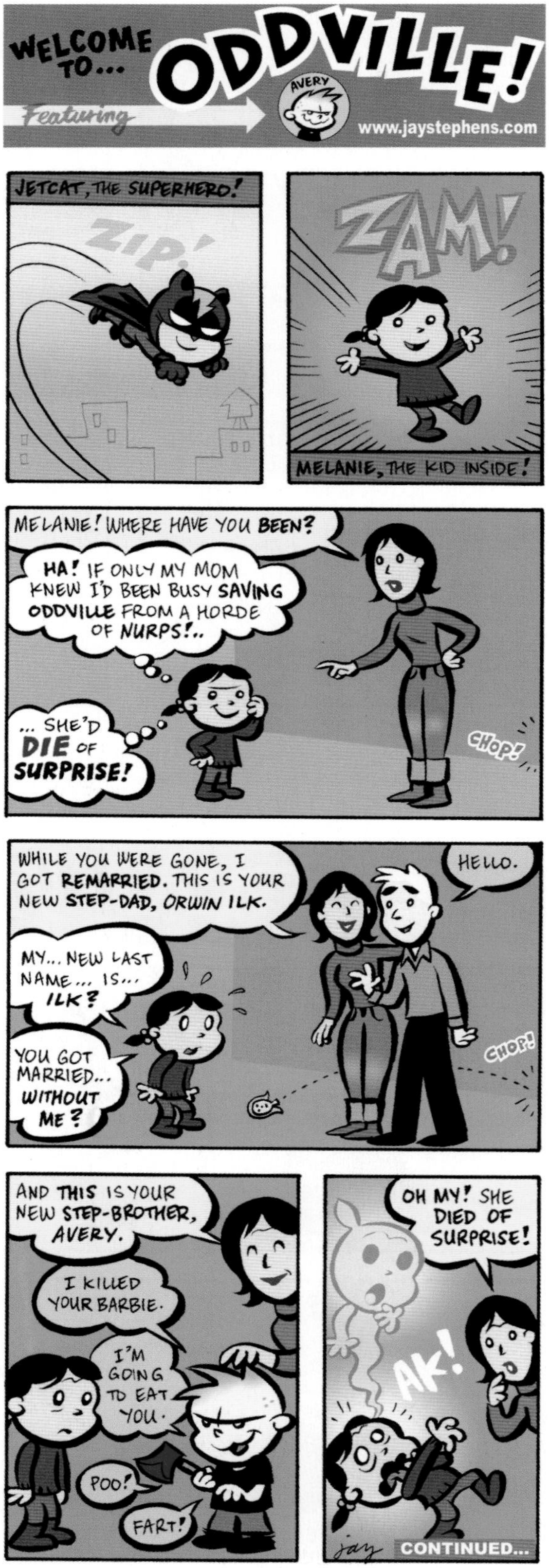
WELCOME TO...
ODDVILLE!
Featuring
AVERY
www.jaystephens.com
JETCAT, THE SUPERHERO!
ZIP!
ZAM!
MELANIE, THE KID INSIDE!
MELANIE! WHERE HAVE YOU BEEN?
HA! IF ONLY MY MOM KNEW I'D BEEN BUSY SAVING ODDVILLE FROM A HORDE OF NURPS!..
... SHE'D DIE OF SURPRISE!
CHOP!
WHILE YOU WERE GONE, I GOT REMARRIED. THIS IS YOUR NEW STEP-DAD, ORWIN ILK.
HELLO.
MY... NEW LAST NAME... IS... ILK?
YOU GOT MARRIED... WITHOUT ME?
CHOP!
AND THIS IS YOUR NEW STEP-BROTHER, AVERY.
I KILLED YOUR BARBIE.
I'M GOING TO EAT YOU.
POO!
FART!
OH MY! SHE DIED OF SURPRISE!
AK!
jay
CONTINUED...

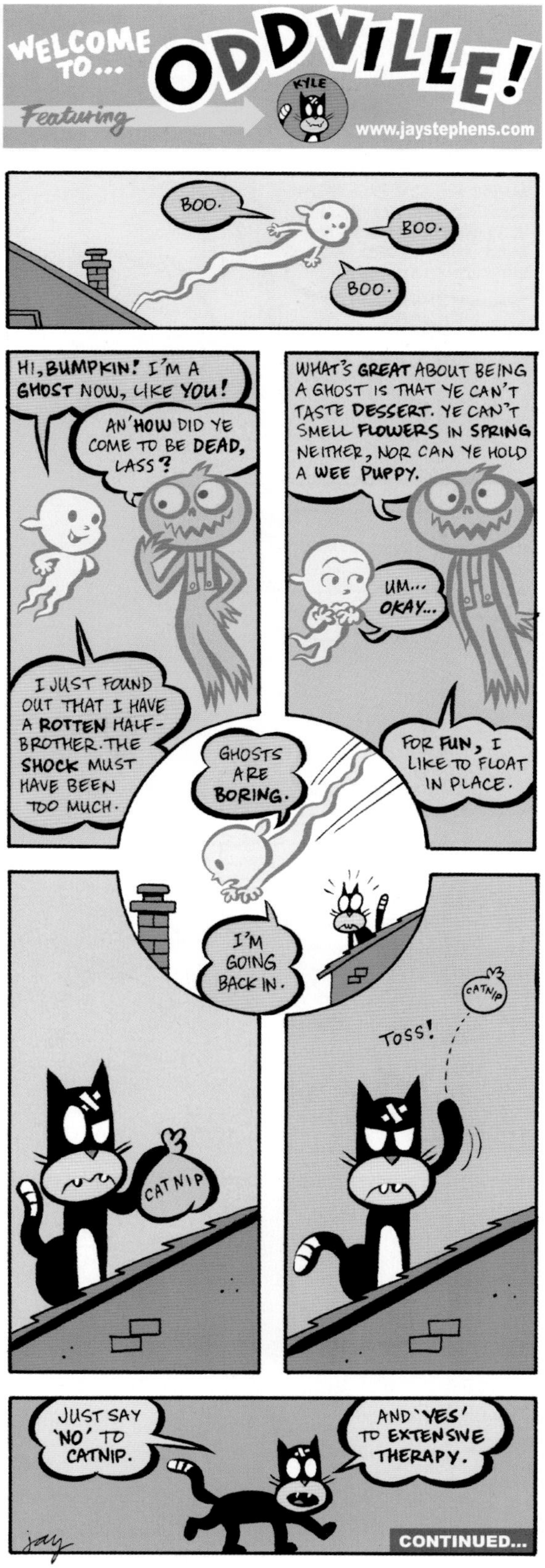

WELCOME TO...
ODDVILLE!
Featuring
KYLE
www.jaystephens.com
BOO.
BOO.
BOO.
HI, BUMPKIN! I'M A GHOST NOW, LIKE YOU!
AN' HOW DID YE COME TO BE DEAD, LASS?
I JUST FOUND OUT THAT I HAVE A ROTTEN HALF-BROTHER. THE SHOCK MUST HAVE BEEN TOO MUCH.
WHAT'S GREAT ABOUT BEING A GHOST IS THAT YE CAN'T TASTE DESSERT. YE CAN'T SMELL FLOWERS IN SPRING NEITHER, NOR CAN YE HOLD A WEE PUPPY.
UM... OKAY...
FOR FUN, I LIKE TO FLOAT IN PLACE.
GHOSTS ARE BORING.
I'M GOING BACK IN.
CATNIP
TOSS!
CATNIP
JUST SAY 'NO' TO CATNIP.
AND 'YES' TO EXTENSIVE THERAPY.
jay
CONTINUED...

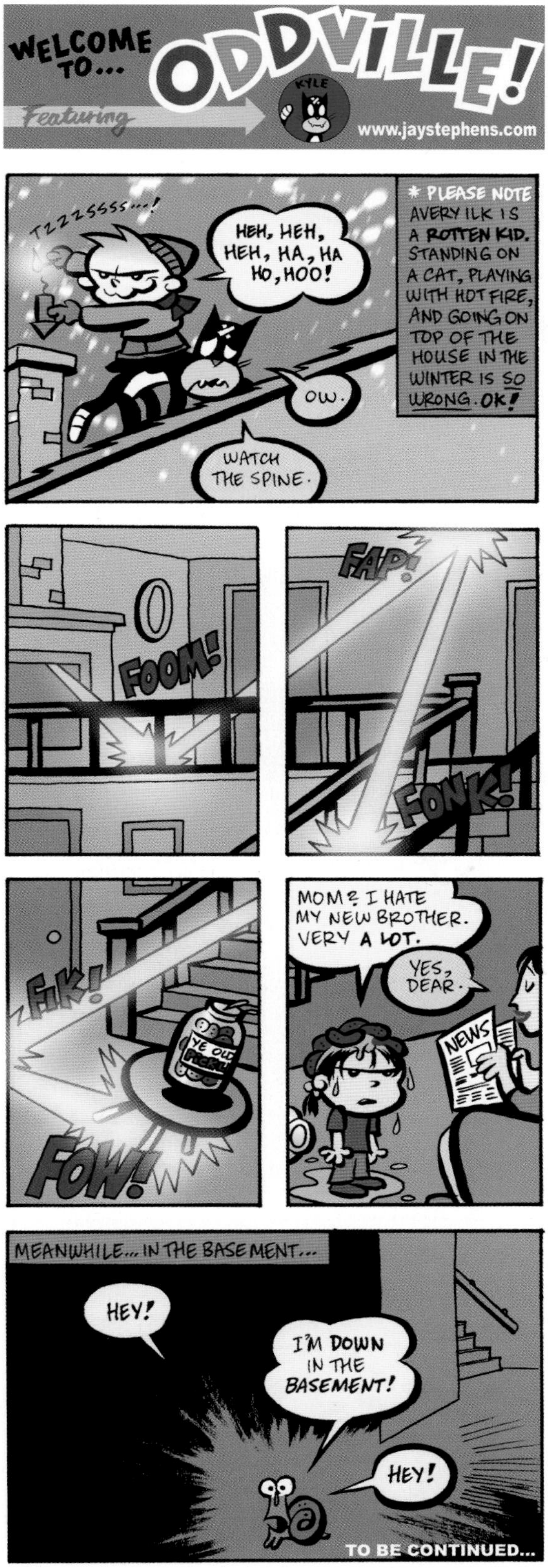

WELCOME TO...
ODDVILLE!
Featuring
KYLE
www.jaystephens.com
TZZZZSSSS...!
HEH, HEH, HEH, HA, HA HO, HOO!
* PLEASE NOTE AVERY ILK IS A ROTTEN KID. STANDING ON A CAT, PLAYING WITH HOT FIRE, AND GOING ON TOP OF THE HOUSE IN THE WINTER IS SO WRONG. OK!
OW.
WATCH THE SPINE.
FOOM!
FAP!
FONK!
FIK!
FOW!
MOM? I HATE MY NEW BROTHER. VERY A LOT.
YES, DEAR.
NEWS
MEANWHILE... IN THE BASEMENT...
HEY!
I'M DOWN IN THE BASEMENT!
HEY!
TO BE CONTINUED...

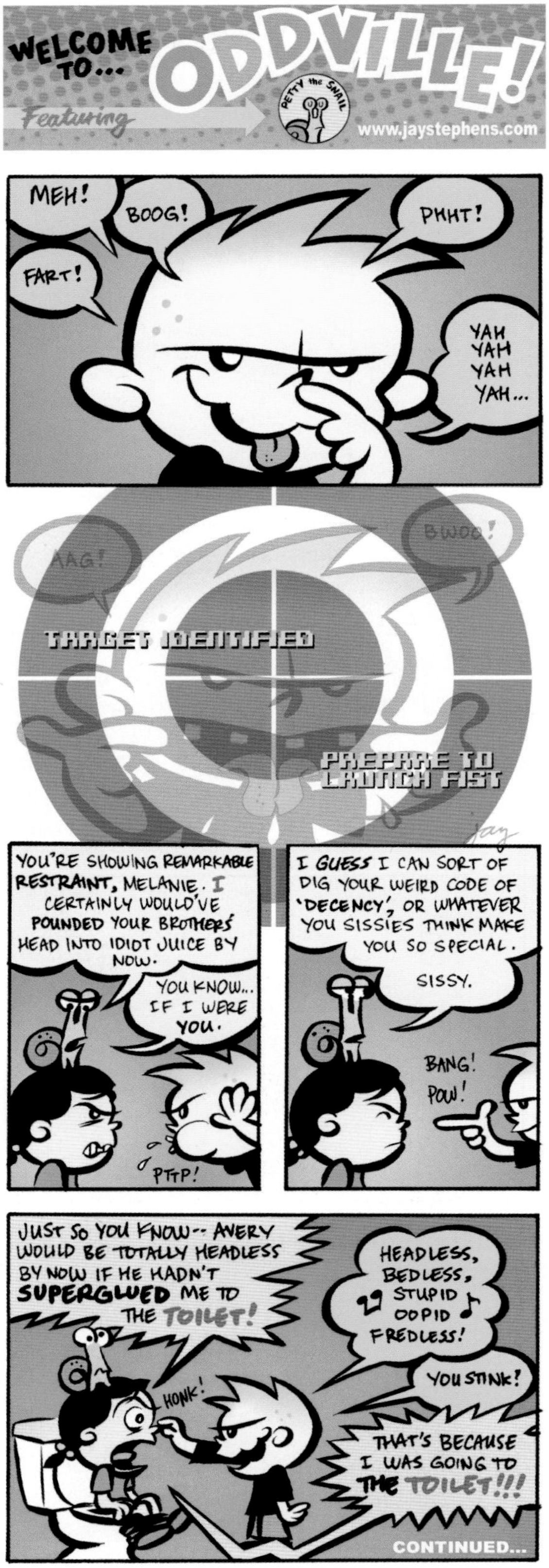

WELCOME TO... ODDVILLE!
Featuring
PETTY the SNAIL
www.jaystephens.com
MEH!
BOOG!
PHHT!
FART!
YAH YAH YAH YAH...
AAG!
BWOO!
TARGET IDENTIFIED
PREPARE TO LAUNCH FIST
YOU'RE SHOWING REMARKABLE RESTRAINT, MELANIE. I CERTAINLY WOULD'VE POUNDED YOUR BROTHERS' HEAD INTO IDIOT JUICE BY NOW.
YOU KNOW... IF I WERE YOU.
PTTP!
I GUESS I CAN SORT OF DIG YOUR WEIRD CODE OF 'DECENCY', OR WHATEVER YOU SISSIES THINK MAKE YOU SO SPECIAL.
SISSY.
BANG! POW!
JUST SO YOU KNOW-- AVERY WOULD BE TOTALLY HEADLESS BY NOW IF HE HADN'T SUPERGLUED ME TO THE TOILET!
HEADLESS, BEDLESS, STUPID OOPID FREDLESS!
YOU STINK!
HONK!
THAT'S BECAUSE I WAS GOING TO THE TOILET!!!
CONTINUED...

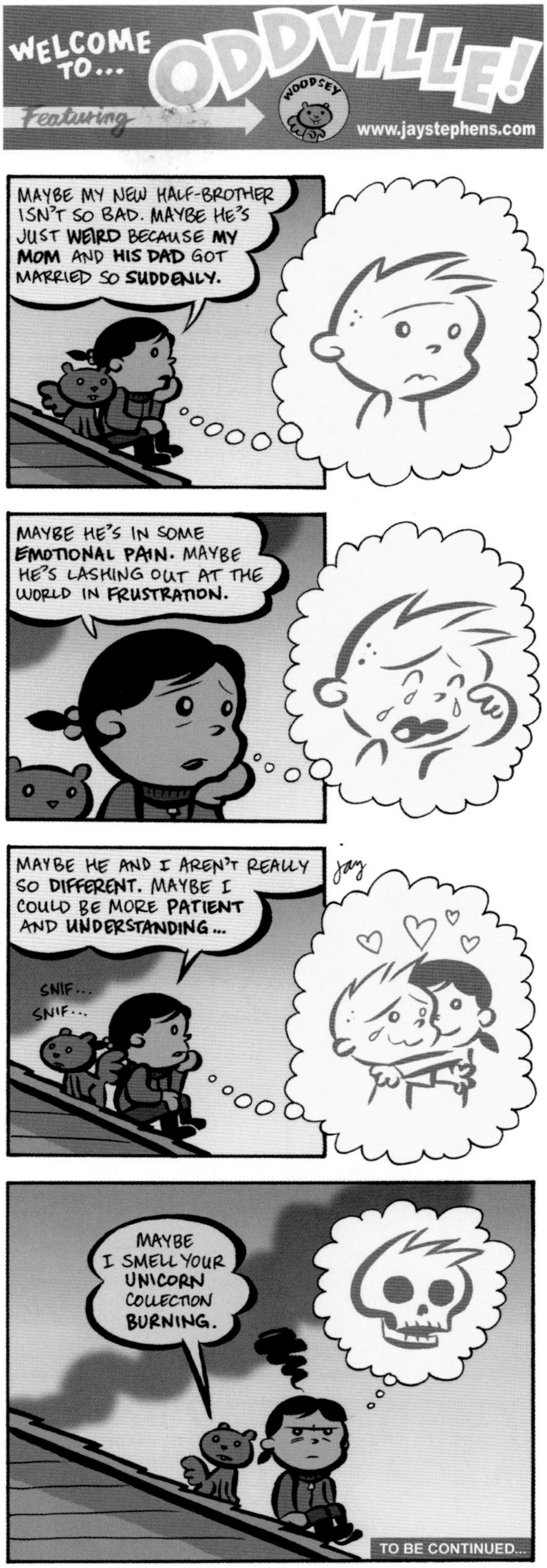

WELCOME TO... ODDVILLE!
Featuring
WOODSEY
www.jaystephens.com
MAYBE MY NEW HALF-BROTHER ISN'T SO BAD. MAYBE HE'S JUST WEIRD BECAUSE MY MOM AND HIS DAD GOT MARRIED SO SUDDENLY.
MAYBE HE'S IN SOME EMOTIONAL PAIN. MAYBE HE'S LASHING OUT AT THE WORLD IN FRUSTRATION.
MAYBE HE AND I AREN'T REALLY SO DIFFERENT. MAYBE I COULD BE MORE PATIENT AND UNDERSTANDING...
SNIF... SNIF...
MAYBE I SMELL YOUR UNICORN COLLECTION BURNING.
TO BE CONTINUED...

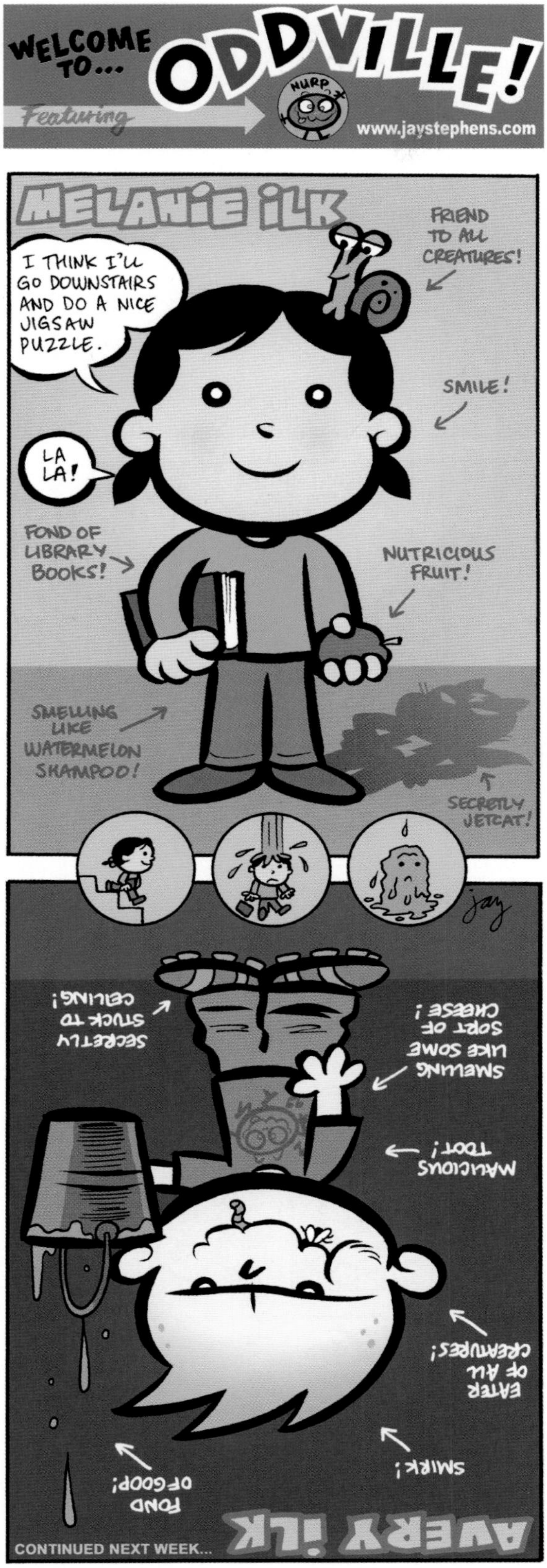
WELCOME TO...
ODDVILLE!
Featuring
NURP
www.jaystephens.com
MELANIE iLK
I THINK I'LL GO DOWNSTAIRS AND DO A NICE JIGSAW PUZZLE.
FRIEND TO ALL CREATURES!
SMILE!
LA LA!
FOND OF LIBRARY BOOKS!
NUTRICIOUS FRUIT!
SMELLING LIKE WATERMELON SHAMPOO!
SECRETLY JETCAT!
jay
SECRETLY STUCK TO CEILING!
SMELLING LIKE SOME SORT OF CHEESE!
MALICIOUS TOOT!
EATER OF ALL CREATURES!
SMIRK!
FOND OF GOOP!
AVERY iLK
CONTINUED NEXT WEEK...

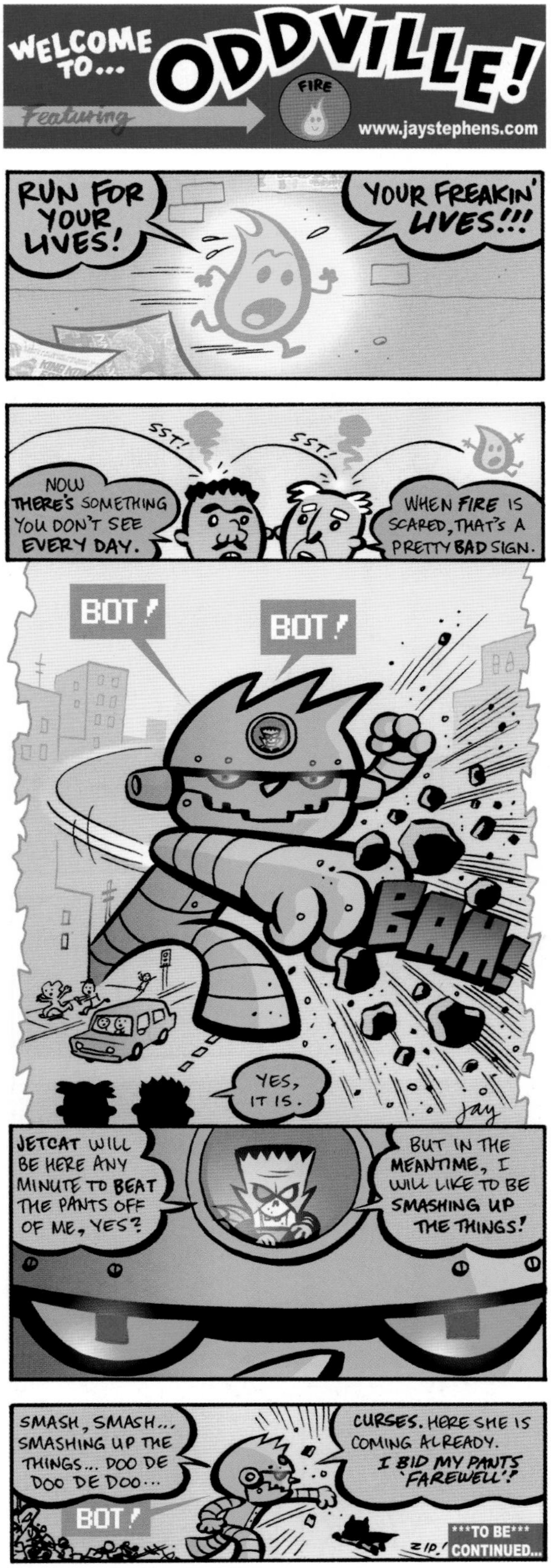
WELCOME TO...
ODDVILLE!
Featuring
FIRE
www.jaystephens.com
RUN FOR YOUR LIVES!
YOUR FREAKIN' LIVES!!!
SST!
SST!
NOW THERE'S SOMETHING YOU DON'T SEE EVERY DAY.
WHEN FIRE IS SCARED, THAT'S A PRETTY BAD SIGN.
BOT!
BOT!
BAM!
YES, IT IS.
jay
JETCAT WILL BE HERE ANY MINUTE TO BEAT THE PANTS OFF OF ME, YES?
BUT IN THE MEANTIME, I WILL LIKE TO BE SMASHING UP THE THINGS!
SMASH, SMASH... SMASHING UP THE THINGS... DOO DE DOO DE DOO...
CURSES. HERE SHE IS COMING ALREADY. I BID MY PANTS 'FAREWELL'!
BOT!
ZIP!
TO BE CONTINUED...

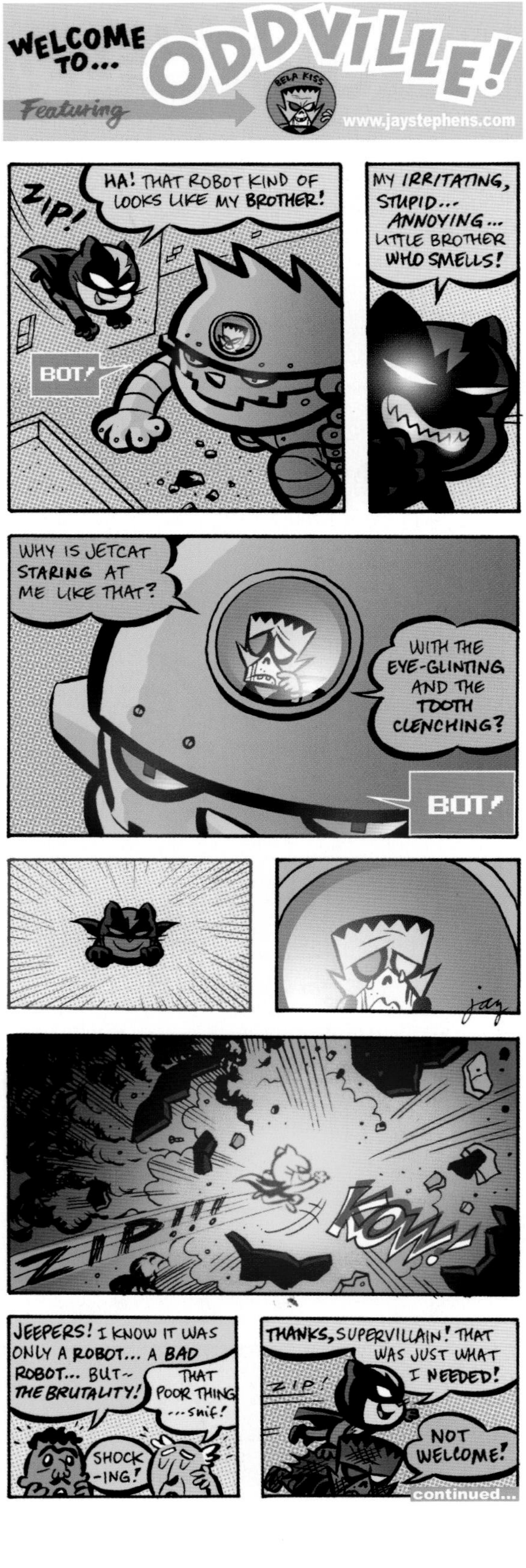

WELCOME TO... ODDVILLE!
Featuring
BELA KISS
www.jaystephens.com
ZIP!
HA! THAT ROBOT KIND OF LOOKS LIKE MY BROTHER!
BOT!
MY IRRITATING, STUPID... ANNOYING... LITTLE BROTHER WHO SMELLS!
WHY IS JETCAT STARING AT ME LIKE THAT?
WITH THE EYE-GLINTING AND THE TOOTH CLENCHING?
BOT!
jay
ZIP!!!
KOW!
JEEPERS! I KNOW IT WAS ONLY A ROBOT... A BAD ROBOT... BUT-- THE BRUTALITY!
THAT POOR THING ...snif!
SHOCK-ING!
THANKS, SUPERVILLAIN! THAT WAS JUST WHAT I NEEDED!
ZIP!
NOT WELCOME!
continued...

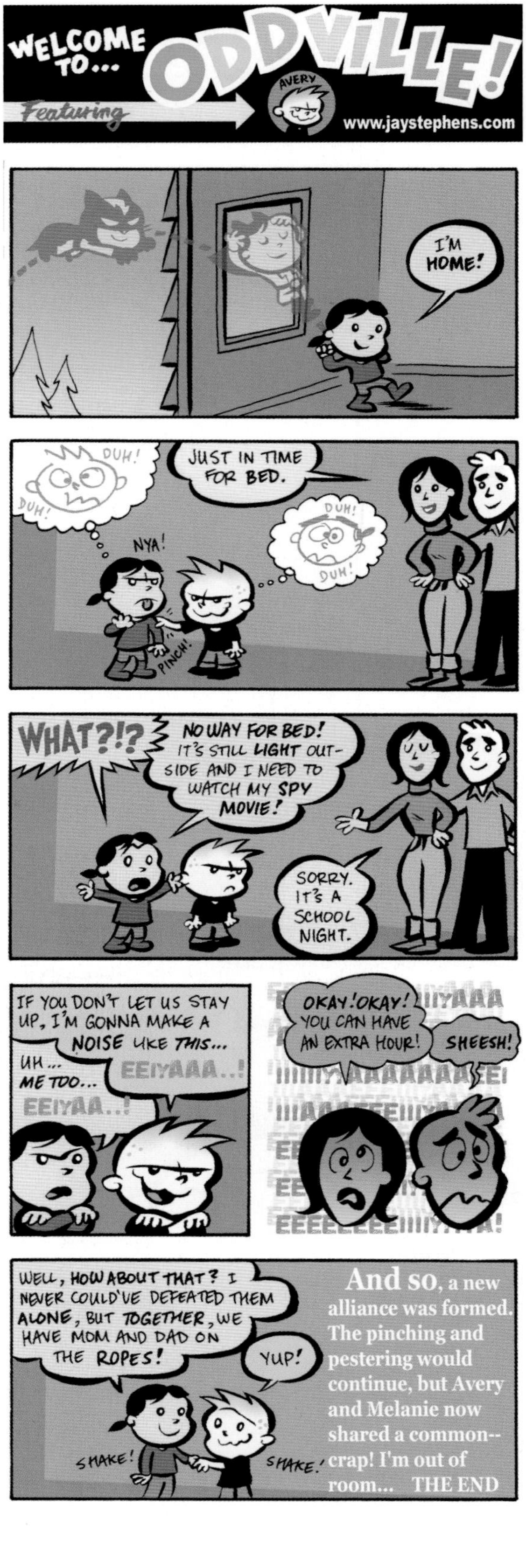

WELCOME TO... ODDVILLE!
Featuring
AVERY
www.jaystephens.com
I'M HOME!
JUST IN TIME FOR BED.
DUH!
DUH!
NYA!
PINCH!
DUH!
DUH!
WHAT?!?
NO WAY FOR BED! IT'S STILL LIGHT OUT-SIDE AND I NEED TO WATCH MY SPY MOVIE!
SORRY. IT'S A SCHOOL NIGHT.
IF YOU DON'T LET US STAY UP, I'M GONNA MAKE A NOISE LIKE THIS...
EEIYAAA..!
UH... ME TOO...
EEIYAA..!
OKAY! OKAY! YOU CAN HAVE AN EXTRA HOUR!
SHEESH!
WELL, HOW ABOUT THAT? I NEVER COULD'VE DEFEATED THEM ALONE, BUT TOGETHER, WE HAVE MOM AND DAD ON THE ROPES!
YUP!
SHAKE!
SHAKE!
And so, a new alliance was formed. The pinching and pestering would continue, but Avery and Melanie now shared a common-- crap! I'm out of room... THE END

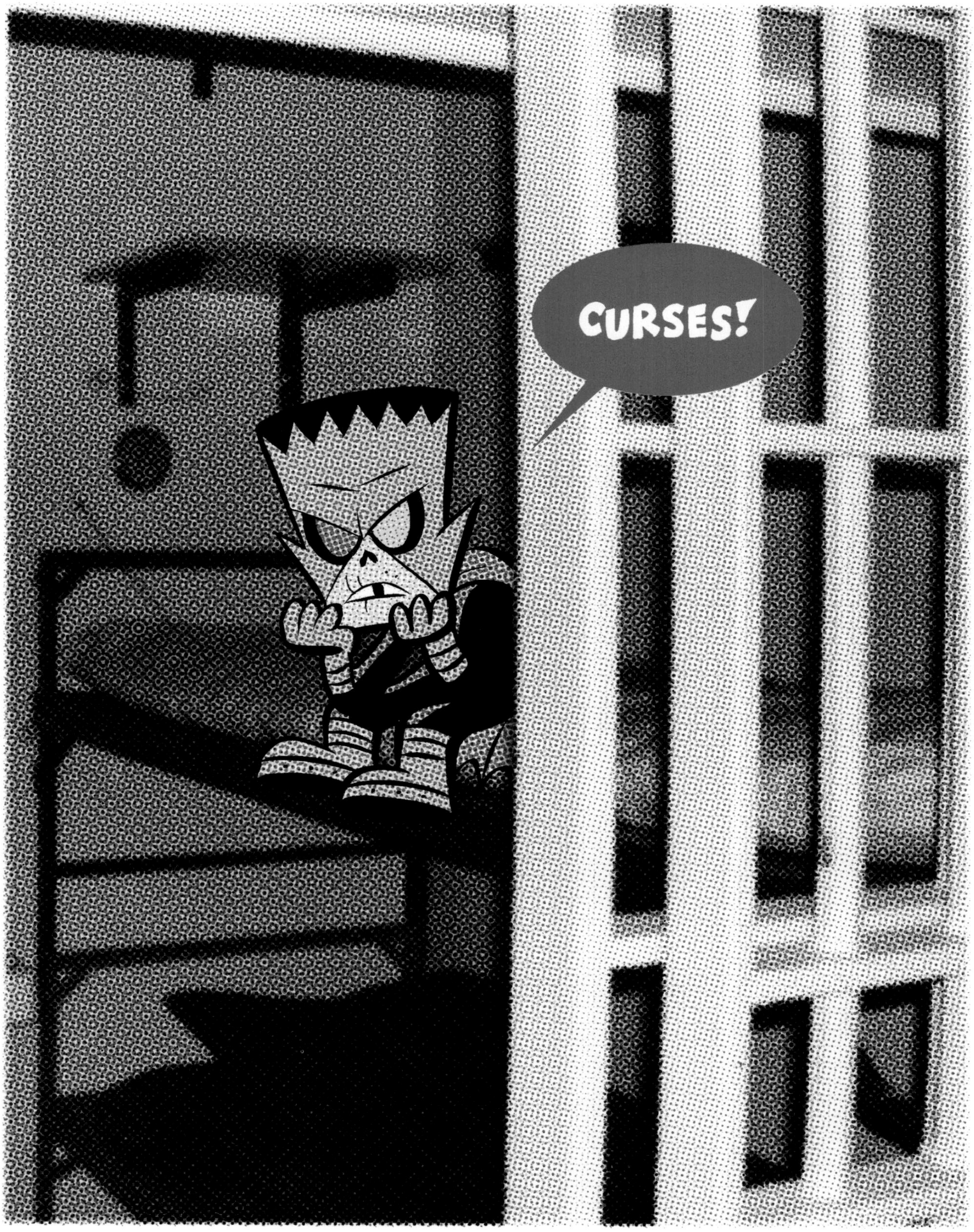
CURSES!

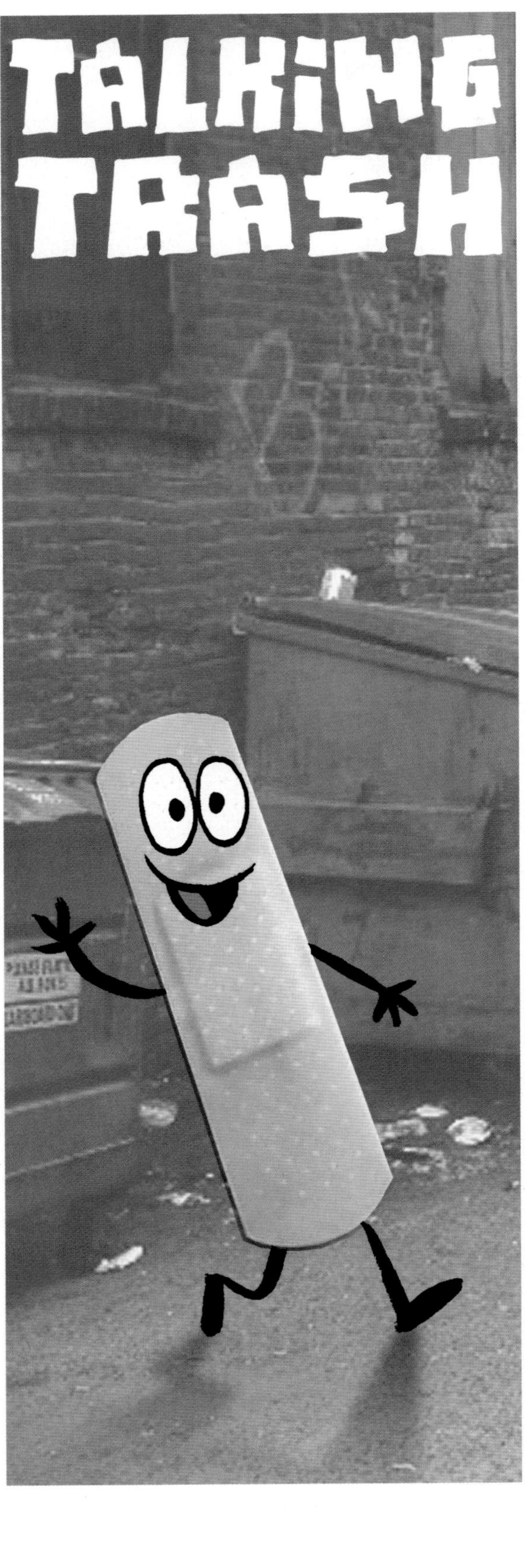
TALKING TRASH

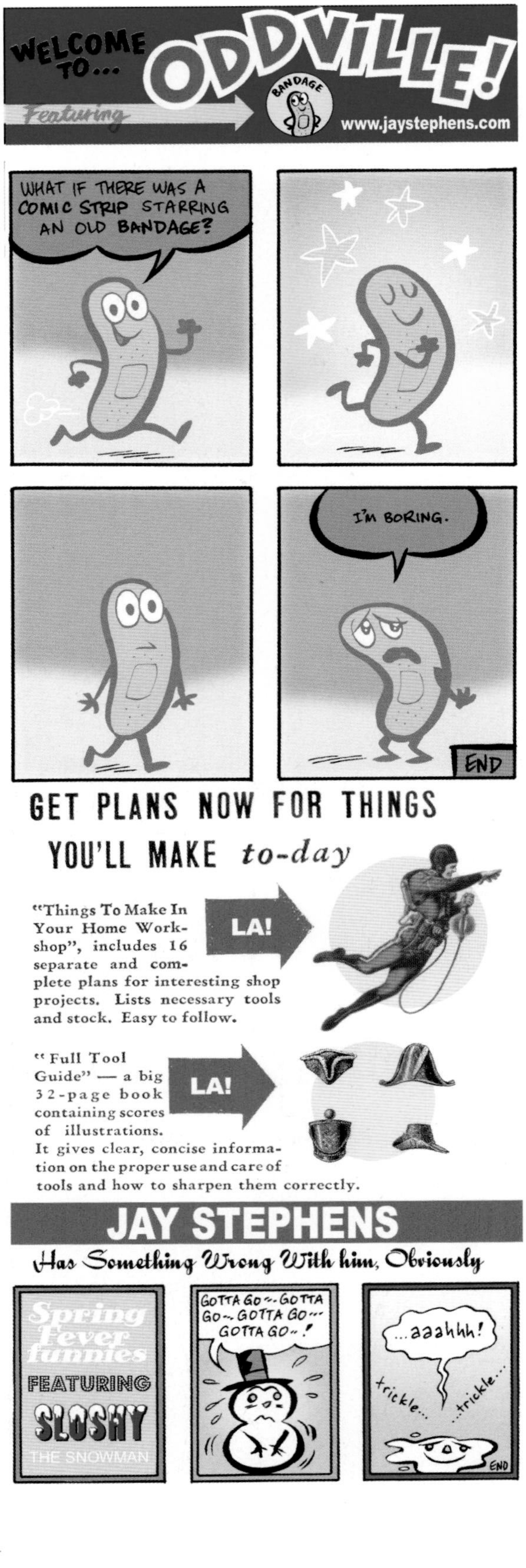
WELCOME TO... ODDVILLE!
Featuring
BANDAGE
www.jaystephens.com
WHAT IF THERE WAS A COMIC STRIP STARRING AN OLD BANDAGE?
I'M BORING.
END
GET PLANS NOW FOR THINGS
YOU'LL MAKE to-day
"Things To Make In Your Home Work-shop", includes 16 separate and com-plete plans for interesting shop projects. Lists necessary tools and stock. Easy to follow.
LA!
"Full Tool Guide" — a big 32-page book containing scores of illustrations. It gives clear, concise informa-tion on the proper use and care of tools and how to sharpen them correctly.
LA!
JAY STEPHENS
Has Something Wrong With him, Obviously
Spring Fever funnies
FEATURING
SLOSHY
THE SNOWMAN
GOTTA GO~-GOTTA GO~-GOTTA GO~-GOTTA GO~!
...aaahhh!
trickle...
...trickle...
END

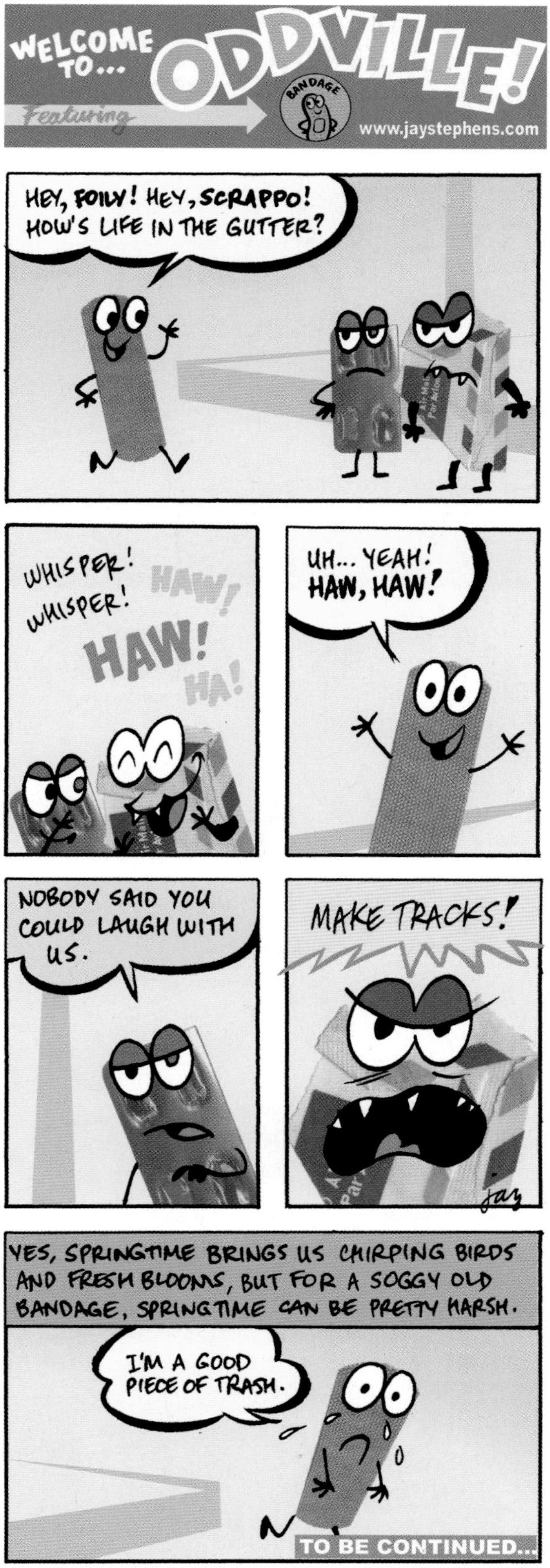

WELCOME TO... ODDVILLE!
Featuring
BANDAGE
www.jaystephens.com
HEY, FOILY! HEY, SCRAPPO! HOW'S LIFE IN THE GUTTER?
WHISPER! WHISPER!
HAW!
HAW!
HA!
UH... YEAH! HAW, HAW!
NOBODY SAID YOU COULD LAUGH WITH US.
MAKE TRACKS!
YES, SPRINGTIME BRINGS US CHIRPING BIRDS AND FRESH BLOOMS, BUT FOR A SOGGY OLD BANDAGE, SPRINGTIME CAN BE PRETTY HARSH.
I'M A GOOD PIECE OF TRASH.
TO BE CONTINUED...

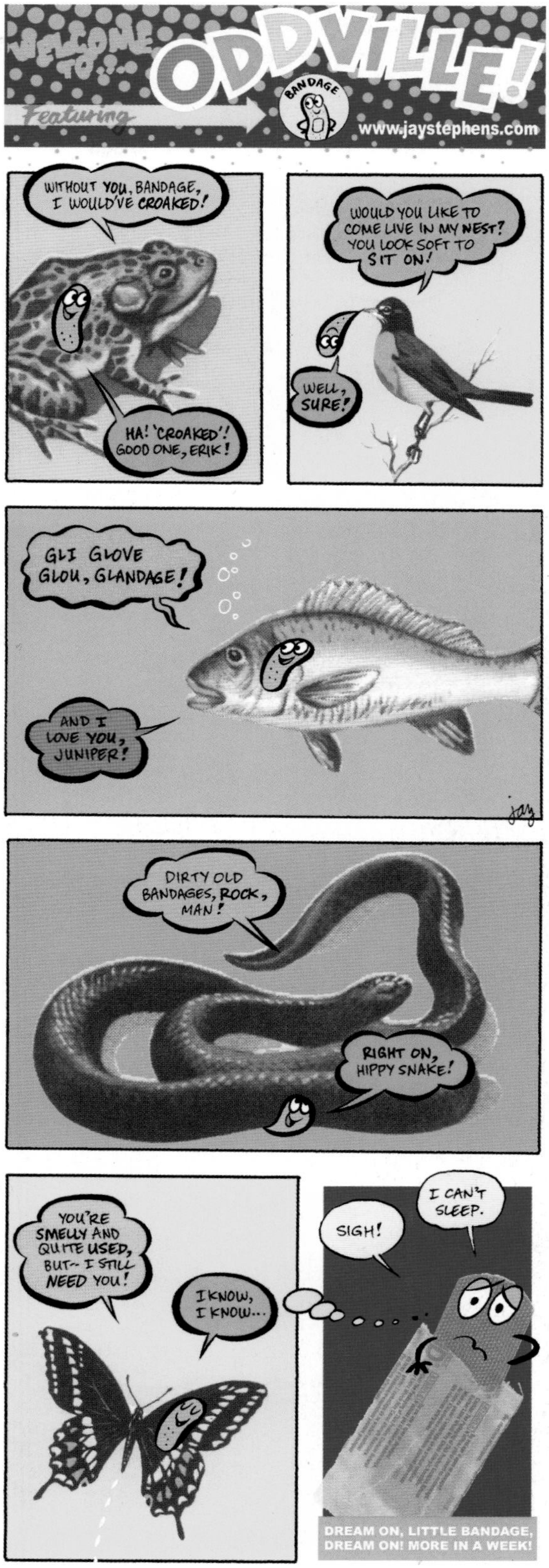

WELCOME TO... ODDVILLE!
Featuring
BANDAGE
www.jaystephens.com
WITHOUT YOU, BANDAGE, I WOULD'VE CROAKED!
HA! 'CROAKED'! GOOD ONE, ERIK!
WOULD YOU LIKE TO COME LIVE IN MY NEST? YOU LOOK SOFT TO SIT ON!
WELL, SURE!
GLI GLOVE GLOU, GLANDAGE!
AND I LOVE YOU, JUNIPER!
DIRTY OLD BANDAGES, ROCK, MAN!
RIGHT ON, HIPPY SNAKE!
YOU'RE SMELLY AND QUITE USED, BUT-- I STILL NEED YOU!
I KNOW, I KNOW...
SIGH!
I CAN'T SLEEP.
DREAM ON, LITTLE BANDAGE, DREAM ON! MORE IN A WEEK!

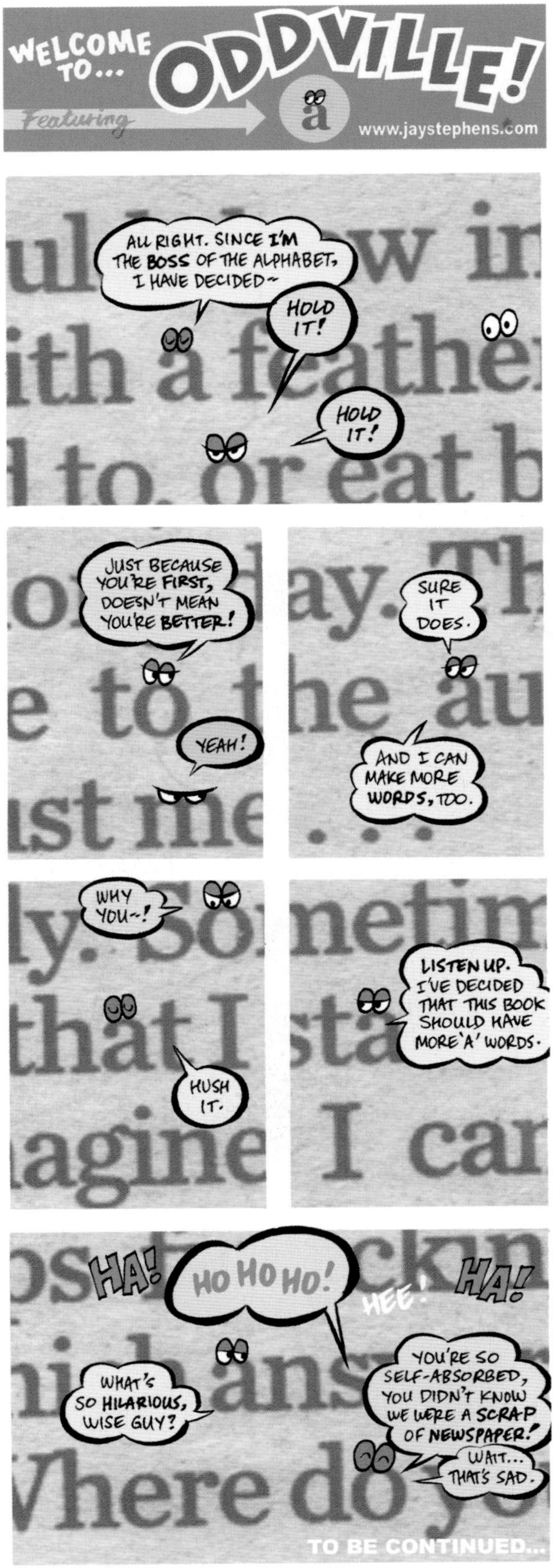
WELCOME TO... ODDVILLE!
Featuring
www.jaystephens.com
ALL RIGHT. SINCE I'M THE BOSS OF THE ALPHABET, I HAVE DECIDED~
HOLD IT!
HOLD IT!
JUST BECAUSE YOU'RE FIRST, DOESN'T MEAN YOU'RE BETTER!
YEAH!
SURE IT DOES.
AND I CAN MAKE MORE WORDS, TOO.
WHY YOU~!
HUSH IT.
LISTEN UP. I'VE DECIDED THAT THIS BOOK SHOULD HAVE MORE 'A' WORDS.
HA!
HO HO HO!
HEE!
HA!
WHAT'S SO HILARIOUS, WISE GUY?
YOU'RE SO SELF-ABSORBED, YOU DIDN'T KNOW WE WERE A SCRAP OF NEWSPAPER!
WAIT... THAT'S SAD.
TO BE CONTINUED...

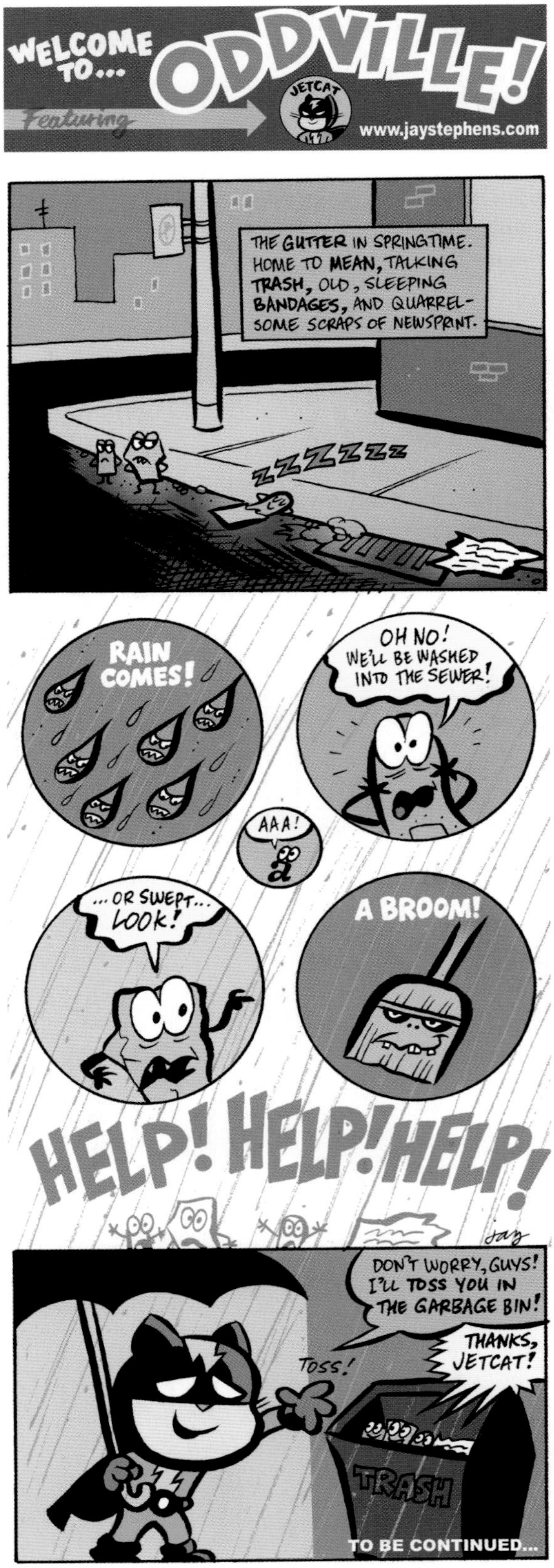
WELCOME TO... ODDVILLE!
Featuring
JETCAT
www.jaystephens.com
THE GUTTER IN SPRINGTIME. HOME TO MEAN, TALKING TRASH, OLD, SLEEPING BANDAGES, AND QUARREL-SOME SCRAPS OF NEWSPRINT.
ZZZZZZZ
RAIN COMES!
OH NO! WE'LL BE WASHED INTO THE SEWER!
AAA!
...OR SWEPT... LOOK!
A BROOM!
HELP! HELP! HELP!
jay
DON'T WORRY, GUYS! I'LL TOSS YOU IN THE GARBAGE BIN!
TOSS!
THANKS, JETCAT!
TRASH
TO BE CONTINUED...

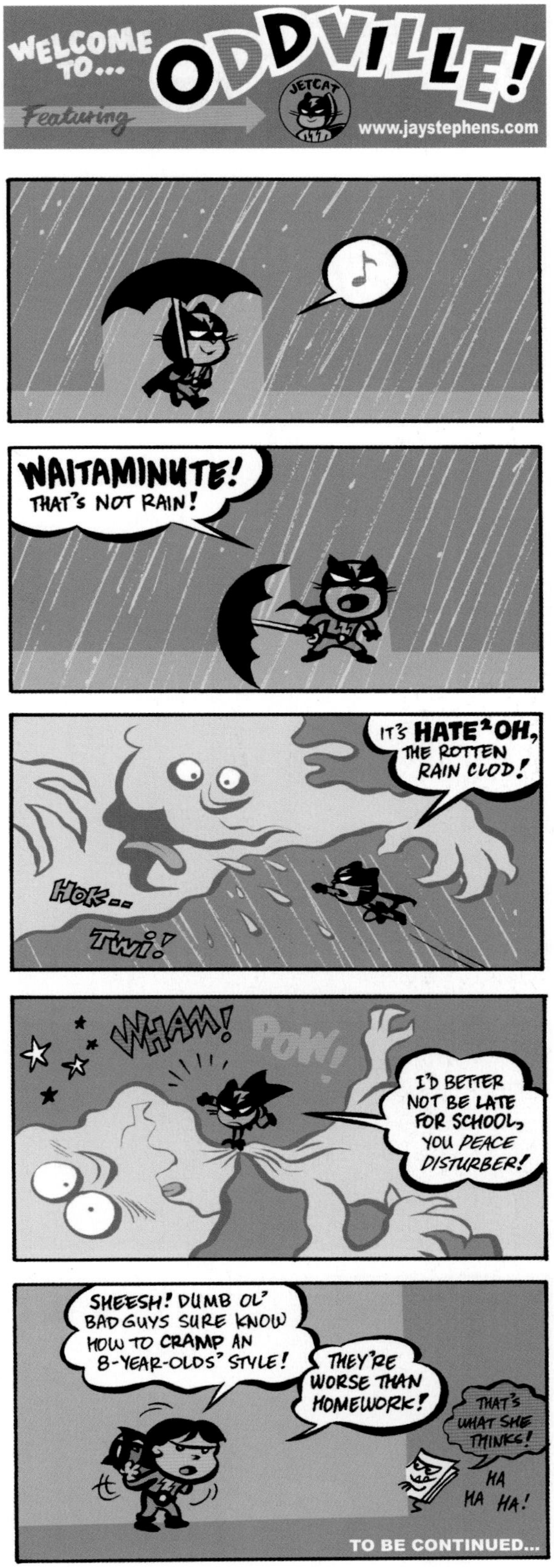

WELCOME TO... ODDVILLE!
Featuring JETCAT
www.jaystephens.com
WAITAMINUTE! THAT'S NOT RAIN!
IT'S HATE²OH, THE ROTTEN RAIN CLOD!
HOK..
TWI!
WHAM!
POW!
I'D BETTER NOT BE LATE FOR SCHOOL, YOU PEACE DISTURBER!
SHEESH! DUMB OL' BAD GUYS SURE KNOW HOW TO CRAMP AN 8-YEAR-OLDS' STYLE!
THEY'RE WORSE THAN HOMEWORK!
THAT'S WHAT SHE THINKS!
HA HA HA!
TO BE CONTINUED...

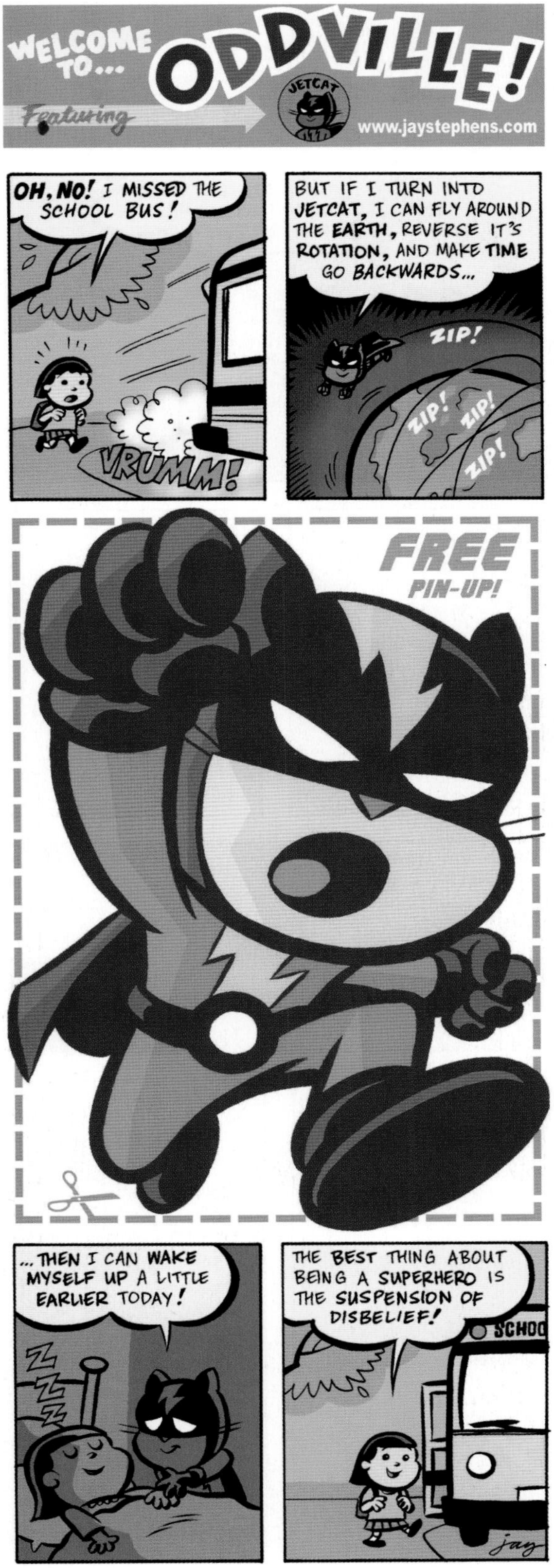

WELCOME TO... ODDVILLE!
Featuring JETCAT
www.jaystephens.com
OH, NO! I MISSED THE SCHOOL BUS!
VRUMM!
BUT IF I TURN INTO JETCAT, I CAN FLY AROUND THE EARTH, REVERSE IT'S ROTATION, AND MAKE TIME GO BACKWARDS...
ZIP!
ZIP!
ZIP!
ZIP!
FREE PIN-UP!
...THEN I CAN WAKE MYSELF UP A LITTLE EARLIER TODAY!
ZZZ
THE BEST THING ABOUT BEING A SUPERHERO IS THE SUSPENSION OF DISBELIEF!
SCHOO
jay

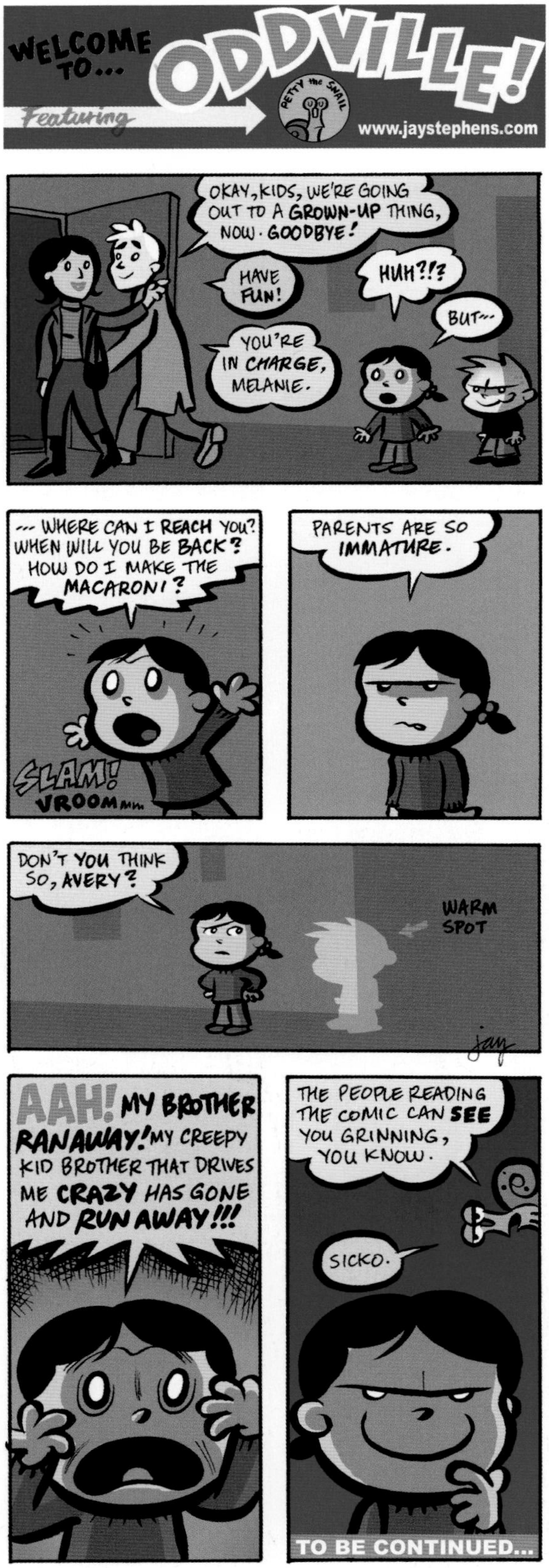
WELCOME TO...
ODDVILLE!
Featuring
PETTY the SNAIL
www.jaystephens.com
OKAY, KIDS, WE'RE GOING OUT TO A GROWN-UP THING, NOW. GOODBYE!
HAVE FUN!
HUH?!?
YOU'RE IN CHARGE, MELANIE.
BUT—
...WHERE CAN I REACH YOU? WHEN WILL YOU BE BACK? HOW DO I MAKE THE MACARONI?
SLAM!
VROOMmm
PARENTS ARE SO IMMATURE.
DON'T YOU THINK SO, AVERY?
WARM SPOT
jay
AAH! MY BROTHER RAN AWAY! MY CREEPY KID BROTHER THAT DRIVES ME CRAZY HAS GONE AND RUN AWAY!!!
THE PEOPLE READING THE COMIC CAN SEE YOU GRINNING, YOU KNOW.
SICKO.
TO BE CONTINUED...

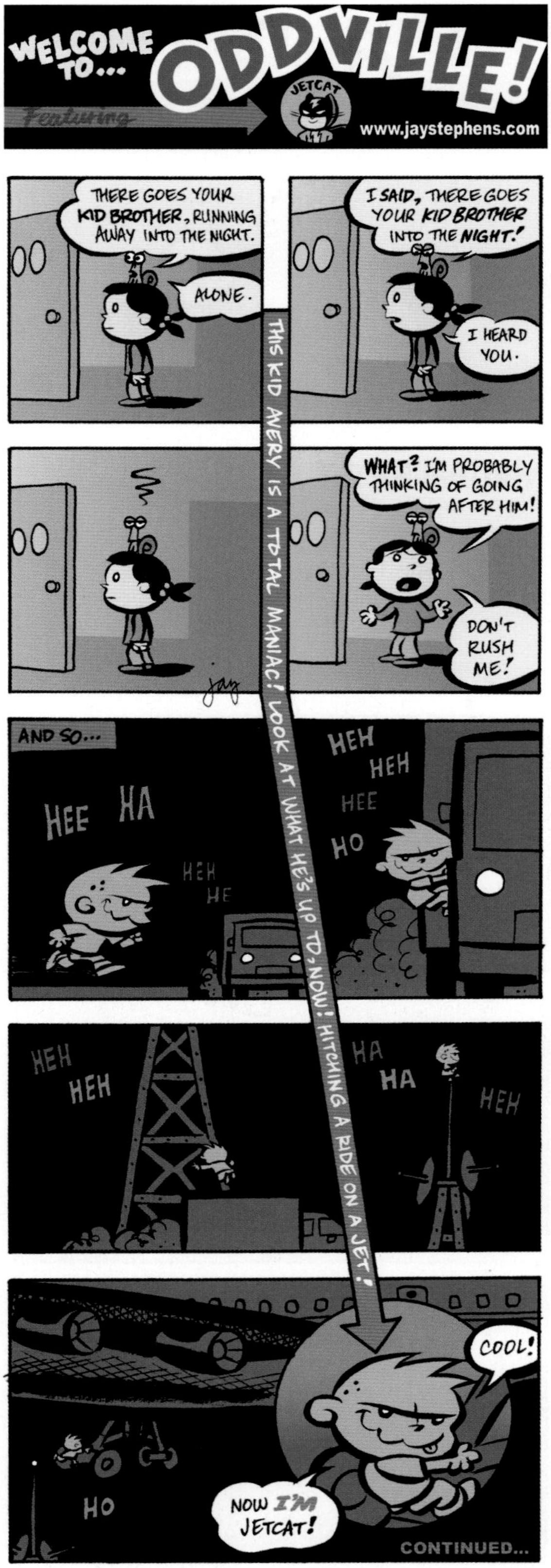
WELCOME TO...
ODDVILLE!
Featuring
JETCAT
www.jaystephens.com
THERE GOES YOUR KID BROTHER, RUNNING AWAY INTO THE NIGHT.
ALONE.
I SAID, THERE GOES YOUR KID BROTHER INTO THE NIGHT!
I HEARD YOU.
WHAT? I'M PROBABLY THINKING OF GOING AFTER HIM!
DON'T RUSH ME!
jay
THIS KID AVERY IS A TOTAL MANIAC! LOOK AT WHAT HE'S UP TO, NOW! HITCHING A RIDE ON A JET!
AND SO...
HEE HA
HEH HE
HEH HEH HEE HO
HEH HEH
HA HA HEH
COOL!
HO
NOW I'M JETCAT!
CONTINUED...

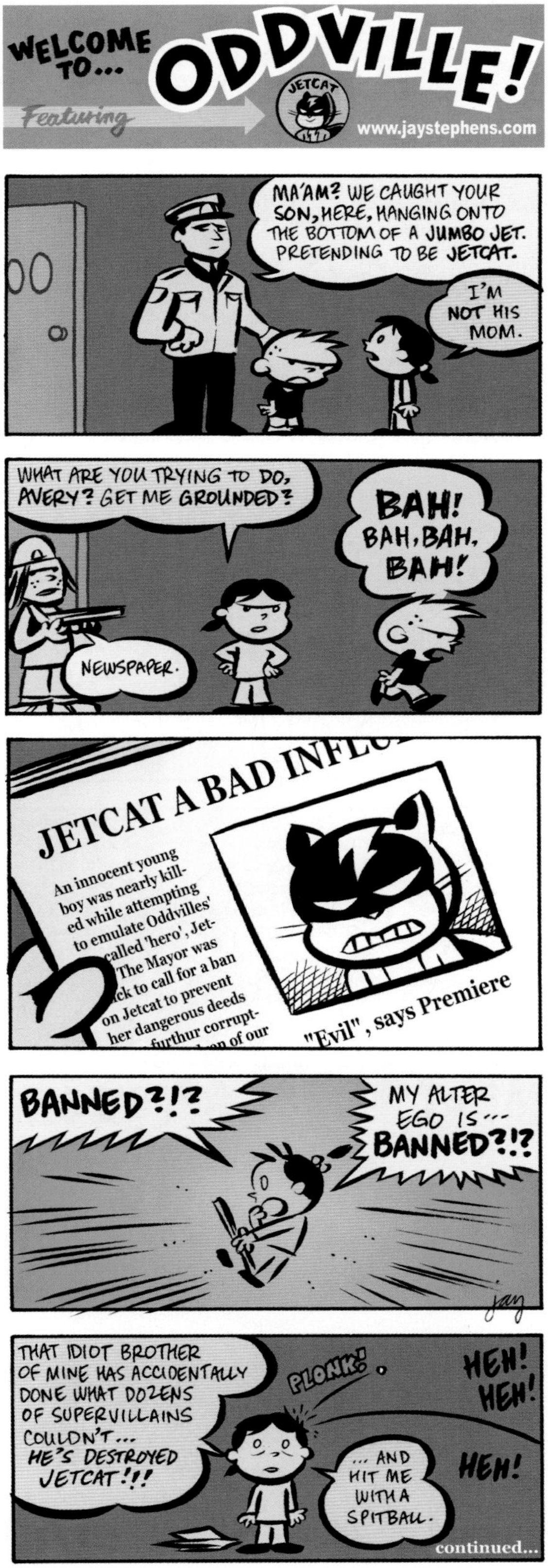

WELCOME TO... ODDVILLE!
Featuring JETCAT
www.jaystephens.com
MA'AM? WE CAUGHT YOUR SON, HERE, HANGING ONTO THE BOTTOM OF A JUMBO JET. PRETENDING TO BE JETCAT.
I'M NOT HIS MOM.
WHAT ARE YOU TRYING TO DO, AVERY? GET ME GROUNDED?
BAH! BAH, BAH, BAH!
NEWSPAPER.
JETCAT A BAD INFLU
An innocent young boy was nearly kill- ed while attempting to emulate Oddvilles' called 'hero', Jet- The Mayor was ck to call for a ban on Jetcat to prevent her dangerous deeds
"Evil", says Premiere
BANNED?!?
MY ALTER EGO IS... BANNED?!?
jay
THAT IDIOT BROTHER OF MINE HAS ACCIDENTALLY DONE WHAT DOZENS OF SUPERVILLAINS COULDN'T... HE'S DESTROYED JETCAT!!!
PLONK!
HEH! HEH!
HEH!
... AND HIT ME WITH A SPITBALL.
continued...

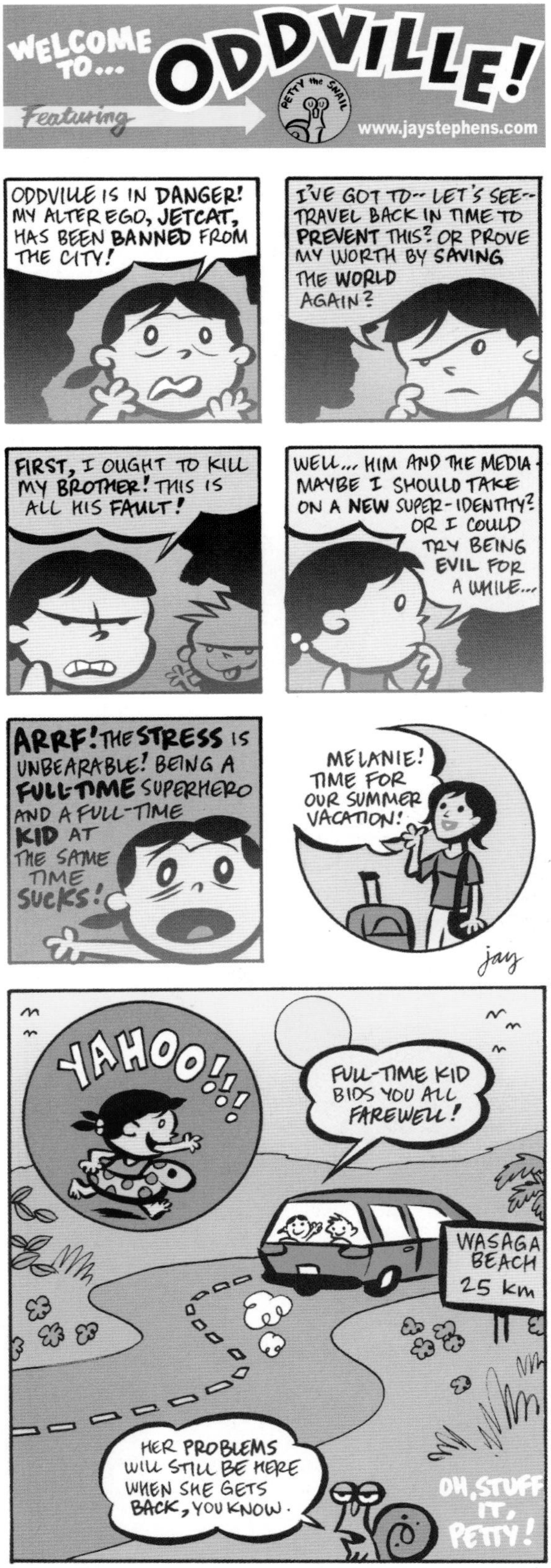

WELCOME TO... ODDVILLE!
Featuring PETTY the SNAIL
www.jaystephens.com
ODDVILLE IS IN DANGER! MY ALTER EGO, JETCAT, HAS BEEN BANNED FROM THE CITY!
I'VE GOT TO-- LET'S SEE-- TRAVEL BACK IN TIME TO PREVENT THIS? OR PROVE MY WORTH BY SAVING THE WORLD AGAIN?
FIRST, I OUGHT TO KILL MY BROTHER! THIS IS ALL HIS FAULT!
WELL... HIM AND THE MEDIA. MAYBE I SHOULD TAKE ON A NEW SUPER-IDENTITY? OR I COULD TRY BEING EVIL FOR A WHILE...
ARRF! THE STRESS IS UNBEARABLE! BEING A FULL-TIME SUPERHERO AND A FULL-TIME KID AT THE SAME TIME SUCKS!
MELANIE! TIME FOR OUR SUMMER VACATION!
jay
YAHOO!!!
FULL-TIME KID BIDS YOU ALL FAREWELL!
WASAGA BEACH 25 km
HER PROBLEMS WILL STILL BE HERE WHEN SHE GETS BACK, YOU KNOW.
OH, STUFF IT, PETTY!

THEM APPLES

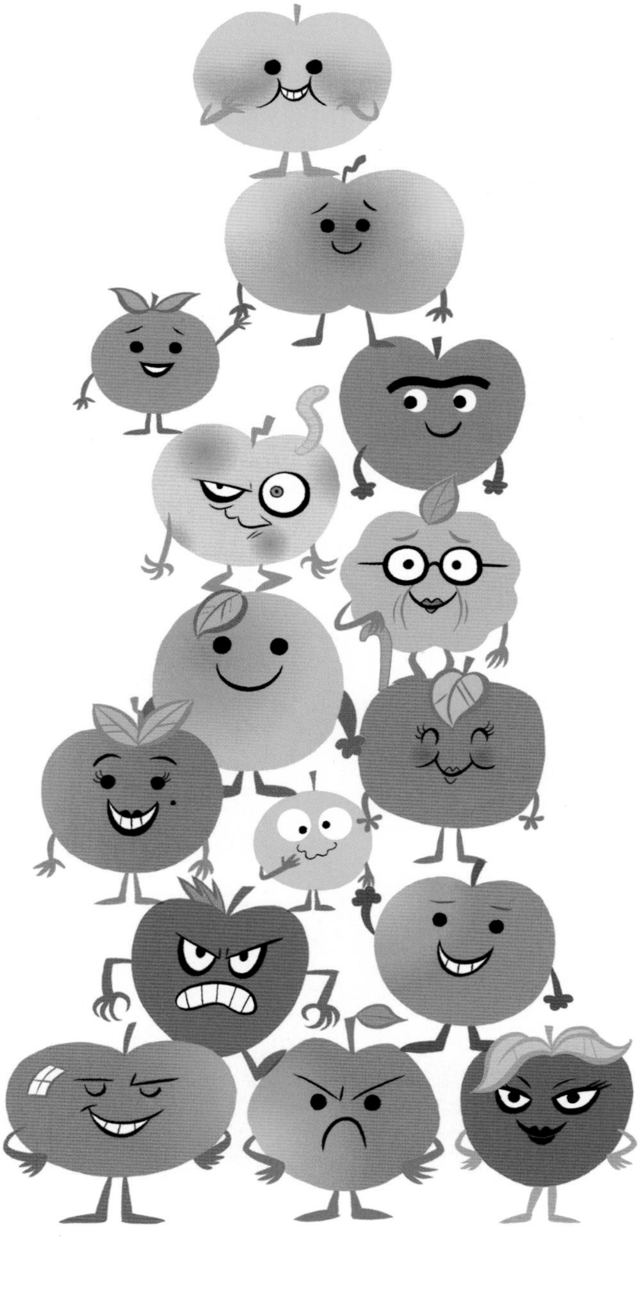

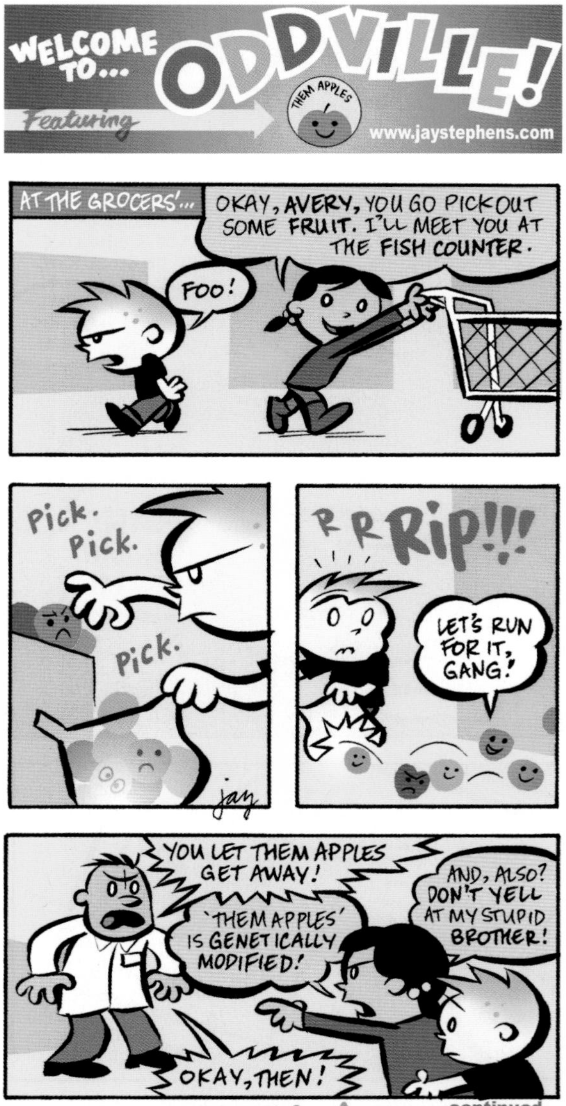
WELCOME TO... ODDVILLE!
Featuring
THEM APPLES
www.jaystephens.com
AT THE GROCERS'...
OKAY, AVERY, YOU GO PICK OUT SOME FRUIT. I'LL MEET YOU AT THE FISH COUNTER.
FOO!
Pick. Pick.
Pick.
jay
R R RIP!!!
LET'S RUN FOR IT, GANG!
YOU LET THEM APPLES GET AWAY!
'THEM APPLES' IS GENETICALLY MODIFIED!
AND, ALSO? DON'T YELL AT MY STUPID BROTHER!
OKAY, THEN!

continued...

MEET THEM APPLES...

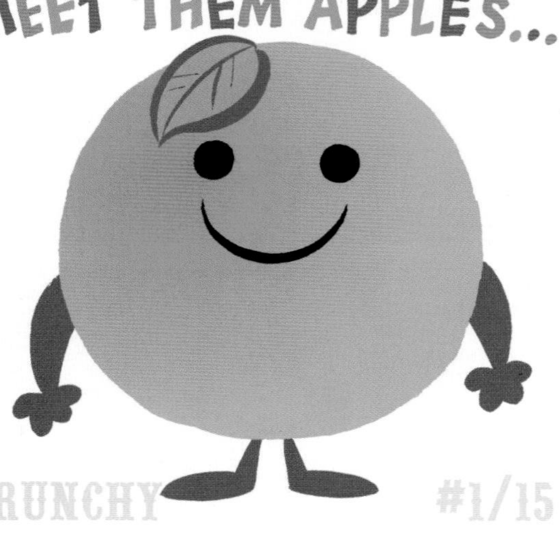

CRUNCHY #1/15

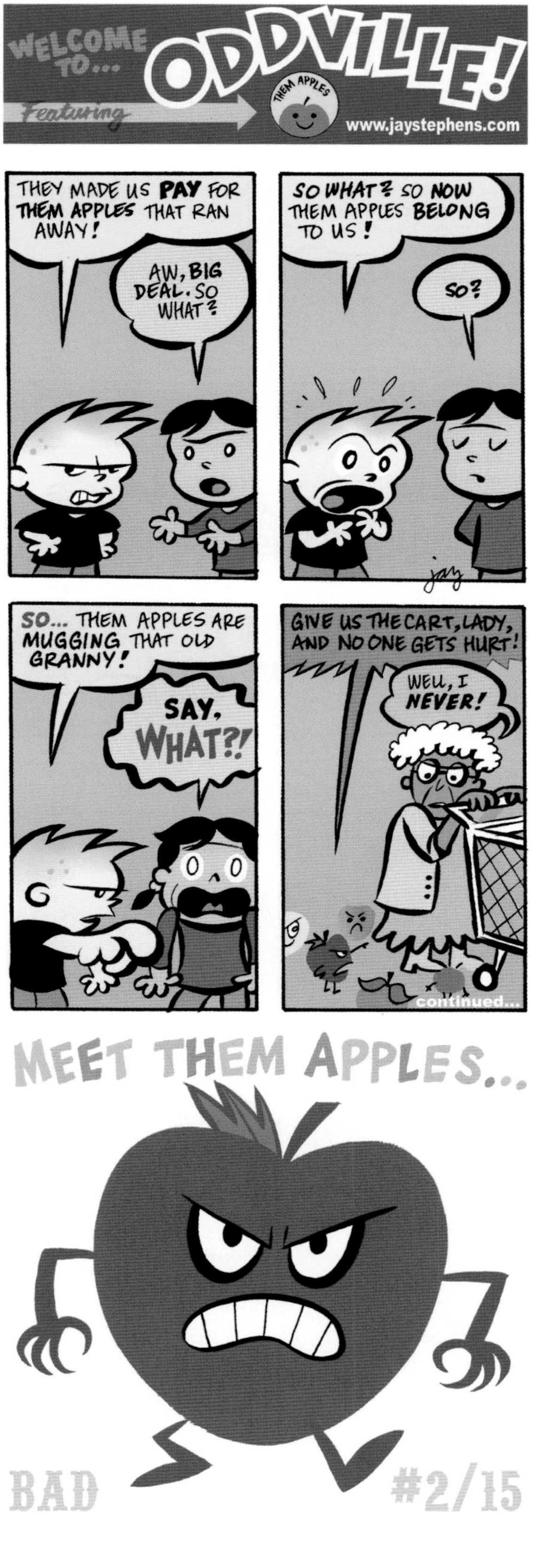
WELCOME TO... ODDVILLE!
Featuring
THEM APPLES
www.jaystephens.com
THEY MADE US PAY FOR THEM APPLES THAT RAN AWAY!
AW, BIG DEAL. SO WHAT?
SO WHAT? SO NOW THEM APPLES BELONG TO US!
SO?
SO... THEM APPLES ARE MUGGING THAT OLD GRANNY!
SAY, WHAT?!
GIVE US THE CART, LADY, AND NO ONE GETS HURT!
WELL, I NEVER!
continued...
MEET THEM APPLES...
BAD
#2/15

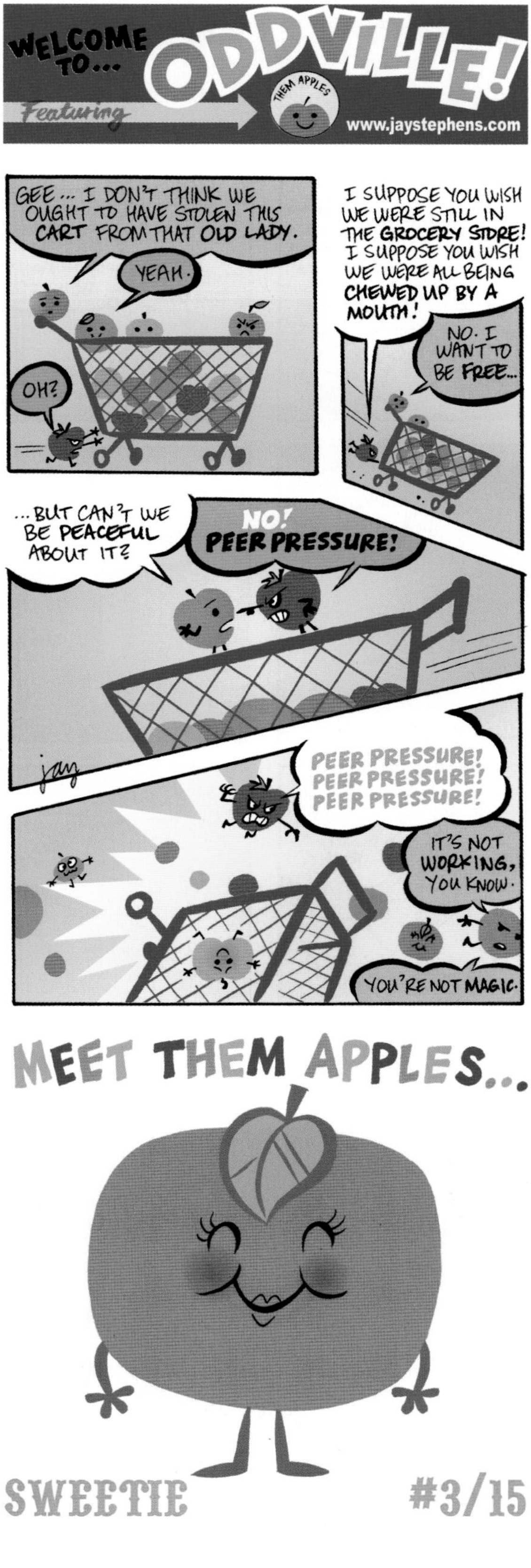
WELCOME TO... ODDVILLE!
Featuring
THEM APPLES
www.jaystephens.com
GEE... I DON'T THINK WE OUGHT TO HAVE STOLEN THIS CART FROM THAT OLD LADY.
YEAH.
OH?
I SUPPOSE YOU WISH WE WERE STILL IN THE GROCERY STORE! I SUPPOSE YOU WISH WE WERE ALL BEING CHEWED UP BY A MOUTH!
NO. I WANT TO BE FREE...
...BUT CAN'T WE BE PEACEFUL ABOUT IT?
NO! PEER PRESSURE!
PEER PRESSURE! PEER PRESSURE! PEER PRESSURE!
IT'S NOT WORKING, YOU KNOW.
YOU'RE NOT MAGIC.
MEET THEM APPLES...
SWEETIE
#3/15

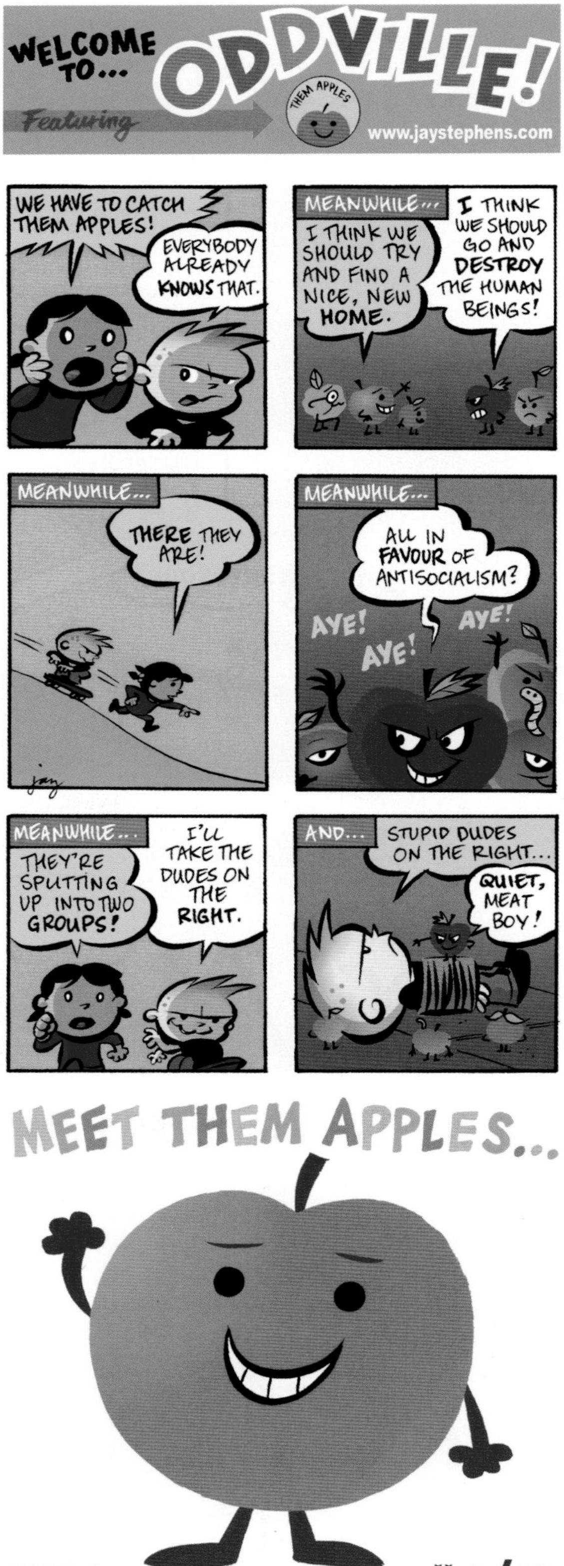
WELCOME TO... ODDVILLE!
Featuring
THEM APPLES
www.jaystephens.com
WE HAVE TO CATCH THEM APPLES!
EVERYBODY ALREADY KNOWS THAT.
MEANWHILE...
I THINK WE SHOULD TRY AND FIND A NICE, NEW HOME.
I THINK WE SHOULD GO AND DESTROY THE HUMAN BEINGS!
MEANWHILE...
THERE THEY ARE!
MEANWHILE...
ALL IN FAVOUR OF ANTISOCIALISM?
AYE!
AYE!
AYE!
MEANWHILE...
THEY'RE SPUTTING UP INTO TWO GROUPS!
I'LL TAKE THE DUDES ON THE RIGHT.
AND...
STUPID DUDES ON THE RIGHT...
QUIET, MEAT BOY!
MEET THEM APPLES...

MAC #4/15

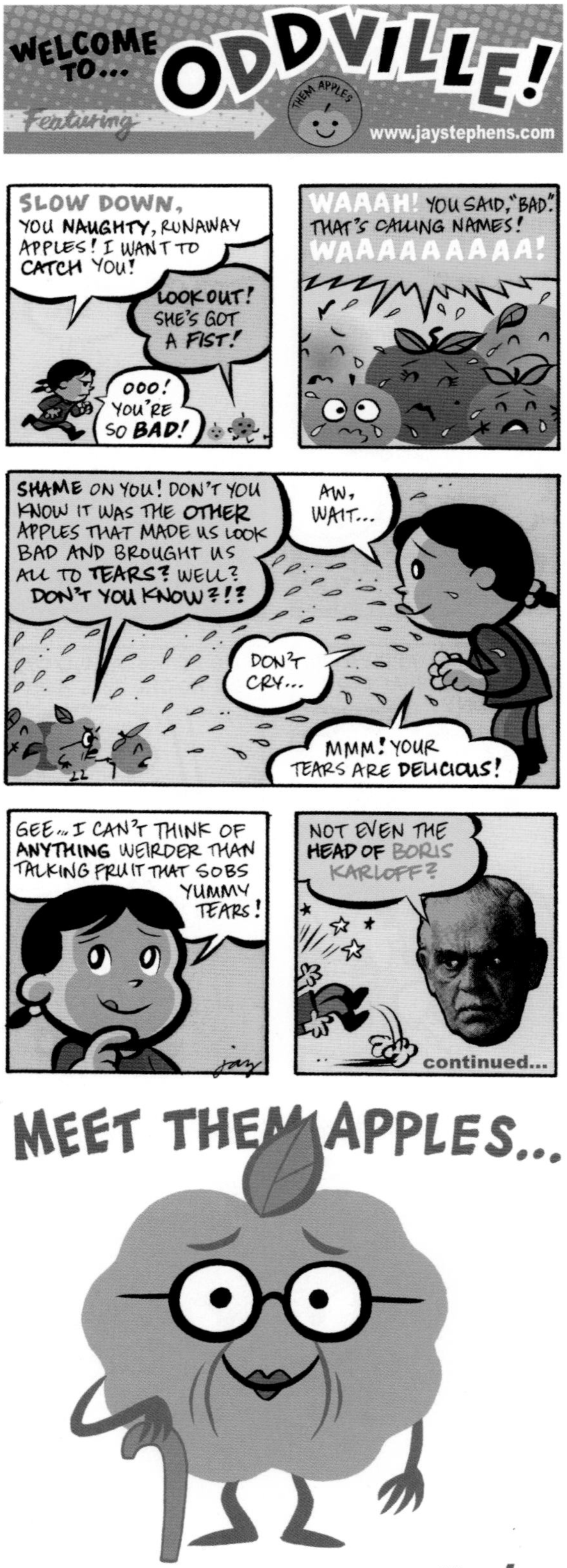
WELCOME TO... ODDVILLE!
Featuring
THEM APPLES
www.jaystephens.com
SLOW DOWN, YOU NAUGHTY, RUNAWAY APPLES! I WANT TO CATCH YOU!
LOOK OUT! SHE'S GOT A FIST!
OOO! YOU'RE SO BAD!
WAAAH! YOU SAID, "BAD". THAT'S CALLING NAMES! WAAAAAAAAA!
SHAME ON YOU! DON'T YOU KNOW IT WAS THE OTHER APPLES THAT MADE US LOOK BAD AND BROUGHT US ALL TO TEARS? WELL? DON'T YOU KNOW?!?
AW, WAIT...
DON'T CRY...
MMM! YOUR TEARS ARE DELICIOUS!
GEE... I CAN'T THINK OF ANYTHING WEIRDER THAN TALKING FRUIT THAT SOBS YUMMY TEARS!
NOT EVEN THE HEAD OF BORIS KARLOFF?
continued...
MEET THEM APPLES...

GRANNY #5/15

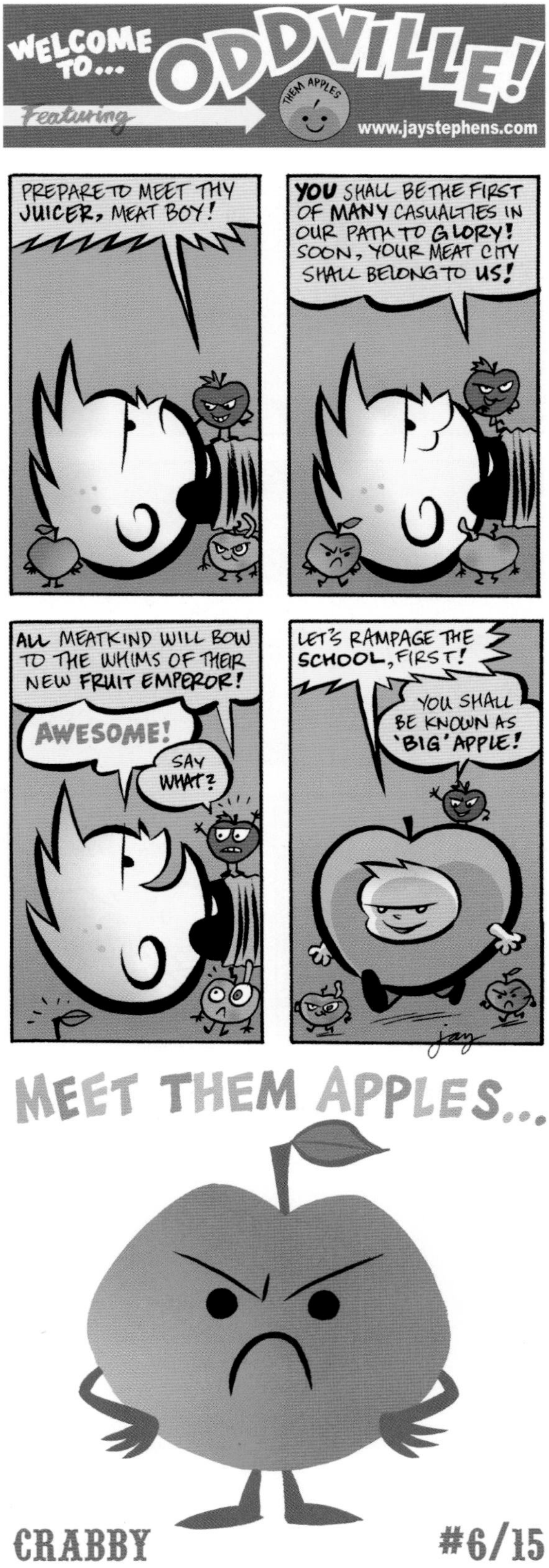
WELCOME TO... ODDVILLE!
Featuring
THEM APPLES
www.jaystephens.com
PREPARE TO MEET THY JUICER, MEAT BOY!
YOU SHALL BE THE FIRST OF MANY CASUALTIES IN OUR PATH TO GLORY! SOON, YOUR MEAT CITY SHALL BELONG TO US!
ALL MEATKIND WILL BOW TO THE WHIMS OF THEIR NEW FRUIT EMPEROR!
AWESOME!
SAY WHAT?
LET'S RAMPAGE THE SCHOOL, FIRST!
YOU SHALL BE KNOWN AS 'BIG' APPLE!
jay
MEET THEM APPLES...
CRABBY
#6/15

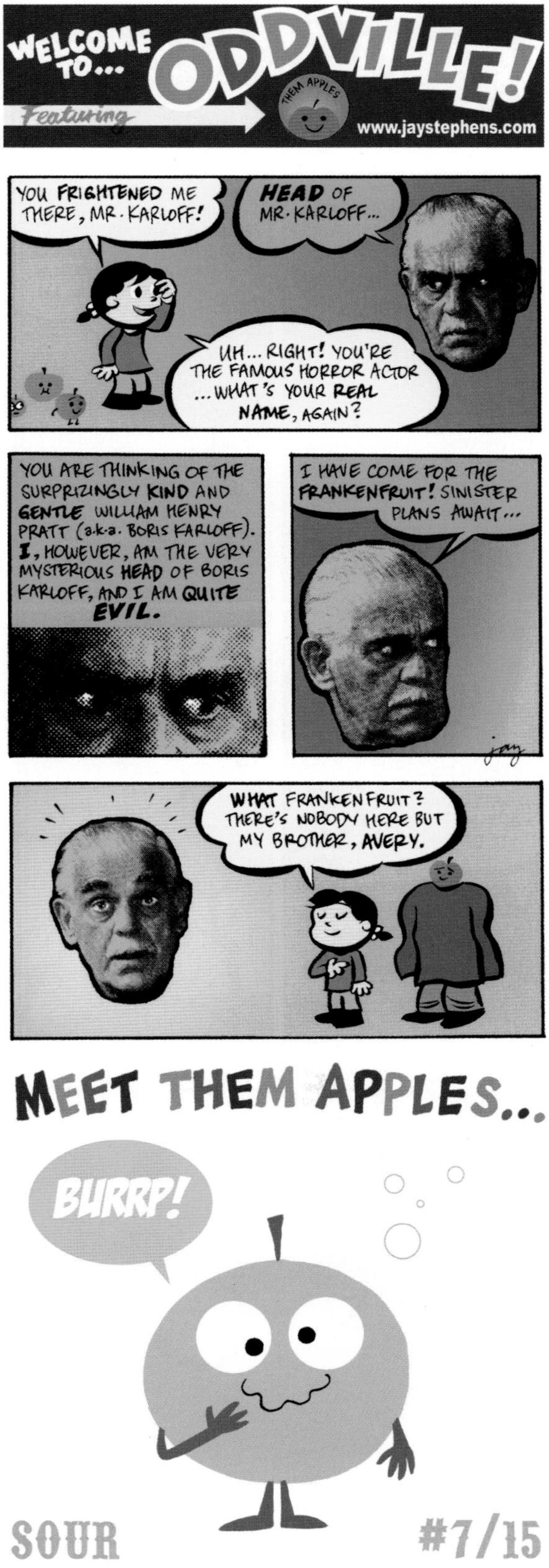
WELCOME TO... ODDVILLE!
Featuring
THEM APPLES
www.jaystephens.com
YOU FRIGHTENED ME THERE, MR. KARLOFF!
HEAD OF MR. KARLOFF...
UH... RIGHT! YOU'RE THE FAMOUS HORROR ACTOR ...WHAT'S YOUR REAL NAME, AGAIN?
YOU ARE THINKING OF THE SURPRIZINGLY KIND AND GENTLE WILLIAM HENRY PRATT (a.k.a. BORIS KARLOFF). I, HOWEVER, AM THE VERY MYSTERIOUS HEAD OF BORIS KARLOFF, AND I AM QUITE EVIL.
I HAVE COME FOR THE FRANKENFRUIT! SINISTER PLANS AWAIT...
jay
WHAT FRANKENFRUIT? THERE'S NOBODY HERE BUT MY BROTHER, AVERY.
MEET THEM APPLES...
BURRP!
SOUR
#7/15

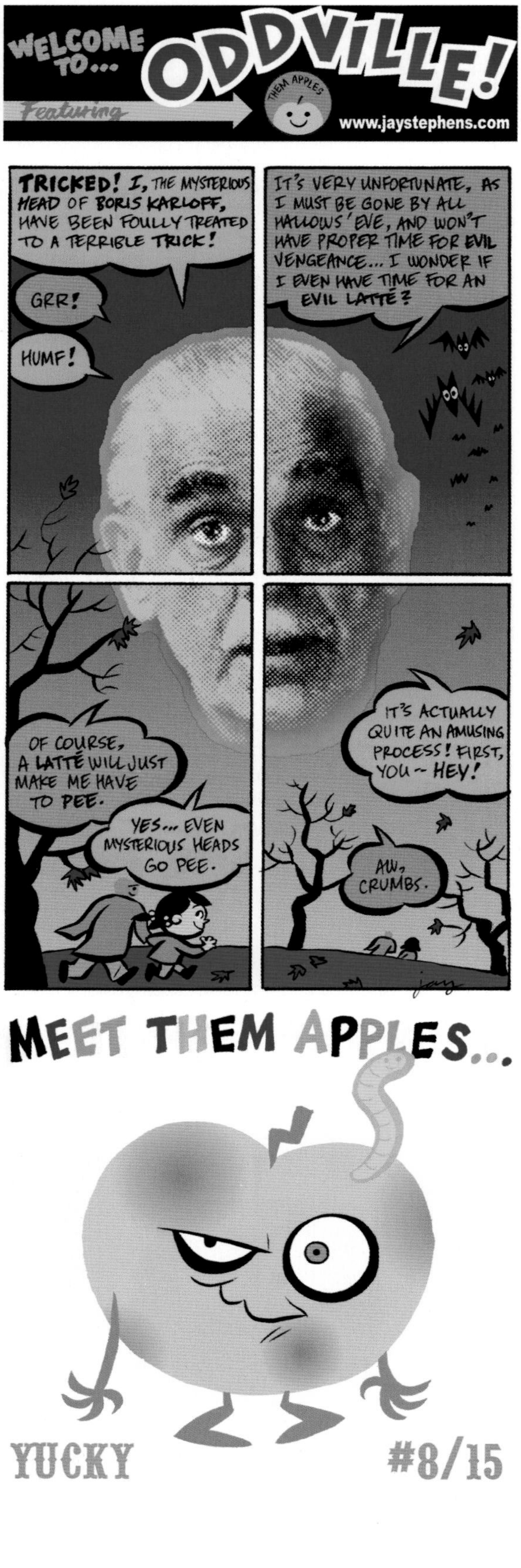
WELCOME TO... ODDVILLE!
Featuring THEM APPLES
www.jaystephens.com
TRICKED! I, THE MYSTERIOUS HEAD OF BORIS KARLOFF, HAVE BEEN FOULLY TREATED TO A TERRIBLE TRICK!
GRR!
HUMF!
IT'S VERY UNFORTUNATE, AS I MUST BE GONE BY ALL HALLOWS' EVE, AND WON'T HAVE PROPER TIME FOR EVIL VENGEANCE... I WONDER IF I EVEN HAVE TIME FOR AN EVIL LATTE?
OF COURSE, A LATTE WILL JUST MAKE ME HAVE TO PEE.
YES... EVEN MYSTERIOUS HEADS GO PEE.
IT'S ACTUALLY QUITE AN AMUSING PROCESS! FIRST, YOU ~ HEY!
AW, CRUMBS.
jay
MEET THEM APPLES...
YUCKY
#8/15

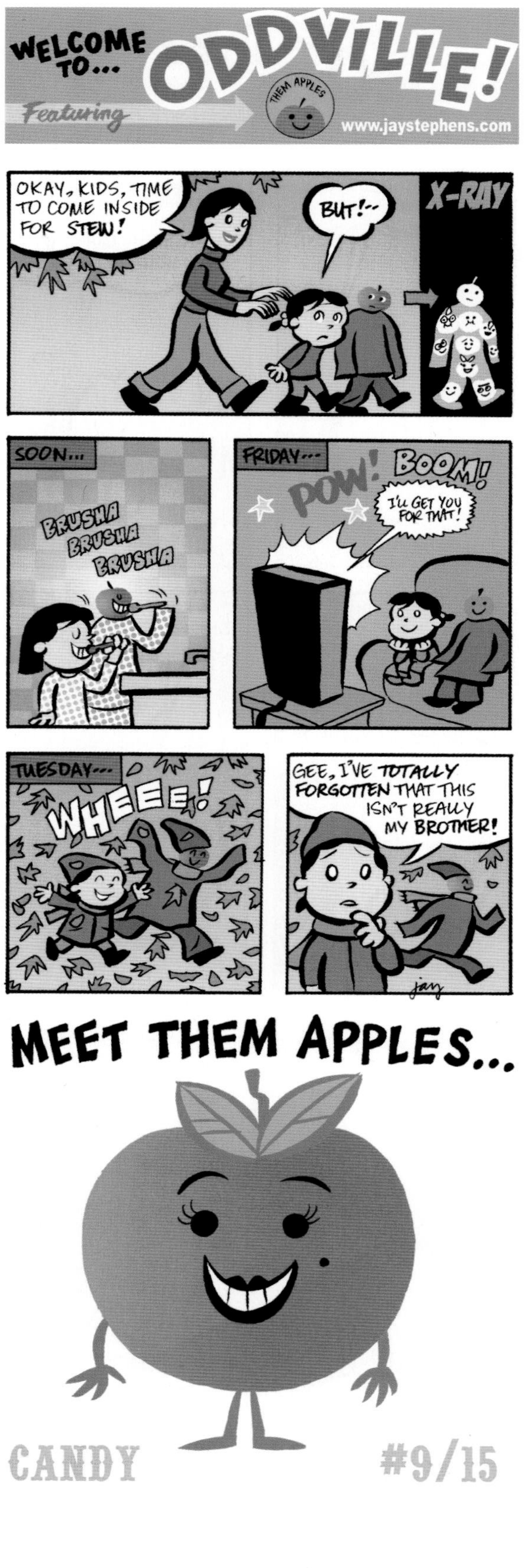
WELCOME TO... ODDVILLE!
Featuring THEM APPLES
www.jaystephens.com
OKAY, KIDS, TIME TO COME INSIDE FOR STEW!
BUT!--
X-RAY
SOON...
BRUSHA BRUSHA BRUSHA
FRIDAY...
POW! BOOM!
I'LL GET YOU FOR THAT!
TUESDAY...
WHEEEE!
GEE, I'VE TOTALLY FORGOTTEN THAT THIS ISN'T REALLY MY BROTHER!
jay
MEET THEM APPLES...
CANDY
#9/15

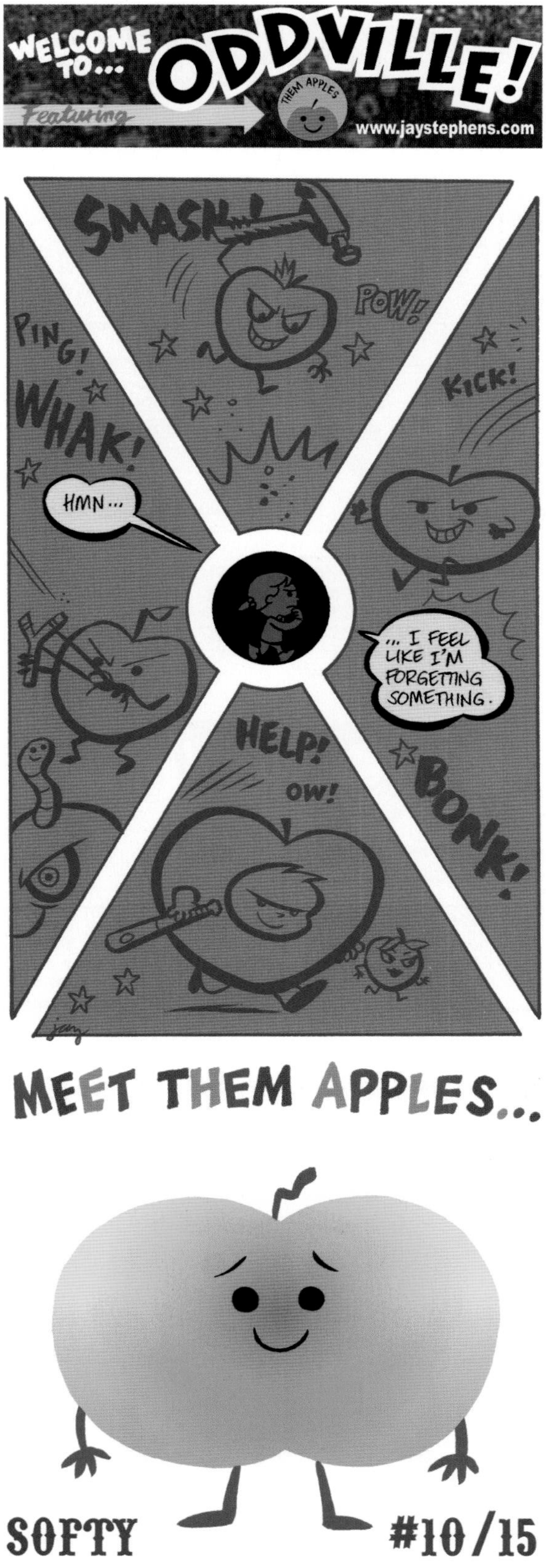
WELCOME TO... ODDVILLE!
Featuring THEM APPLES
www.jaystephens.com
SMASH!
POW!
PING!
WHAK!
KICK!
HMN...
... I FEEL LIKE I'M FORGETTING SOMETHING.
HELP!
OW!
BONK!
MEET THEM APPLES...
SOFTY
#10/15

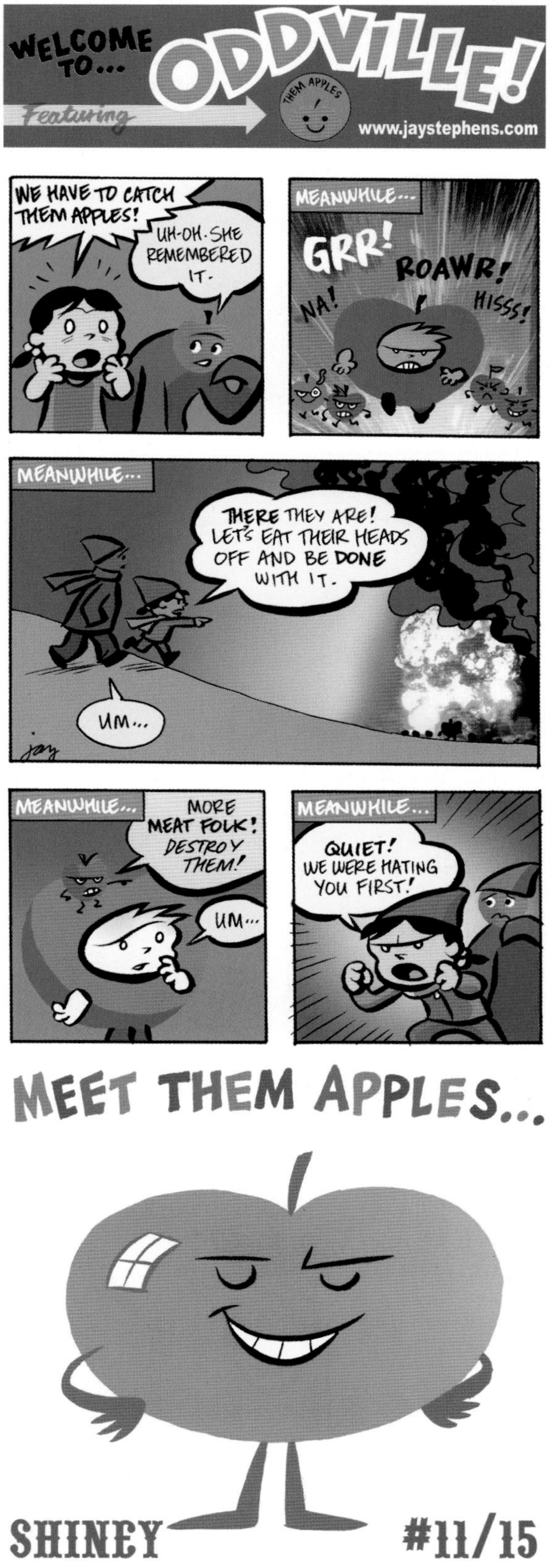
WELCOME TO... ODDVILLE!
Featuring THEM APPLES
www.jaystephens.com
WE HAVE TO CATCH THEM APPLES!
UH-OH. SHE REMEMBERED IT.
MEANWHILE...
GRR!
ROAWR!
NA!
HISSS!
MEANWHILE...
THERE THEY ARE! LET'S EAT THEIR HEADS OFF AND BE DONE WITH IT.
UM...
MEANWHILE...
MORE MEAT FOLK! DESTROY THEM!
UM...
MEANWHILE...
QUIET! WE WERE HATING YOU FIRST!
MEET THEM APPLES...
SHINEY
#11/15

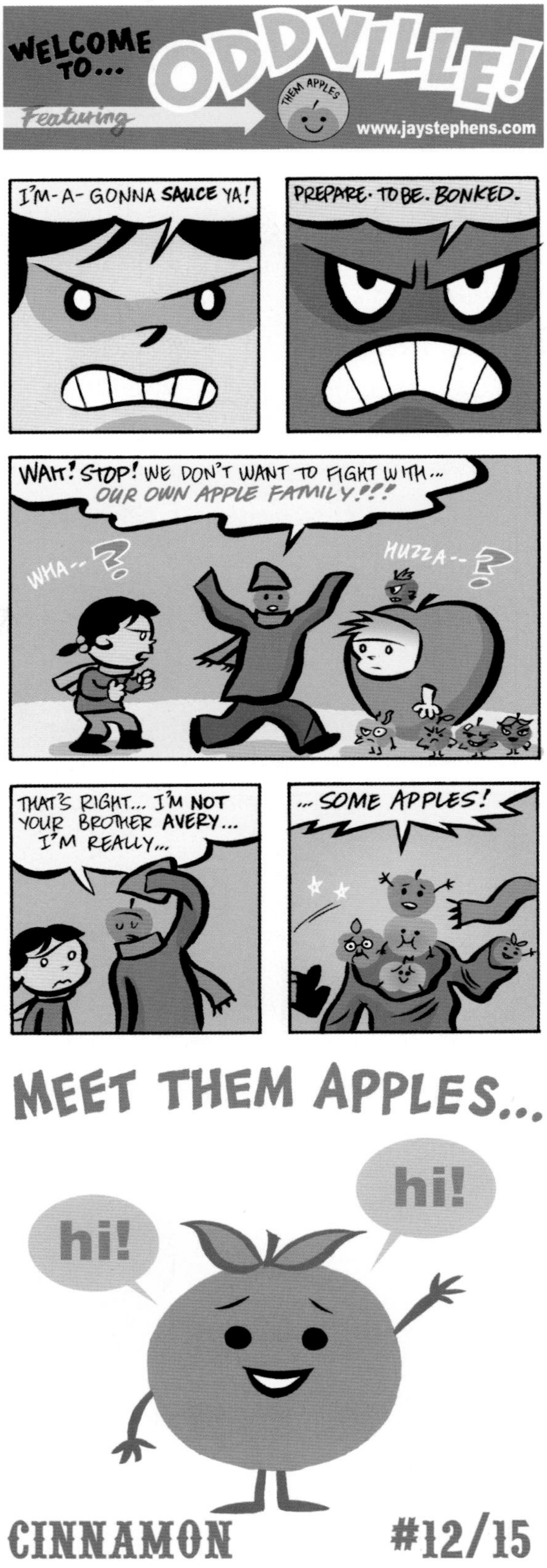
WELCOME TO... ODDVILLE!
Featuring THEM APPLES
www.jaystephens.com
I'M-A- GONNA SAUCE YA!
PREPARE. TO BE. BONKED.
WAIT! STOP! WE DON'T WANT TO FIGHT WITH... OUR OWN APPLE FAMILY!!!
WHA--?
HUZZA--?
THAT'S RIGHT... I'M NOT YOUR BROTHER AVERY... I'M REALLY...
...SOME APPLES!
MEET THEM APPLES...
hi!
hi!
CINNAMON
#12/15

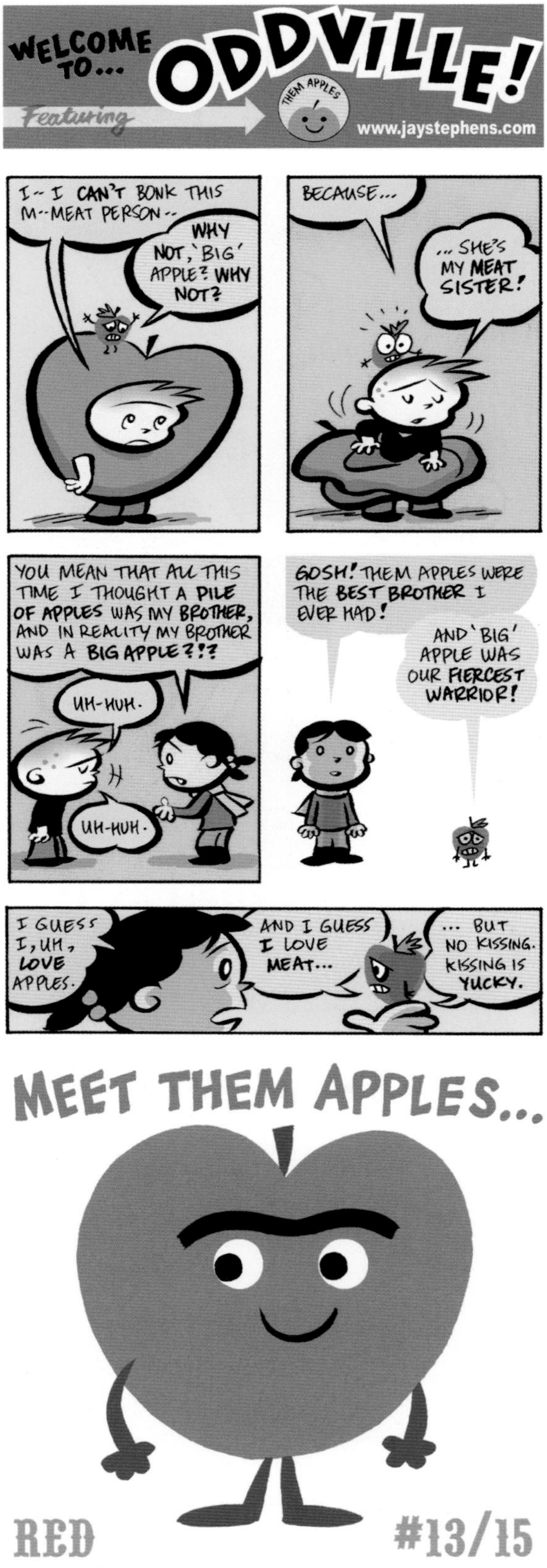
WELCOME TO... ODDVILLE!
Featuring THEM APPLES
www.jaystephens.com
I-- I CAN'T BONK THIS M--MEAT PERSON--
WHY NOT, 'BIG' APPLE? WHY NOT?
BECAUSE...
...SHE'S MY MEAT SISTER!
YOU MEAN THAT ALL THIS TIME I THOUGHT A PILE OF APPLES WAS MY BROTHER, AND IN REALITY MY BROTHER WAS A BIG APPLE?!?
UH-HUH.
UH-HUH.
GOSH! THEM APPLES WERE THE BEST BROTHER I EVER HAD!
AND 'BIG' APPLE WAS OUR FIERCEST WARRIOR!
I GUESS I, UH, LOVE APPLES.
AND I GUESS I LOVE MEAT...
... BUT NO KISSING. KISSING IS YUCKY.
MEET THEM APPLES...
RED
#13/15

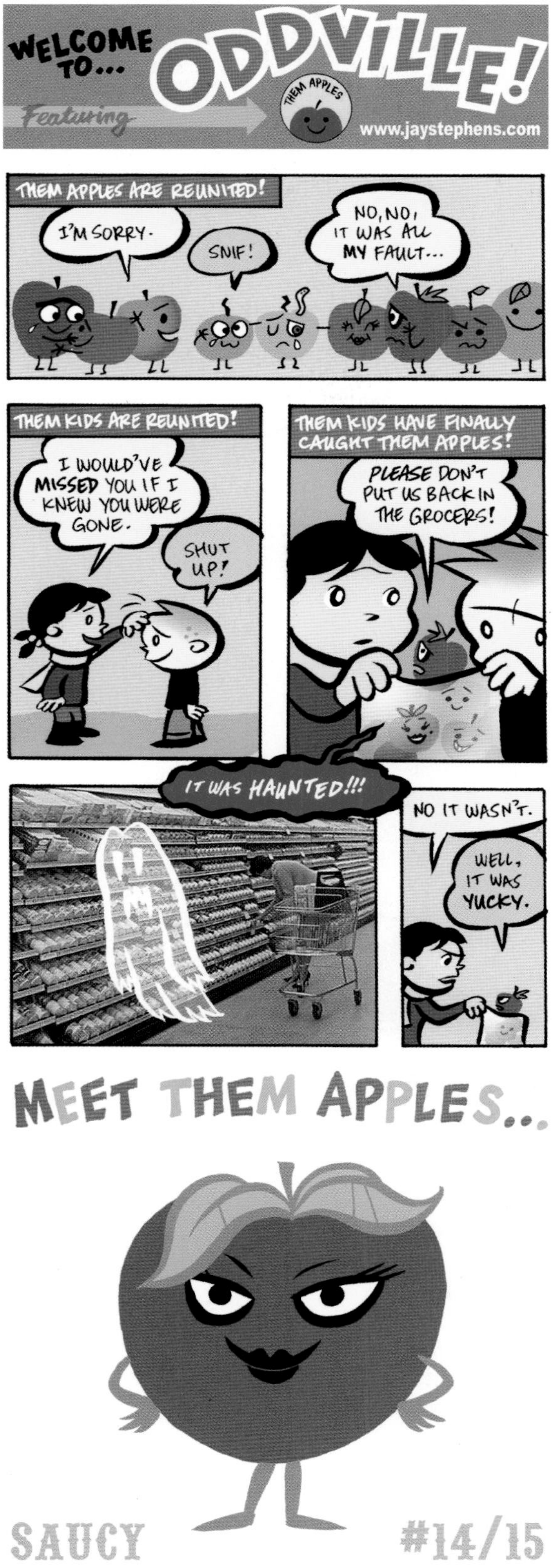
WELCOME TO... ODDVILLE!
Featuring THEM APPLES
www.jaystephens.com
THEM APPLES ARE REUNITED!
I'M SORRY.
SNIF!
NO, NO, IT WAS ALL MY FAULT...
THEM KIDS ARE REUNITED!
I WOULD'VE MISSED YOU IF I KNEW YOU WERE GONE.
SHUT UP!
THEM KIDS HAVE FINALLY CAUGHT THEM APPLES!
PLEASE DON'T PUT US BACK IN THE GROCERS!
IT WAS HAUNTED!!!
NO IT WASN'T.
WELL, IT WAS YUCKY.
MEET THEM APPLES...
SAUCY
#14/15

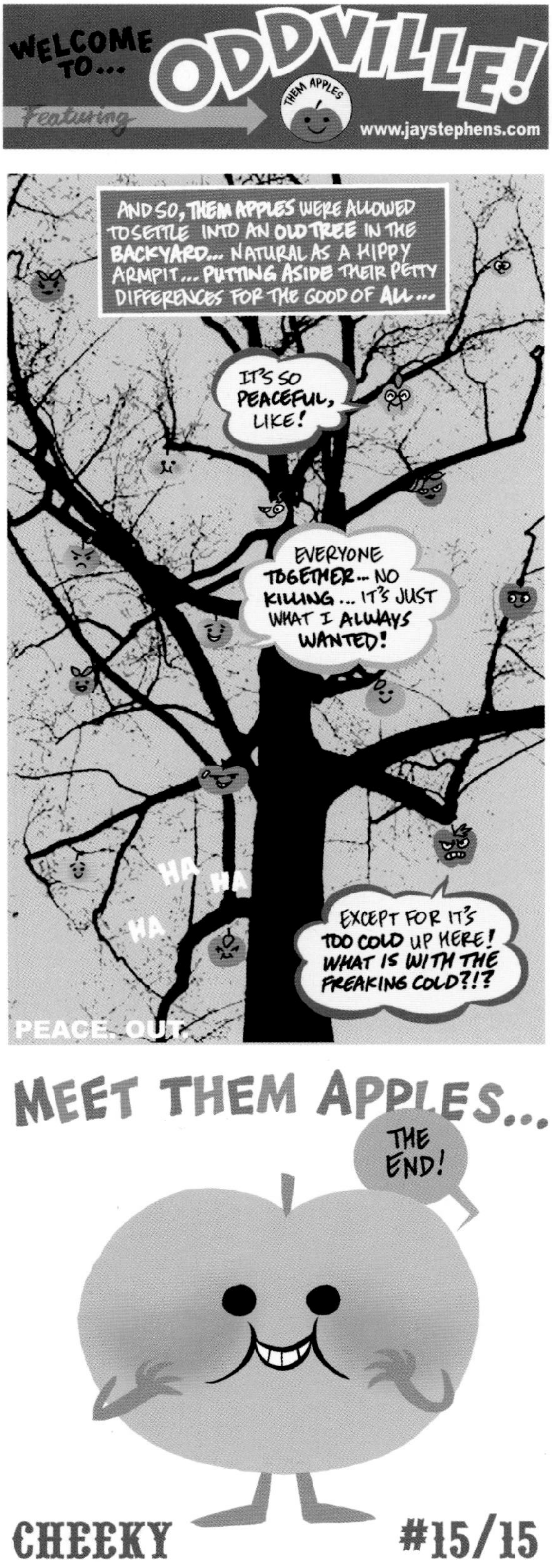
WELCOME TO... ODDVILLE!
Featuring THEM APPLES
www.jaystephens.com
AND SO, THEM APPLES WERE ALLOWED TO SETTLE INTO AN OLD TREE IN THE BACKYARD... NATURAL AS A HIPPY ARMPIT... PUTTING ASIDE THEIR PETTY DIFFERENCES FOR THE GOOD OF ALL...
IT'S SO PEACEFUL, LIKE!
EVERYONE TOGETHER... NO KILLING... IT'S JUST WHAT I ALWAYS WANTED!
HA HA HA
EXCEPT FOR IT'S TOO COLD UP HERE! WHAT IS WITH THE FREAKING COLD?!?
PEACE. OUT.
MEET THEM APPLES...
THE END!
CHEEKY
#15/15

COOTIES

WELCOME TO... LI'L ODDVILLE!
Featuring
LUNGS
www.jaystephens.com
CAFF! CAFF!
HORK--
PTU!
SPLOOTCH.
SMEAR--
LICK
LICK
LICK
AWW-- KITTY WITTY WITTY...
AAH! COOTIES! RUN FOR IT, LEFTY!

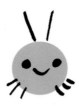

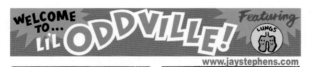

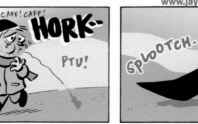

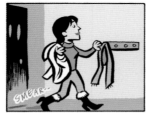

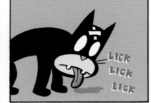

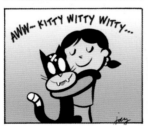

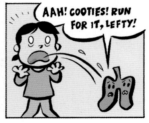

WELCOME TO... LI'L ODDVILLE!
Featuring
PETTY the SNAIL
www.jaystephens.com
HEY! IDIOT! WHERE'S THE DAILY LETTUCE, HUH?
LET'S BUST A MOVE!
I GOTS A RUMBLY IN MY TUMBLY!
S--SORRY PETTY... I'M NOT FEELING SO W--WELL. I THINK I NEED TO GET TO THE HOSPITAL...
DRAMA QUEEN.
USED GARMENTS
FOR AID IN THE AVOIDANCE OF VAMPIRES
SO PUNGENT
AS TO REPEL EVEN THE UNQUIET DEAD
$10,000.00 or best offer
jay

WELCOME TO... LI'L ODDVILLE!
Featuring
COOTIES
www.jaystephens.com
HEY, NO FAIR! YOU HAVE COOTIES!
EVERYONE KNOWS HOW MUCH I LOVE COOTIES AND EVERYTHING... WHY DID YOU HAVE TO GO AND FLAUNT OFF YOUR COOTIES RIGHT IN FRONT OF ME?
HA-CHOOOM!
jay
LOOK! NOW I HAVE SOME!
THANKS!
THIS ONE'S NAME IS "STUPID".

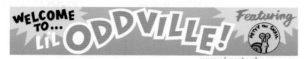

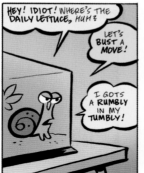

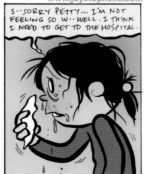

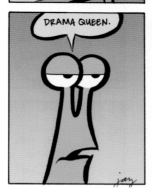

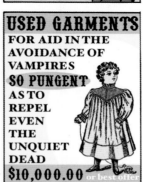

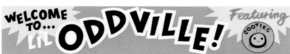

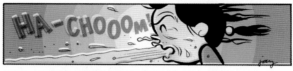

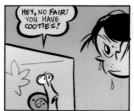

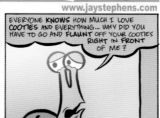

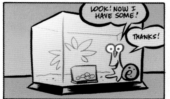

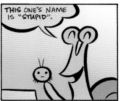

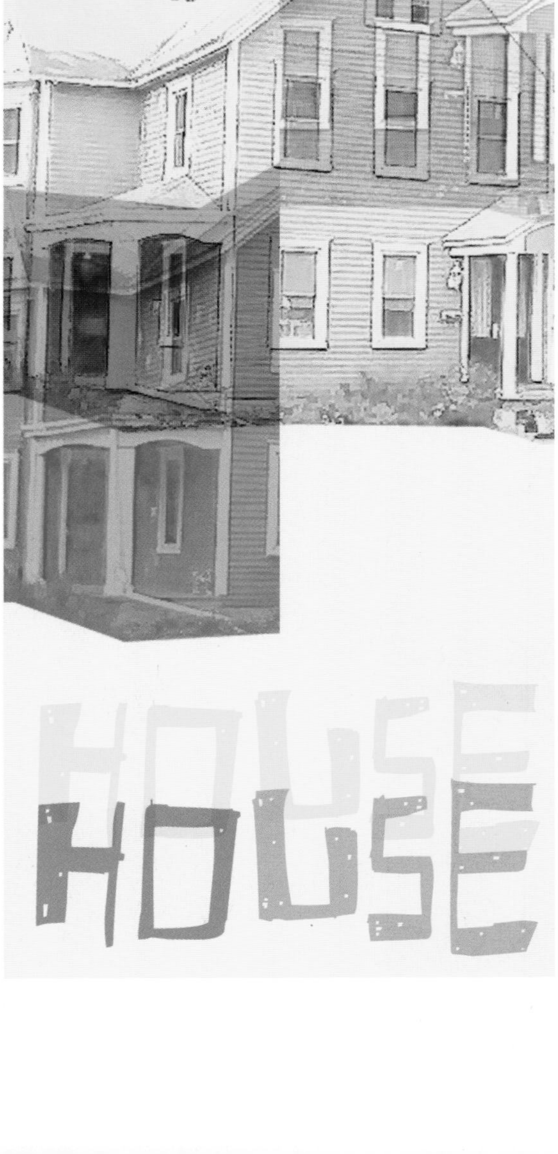
HALFWAY
HOUSE

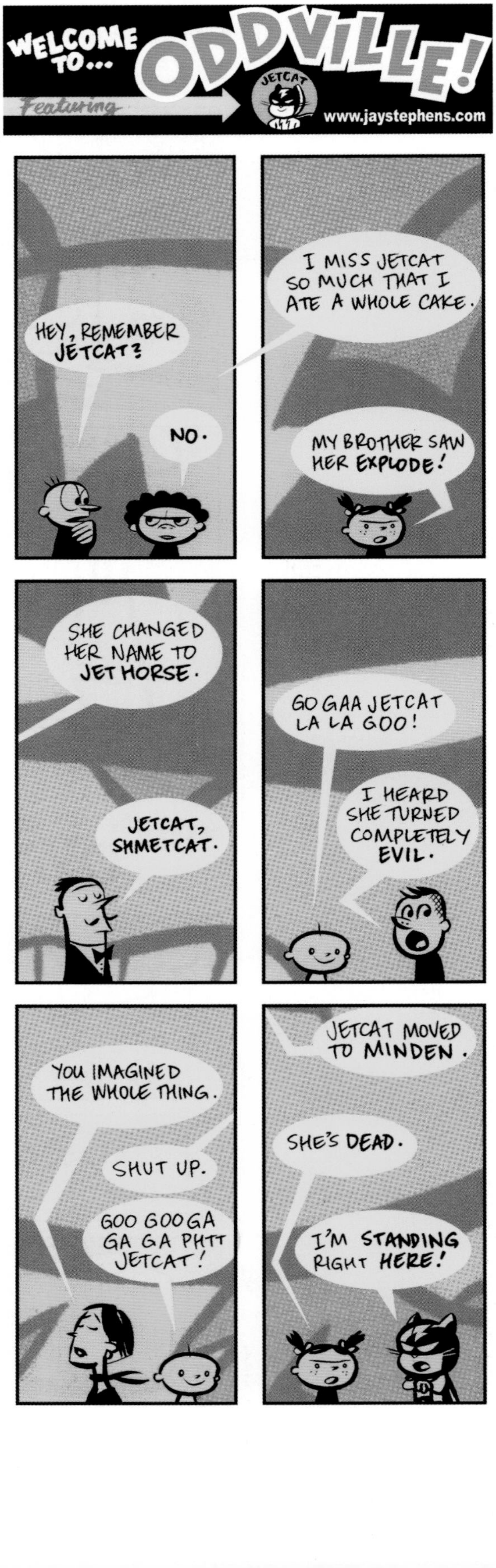
WELCOME TO...
ODDVILLE!
Featuring
JETCAT
www.jaystephens.com
HEY, REMEMBER JETCAT?
NO.
I MISS JETCAT SO MUCH THAT I ATE A WHOLE CAKE.
MY BROTHER SAW HER EXPLODE!
SHE CHANGED HER NAME TO JET HORSE.
JETCAT, SHMETCAT.
GO GAA JETCAT LA LA GOO!
I HEARD SHE TURNED COMPLETELY EVIL.
YOU IMAGINED THE WHOLE THING.
SHUT UP.
GOO GOO GA GA GA PHTT JETCAT!
JETCAT MOVED TO MINDEN.
SHE'S DEAD.
I'M STANDING RIGHT HERE!

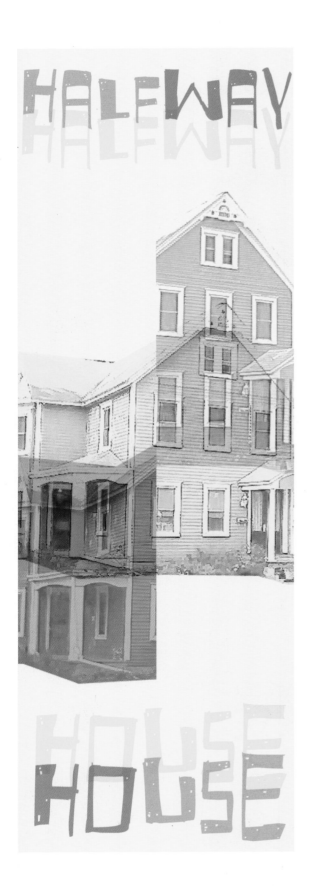

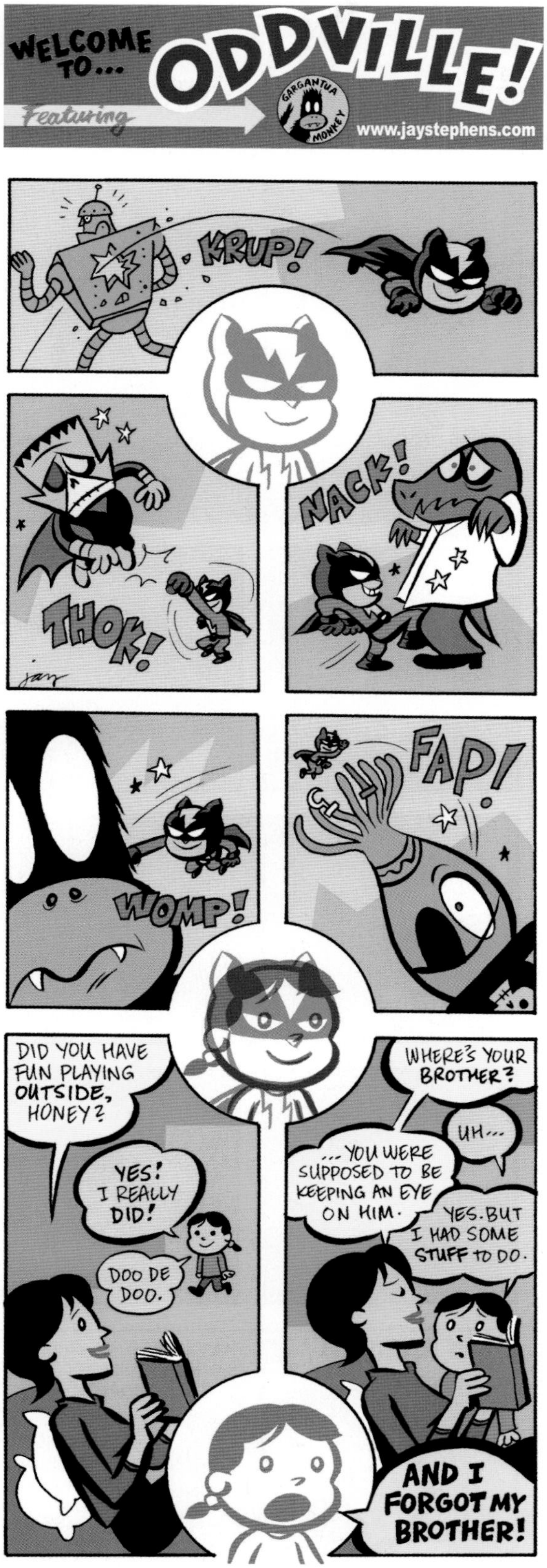
WELCOME TO... ODDVILLE!
Featuring
GARGANTUA MONKEY
www.jaystephens.com
KRUP!
NACK!
THOK!
WOMP!
FAP!
DID YOU HAVE FUN PLAYING OUTSIDE, HONEY?
YES! I REALLY DID!
DOO DE DOO.
WHERE'S YOUR BROTHER?
UH...
...YOU WERE SUPPOSED TO BE KEEPING AN EYE ON HIM.
YES. BUT I HAD SOME STUFF TO DO.
AND I FORGOT MY BROTHER!

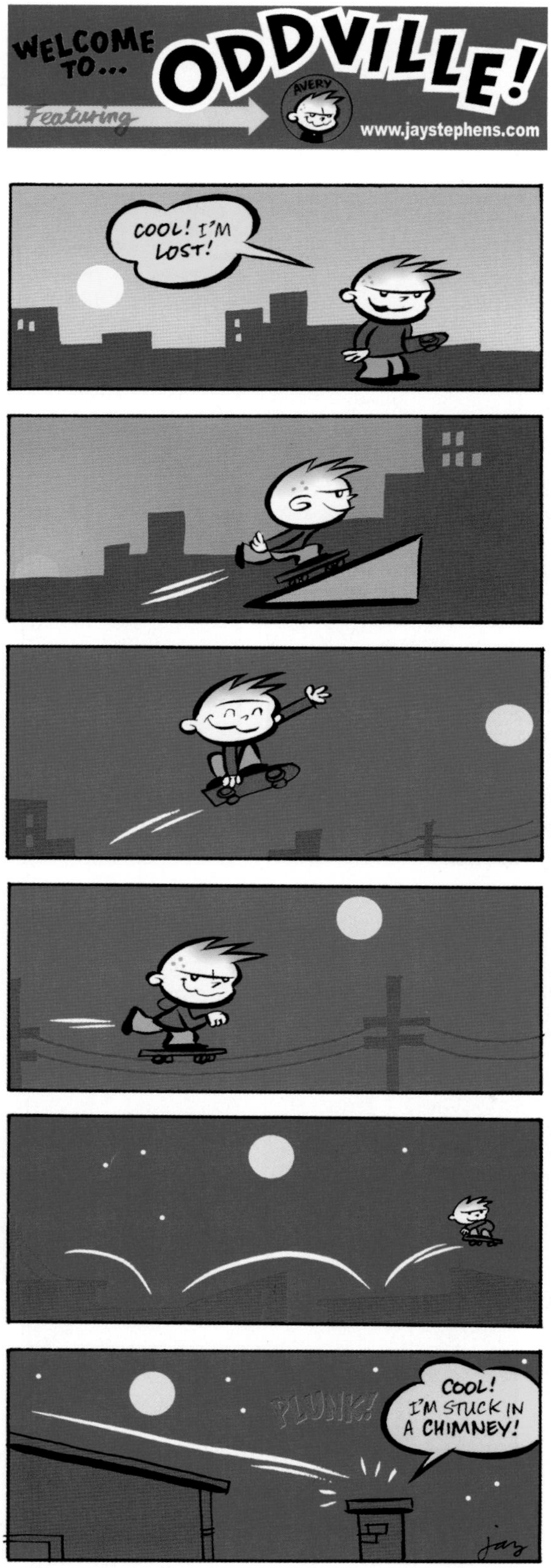
WELCOME TO... ODDVILLE!
Featuring
AVERY
www.jaystephens.com
COOL! I'M LOST!
PLUNK!
COOL! I'M STUCK IN A CHIMNEY!

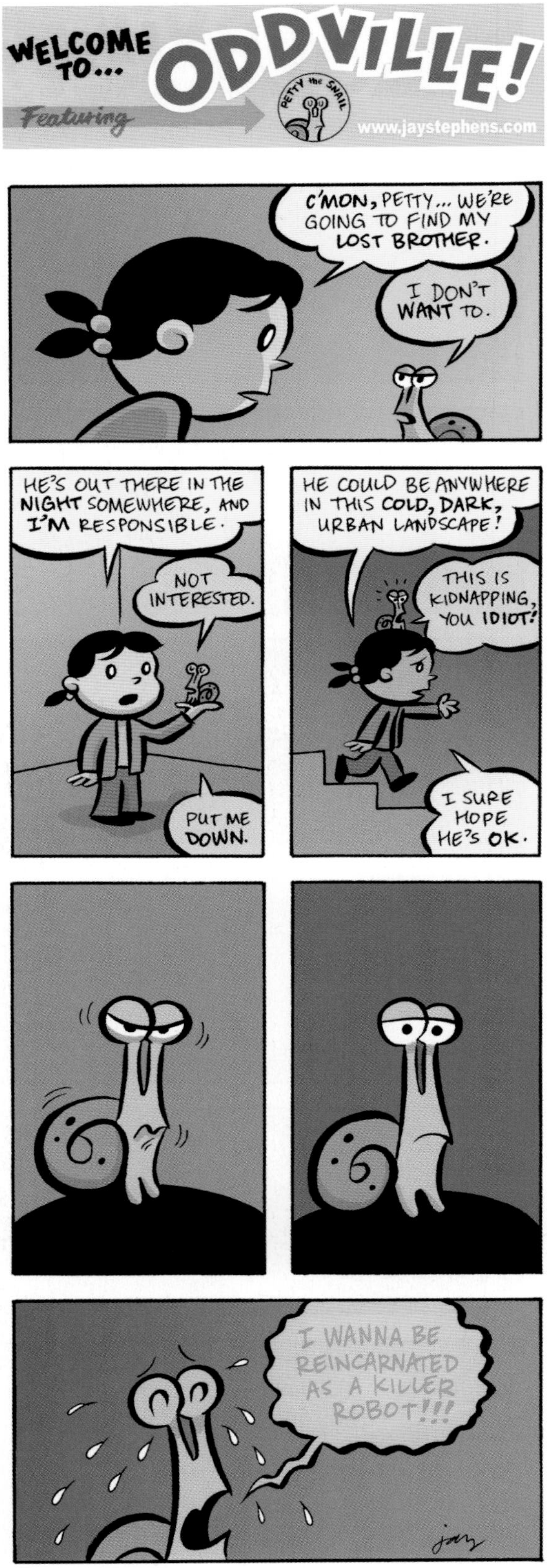
WELCOME TO... ODDVILLE!
Featuring
PETTY the SNAIL
www.jaystephens.com
C'MON, PETTY... WE'RE GOING TO FIND MY LOST BROTHER.
I DON'T WANT TO.
HE'S OUT THERE IN THE NIGHT SOMEWHERE, AND I'M RESPONSIBLE.
NOT INTERESTED.
PUT ME DOWN.
HE COULD BE ANYWHERE IN THIS COLD, DARK, URBAN LANDSCAPE!
THIS IS KIDNAPPING, YOU IDIOT!
I SURE HOPE HE'S OK.
I WANNA BE REINCARNATED AS A KILLER ROBOT!!!
jay

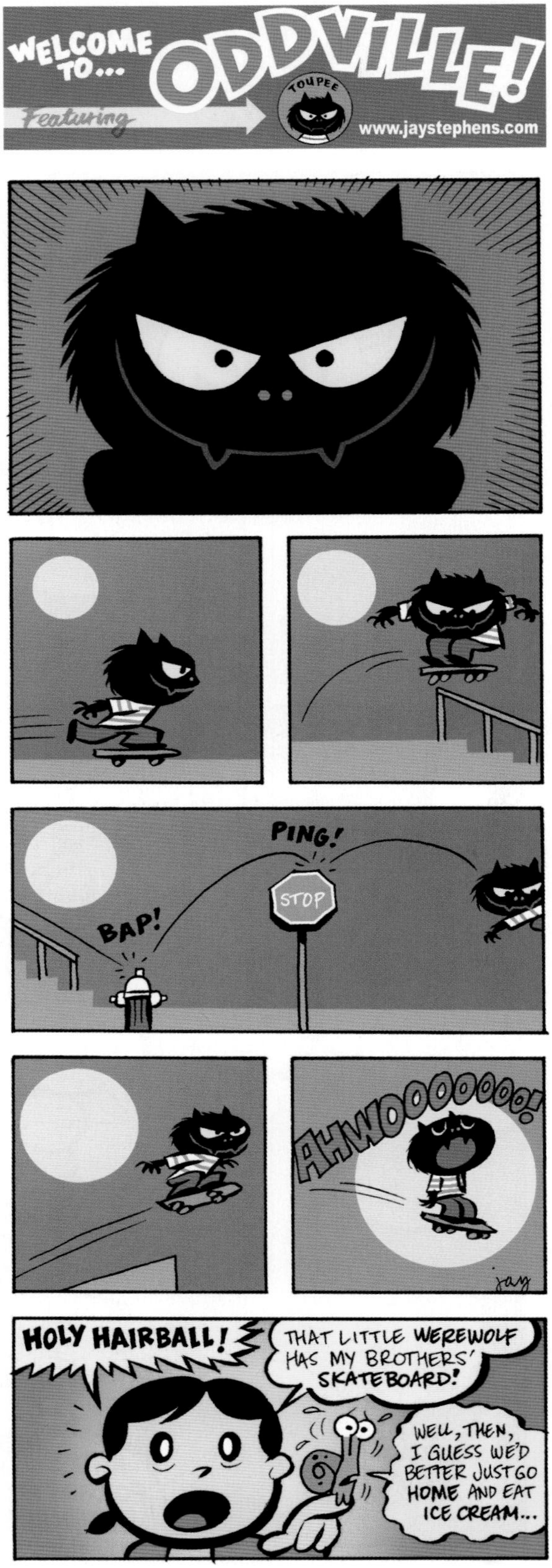
WELCOME TO... ODDVILLE!
Featuring
TOUPEE
www.jaystephens.com
PING!
BAP!
STOP
AHWOOOOOOO!
jay
HOLY HAIRBALL!
THAT LITTLE WEREWOLF HAS MY BROTHERS' SKATEBOARD!
WELL, THEN, I GUESS WE'D BETTER JUST GO HOME AND EAT ICE CREAM...

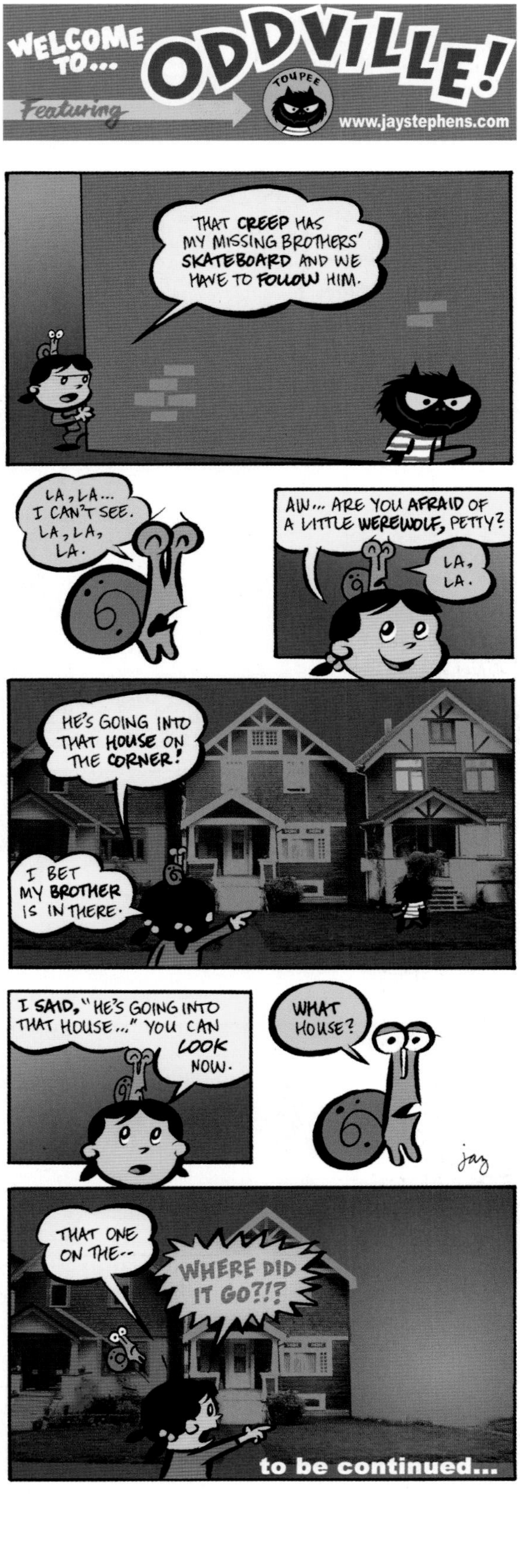
WELCOME TO... ODDVILLE!
Featuring
TOUPEE
www.jaystephens.com
THAT CREEP HAS MY MISSING BROTHERS' SKATEBOARD AND WE HAVE TO FOLLOW HIM.
LA, LA... I CAN'T SEE. LA, LA, LA.
AW... ARE YOU AFRAID OF A LITTLE WEREWOLF, PETTY?
LA, LA.
HE'S GOING INTO THAT HOUSE ON THE CORNER!
I BET MY BROTHER IS IN THERE.
I SAID, "HE'S GOING INTO THAT HOUSE..." YOU CAN LOOK NOW.
WHAT HOUSE?
jay
THAT ONE ON THE--
WHERE DID IT GO?!?
to be continued...

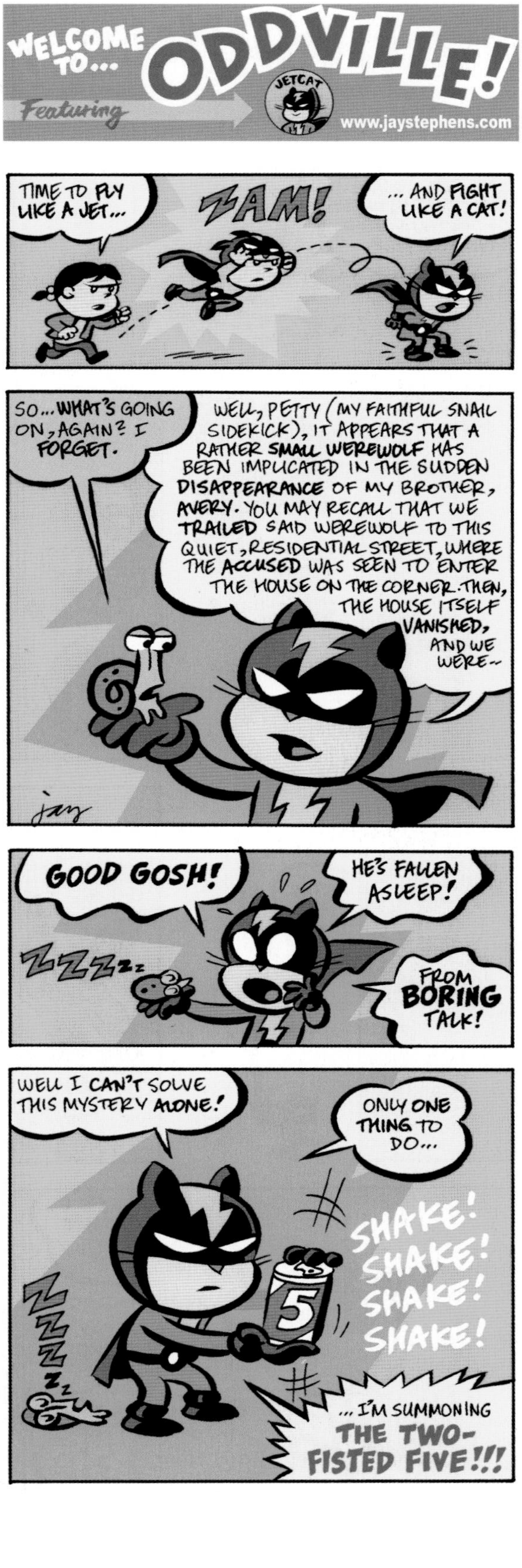
WELCOME TO... ODDVILLE!
Featuring
JETCAT
www.jaystephens.com
TIME TO FLY LIKE A JET...
ZAM!
... AND FIGHT LIKE A CAT!
SO... WHAT'S GOING ON, AGAIN? I FORGET.
WELL, PETTY (MY FAITHFUL SNAIL SIDEKICK), IT APPEARS THAT A RATHER SMALL WEREWOLF HAS BEEN IMPLICATED IN THE SUDDEN DISAPPEARANCE OF MY BROTHER, AVERY. YOU MAY RECALL THAT WE TRAILED SAID WEREWOLF TO THIS QUIET, RESIDENTIAL STREET, WHERE THE ACCUSED WAS SEEN TO ENTER THE HOUSE ON THE CORNER. THEN, THE HOUSE ITSELF VANISHED, AND WE WERE--
jay
GOOD GOSH!
HE'S FALLEN ASLEEP!
ZZZzz
FROM BORING TALK!
WELL I CAN'T SOLVE THIS MYSTERY ALONE!
ONLY ONE THING TO DO...
SHAKE! SHAKE! SHAKE! SHAKE!
5
... I'M SUMMONING THE TWO-FISTED FIVE!!!

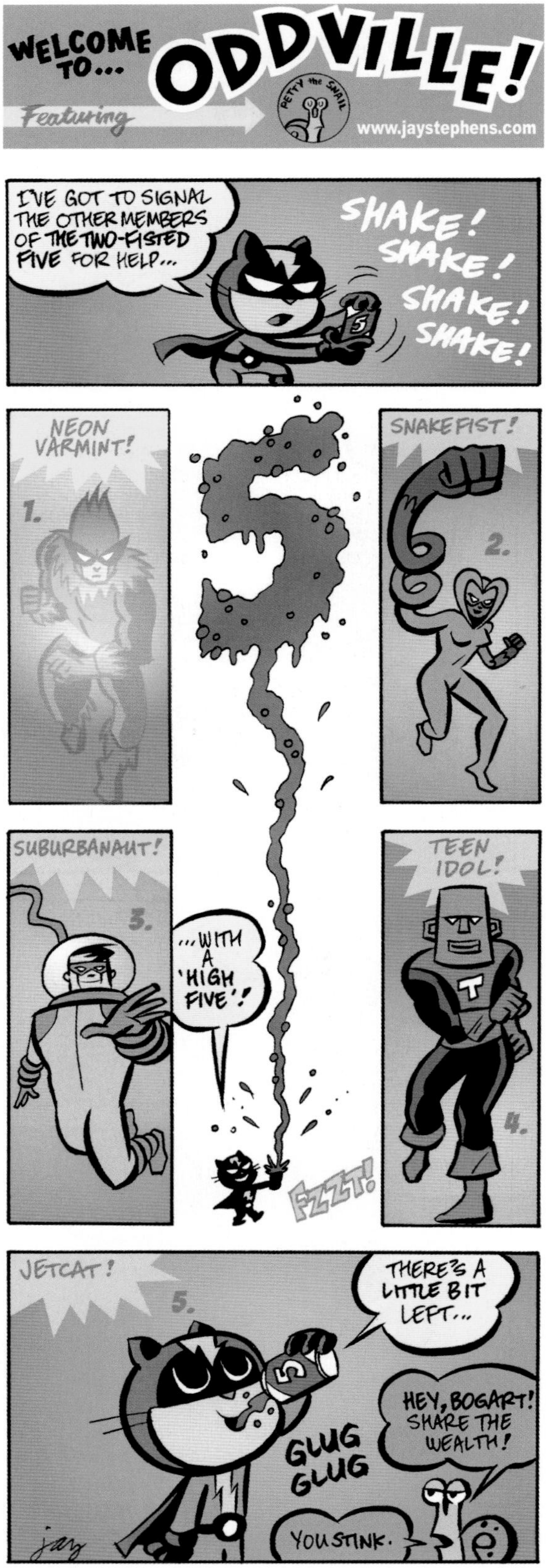
WELCOME TO... ODDVILLE!
Featuring PETTY the SNAIL
www.jaystephens.com
I'VE GOT TO SIGNAL THE OTHER MEMBERS OF THE TWO-FISTED FIVE FOR HELP...
SHAKE! SHAKE! SHAKE! SHAKE!
NEON VARMINT!
1.
SNAKEFIST!
2.
SUBURBANAUT!
3.
...WITH A 'HIGH FIVE'!
TEEN IDOL!
4.
FZZZT!
JETCAT!
5.
THERE'S A LITTLE BIT LEFT...
GLUG GLUG
HEY, BOGART! SHARE THE WEALTH!
YOU STINK.
jay

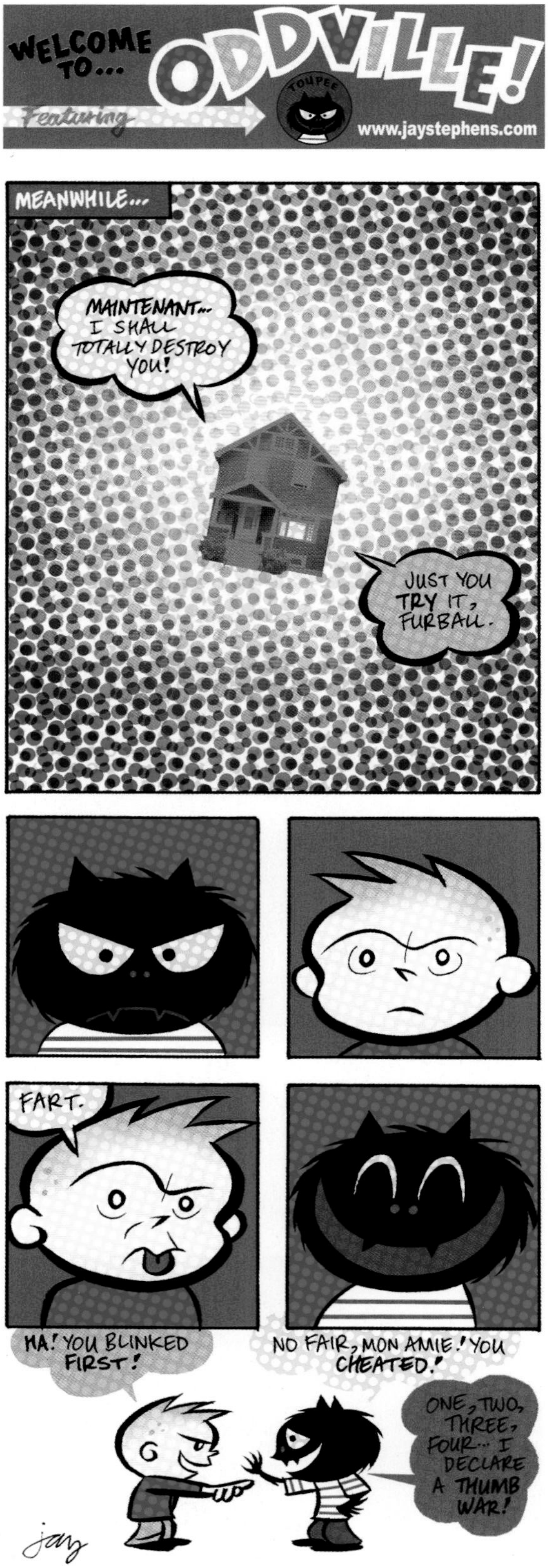
WELCOME TO... ODDVILLE!
Featuring TOUPEE
www.jaystephens.com
MEANWHILE...
MAINTENANT... I SHALL TOTALLY DESTROY YOU!
JUST YOU TRY IT, FURBALL.
FART.
HA! YOU BLINKED FIRST!
NO FAIR, MON AMIE! YOU CHEATED!
ONE, TWO, THREE, FOUR... I DECLARE A THUMB WAR!
jay

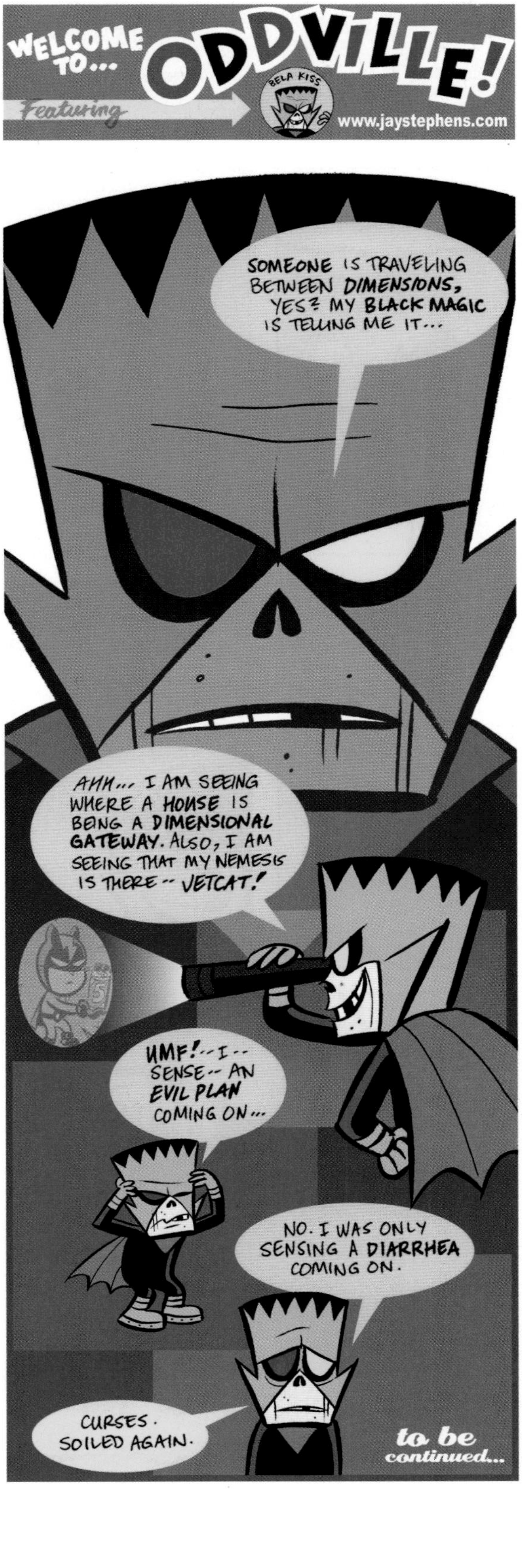
WELCOME TO... ODDVILLE!
Featuring
BELA KISS
www.jaystephens.com
SOMEONE IS TRAVELING BETWEEN DIMENSIONS, YES? MY BLACK MAGIC IS TELLING ME IT...
AHH... I AM SEEING WHERE A HOUSE IS BEING A DIMENSIONAL GATEWAY. ALSO, I AM SEEING THAT MY NEMESIS IS THERE -- JETCAT!
UMF! -- I -- SENSE -- AN EVIL PLAN COMING ON...
NO. I WAS ONLY SENSING A DIARRHEA COMING ON.
CURSES. SOILED AGAIN.
to be continued...

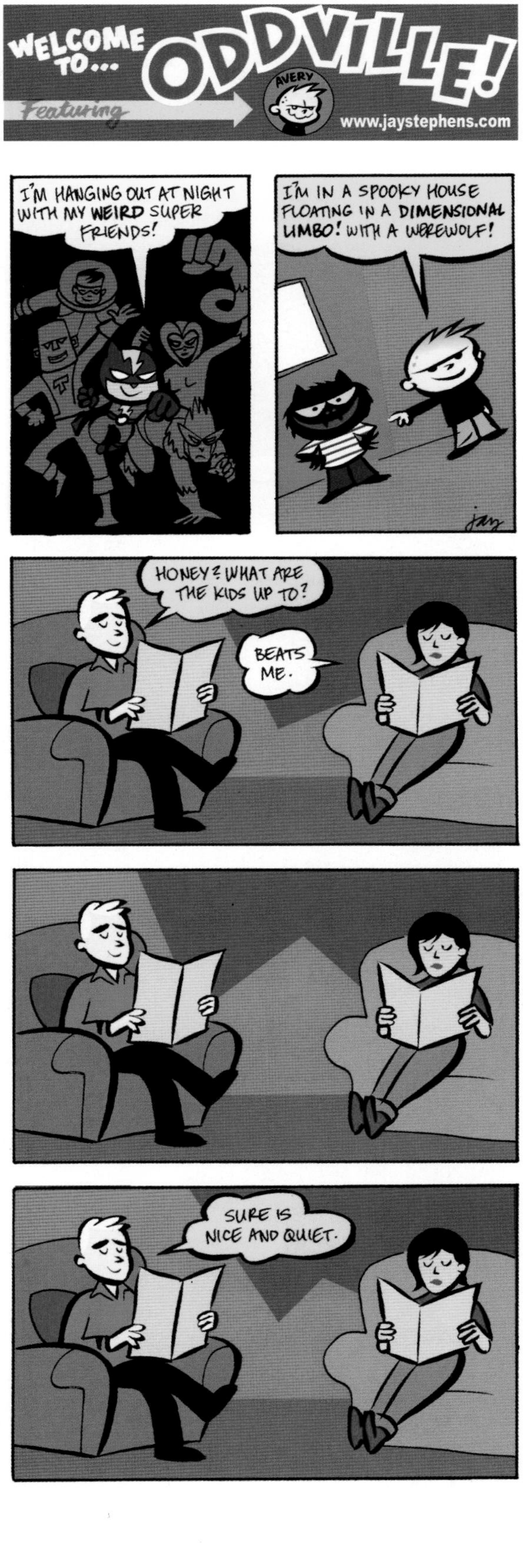
WELCOME TO... ODDVILLE!
Featuring
AVERY
www.jaystephens.com
I'M HANGING OUT AT NIGHT WITH MY WEIRD SUPER FRIENDS!
I'M IN A SPOOKY HOUSE FLOATING IN A DIMENSIONAL LIMBO! WITH A WEREWOLF!
jay
HONEY? WHAT ARE THE KIDS UP TO?
BEATS ME.
SURE IS NICE AND QUIET.

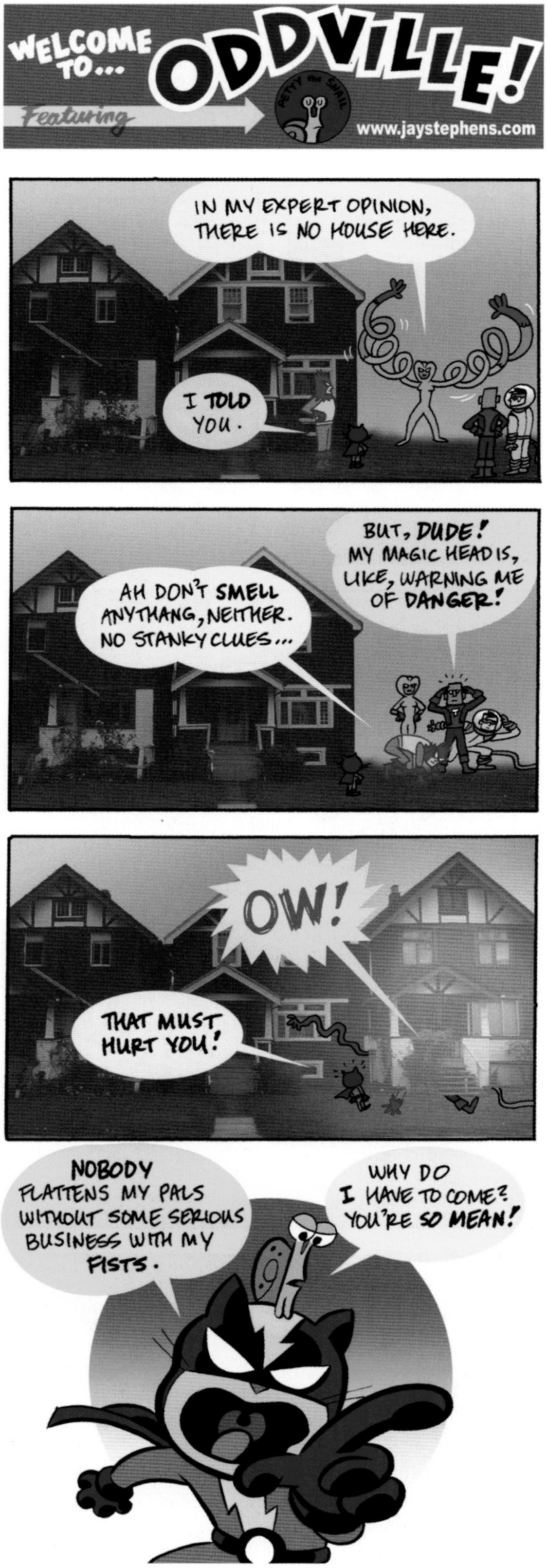
WELCOME TO... ODDVILLE!
Featuring
BETTY the SNAIL
www.jaystephens.com
IN MY EXPERT OPINION, THERE IS NO HOUSE HERE.
I TOLD YOU.
BUT, DUDE! MY MAGIC HEAD IS, LIKE, WARNING ME OF DANGER!
AH DON'T SMELL ANYTHANG, NEITHER. NO STANKY CLUES...
OW!
THAT MUST HURT YOU!
NOBODY FLATTENS MY PALS WITHOUT SOME SERIOUS BUSINESS WITH MY FISTS.
WHY DO I HAVE TO COME? YOU'RE SO MEAN!

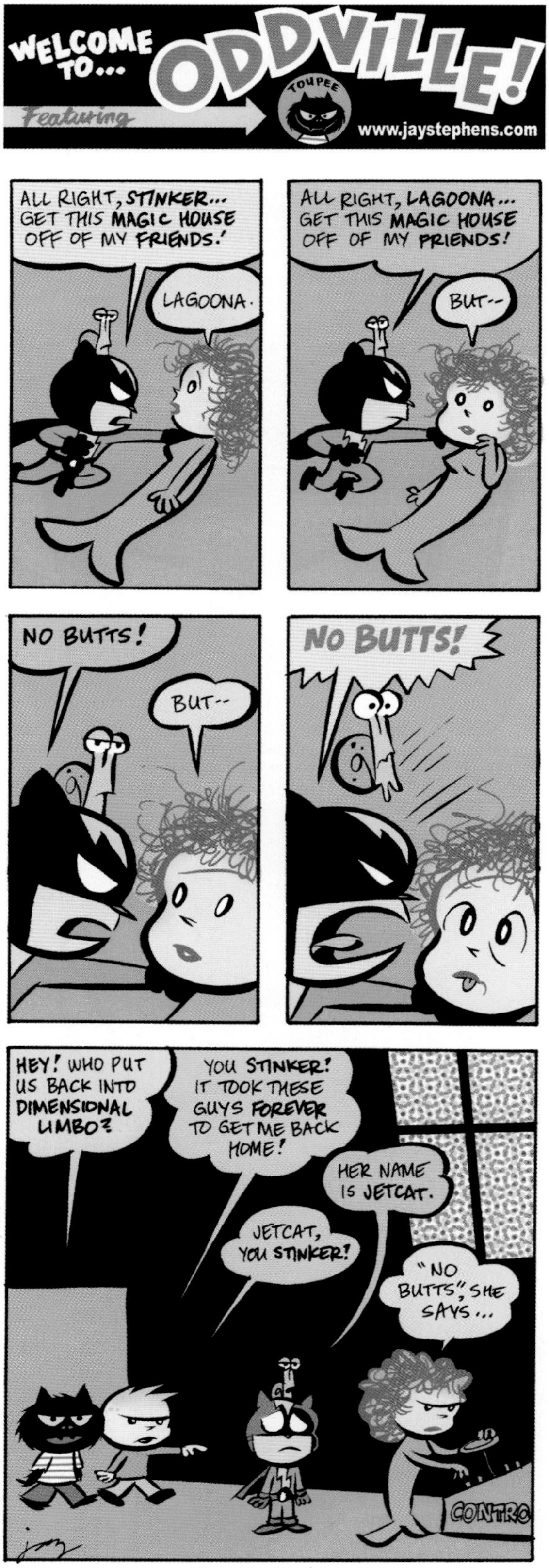
WELCOME TO... ODDVILLE!
Featuring
TOUPEE
www.jaystephens.com
ALL RIGHT, STINKER... GET THIS MAGIC HOUSE OFF OF MY FRIENDS!
LAGOONA.
ALL RIGHT, LAGOONA... GET THIS MAGIC HOUSE OFF OF MY FRIENDS!
BUT--
NO BUTTS!
BUT--
NO BUTTS!
HEY! WHO PUT US BACK INTO DIMENSIONAL LIMBO?
YOU STINKER! IT TOOK THESE GUYS FOREVER TO GET ME BACK HOME!
HER NAME IS JETCAT.
JETCAT, YOU STINKER!
"NO BUTTS," SHE SAYS...
CONTRO

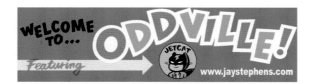

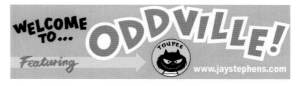

WELCOME TO... ODDVILLE!
Featuring
JETCAT
www.jaystephens.com
BEHOLD, IF YOU WILL, THE UNCANNY HALF-WAY HOUSE...
...HOVERING, AS IT DOES, BETWEEN THE DIMENSIONS.
HOVER
HOVER
INSIDE, WE FIND TOUPÉE... HALF BOY, HALF WOLF...
GRR!
LAGOONA... HALF GIRL, HALF FISH...
GLUB!
...AND EUGENE... HALF PHOTO, HALF DOODLE.
GAH!
THE LITTLE SUPERHERO, JETCAT, DOESN'T THINK EUGENE IS A VERY GOOD CHARACTER, AND SENDS HIM OFF TO SULK IN THE LAUNDRY ROOM.
GOWAN... GET GOIN'!
AW, MAN!
PETTY THE SNAIL HAS SOMETHING TO SAY...
YOU'RE AN IDIOT.
GET US HOME RIGHT NOW, IDIOT.
HEY!

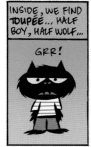

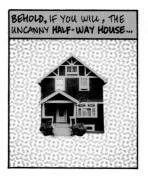

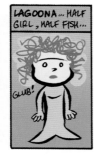

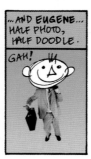

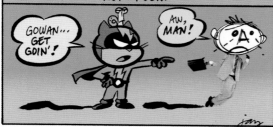

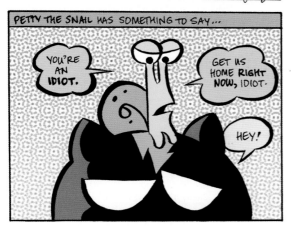

WELCOME TO... ODDVILLE!
Featuring
TOUPEE
www.jaystephens.com
STOP SUCKING OUT, YOU BIG BABIES WITH POOPY DIAPERS ON...
...YOU KNOW I'M GOING TO SAVE OUR LIVES AS USUAL.
PAIRHAPS EEF YOU WERE A ROBOT, OR ALSO A ST. BERNARD, ZIS WOULD BE TRUE... BUT YOU ARE ONLY A ~ HOW-YOU-SAY? ~ 'SUPERHERO'... ZE PUNCHING OUT EES OF NO USE TO US ERE IN LIMBO.
PARASOLS.
I'M SORRY, WHAT WAS THAT? I WAS THINKING ABOUT PARASOLS.
LE FAINT!

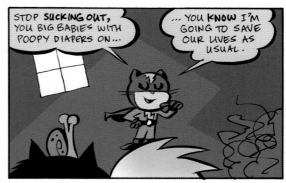

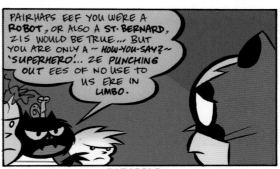

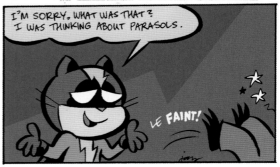

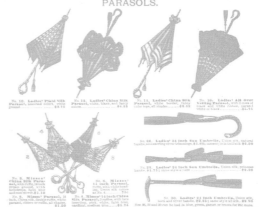

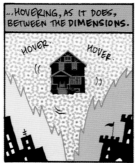

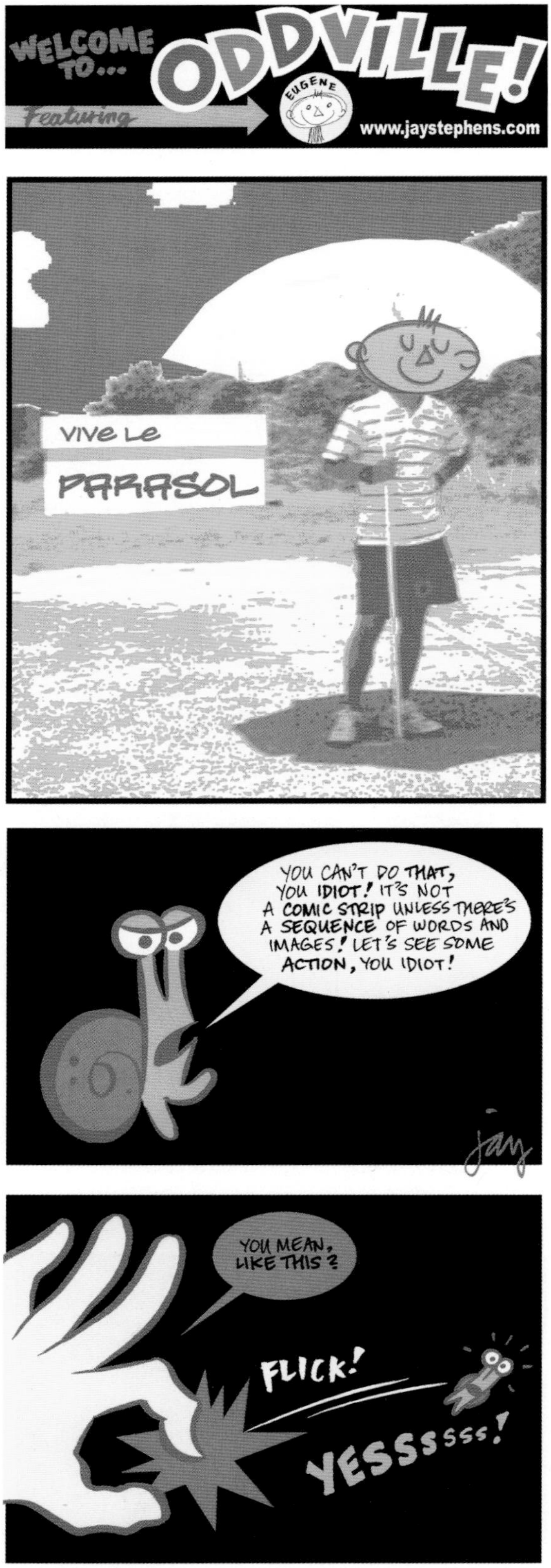
WELCOME TO... ODDVILLE!
Featuring
EUGENE
www.jaystephens.com
VIVE LE
PARASOL
YOU CAN'T DO THAT, YOU IDIOT! IT'S NOT A COMIC STRIP UNLESS THERE'S A SEQUENCE OF WORDS AND IMAGES! LET'S SEE SOME ACTION, YOU IDIOT!
YOU MEAN, LIKE THIS?
FLICK!
YESSSsss!

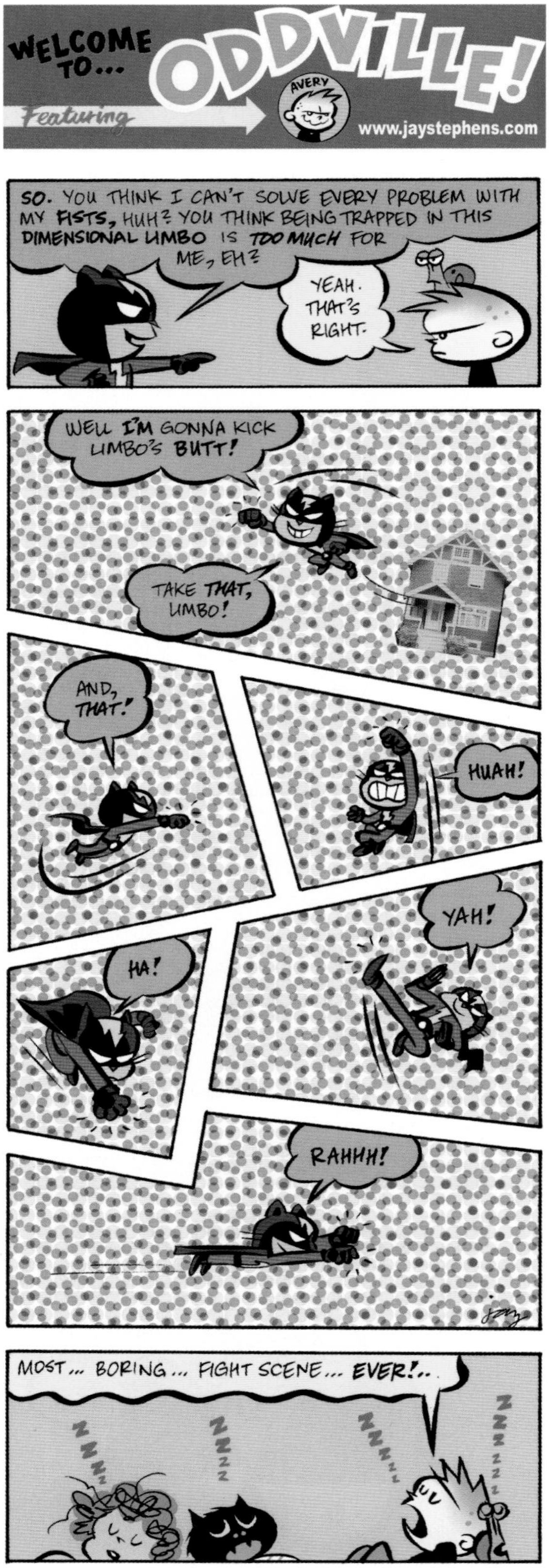
WELCOME TO... ODDVILLE!
Featuring
AVERY
www.jaystephens.com
SO. YOU THINK I CAN'T SOLVE EVERY PROBLEM WITH MY FISTS, HUH? YOU THINK BEING TRAPPED IN THIS DIMENSIONAL LIMBO IS TOO MUCH FOR ME, EH?
YEAH. THAT'S RIGHT.
WELL I'M GONNA KICK LIMBO'S BUTT!
TAKE THAT, LIMBO!
AND, THAT!
HUAH!
YAH!
HA!
RAHHH!
MOST... BORING... FIGHT SCENE... EVER!..

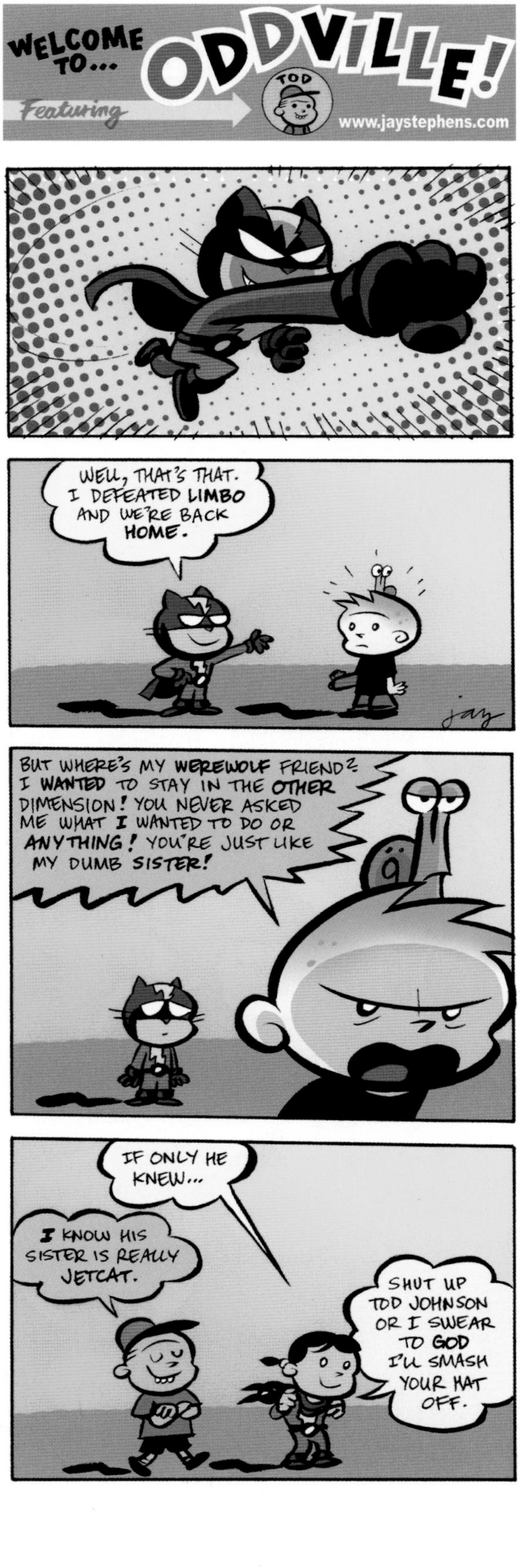
WELCOME TO... ODDVILLE!
Featuring TOD
www.jaystephens.com
WELL, THAT'S THAT. I DEFEATED LIMBO AND WE'RE BACK HOME.
BUT WHERE'S MY WEREWOLF FRIEND? I WANTED TO STAY IN THE OTHER DIMENSION! YOU NEVER ASKED ME WHAT I WANTED TO DO OR ANYTHING! YOU'RE JUST LIKE MY DUMB SISTER!
IF ONLY HE KNEW...
I KNOW HIS SISTER IS REALLY JETCAT.
SHUT UP TOD JOHNSON OR I SWEAR TO GOD I'LL SMASH YOUR HAT OFF.

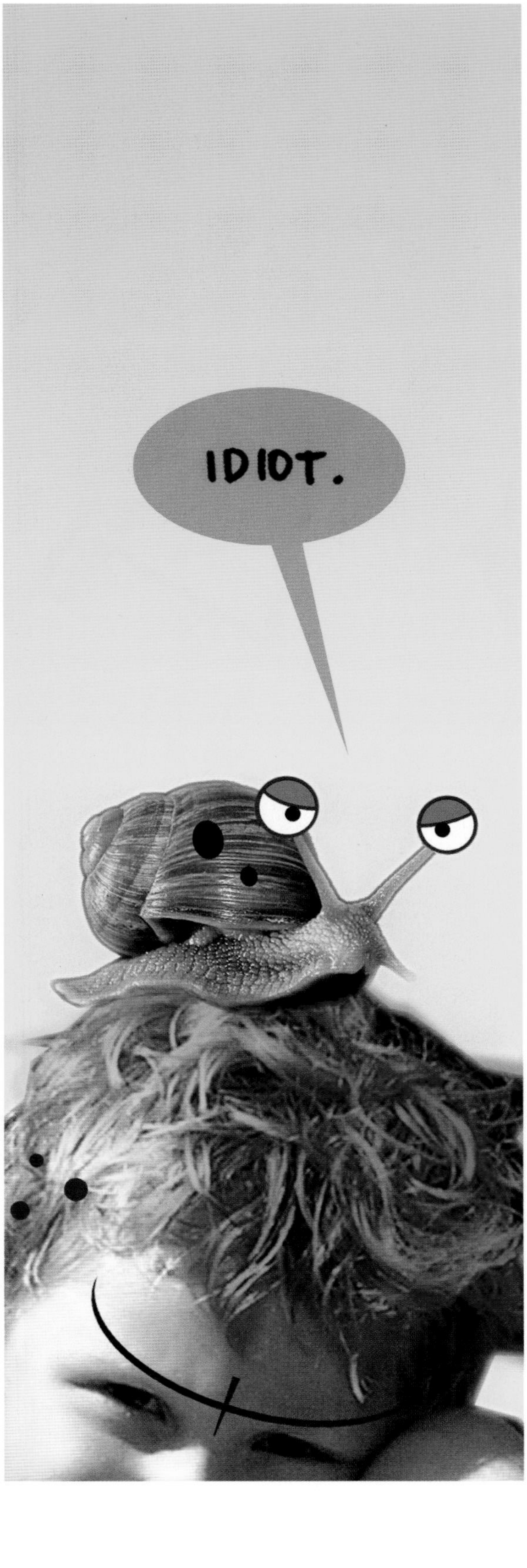
IDIOT.

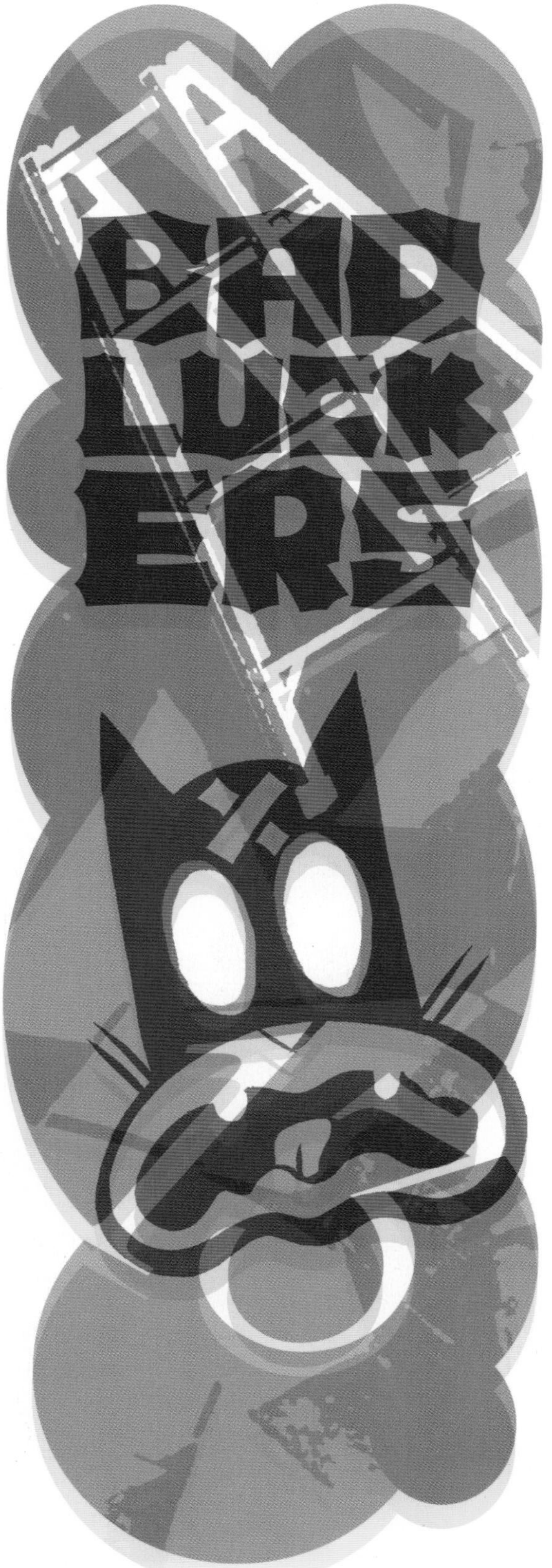
BAD LUCK ERS

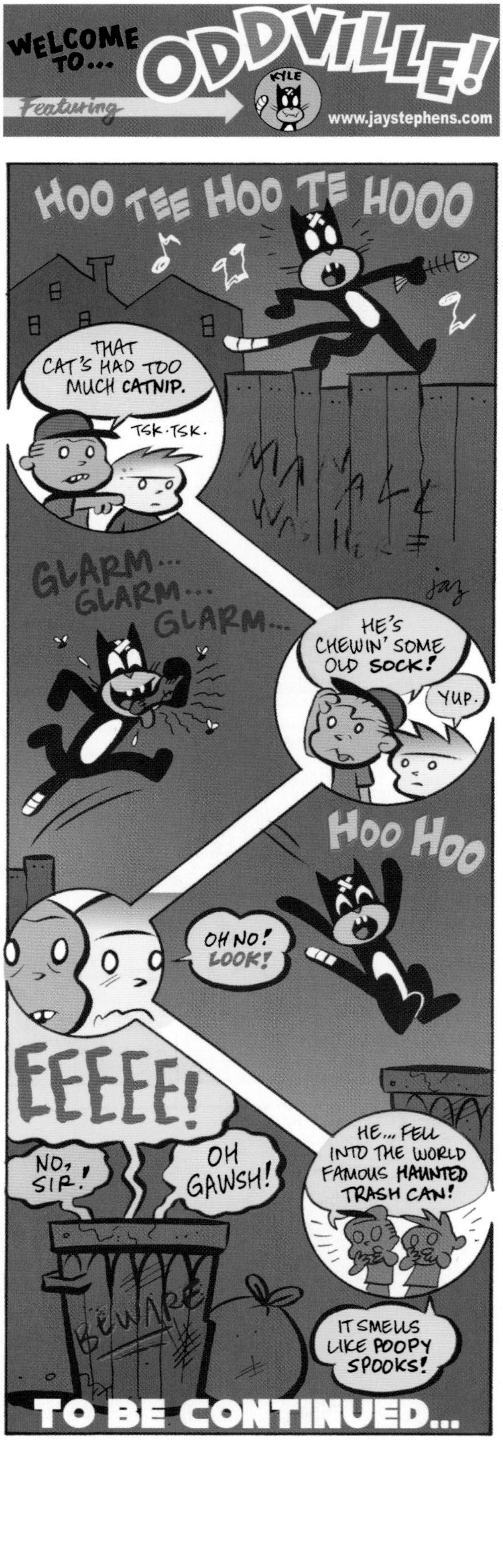
WELCOME TO... ODDVILLE!
Featuring KYLE
www.jaystephens.com
HOO TEE HOO TE HOOO
THAT CAT'S HAD TOO MUCH CATNIP.
TSK·TSK.
GLARM... GLARM... GLARM...
HE'S CHEWIN' SOME OLD SOCK!
YUP.
HOO HOO
OH NO! LOOK!
EEEEE!
NO, SIR!
OH GAWSH!
HE... FELL INTO THE WORLD FAMOUS HAUNTED TRASH CAN!
BEWARE
IT SMELLS LIKE POOPY SPOOKS!
TO BE CONTINUED...

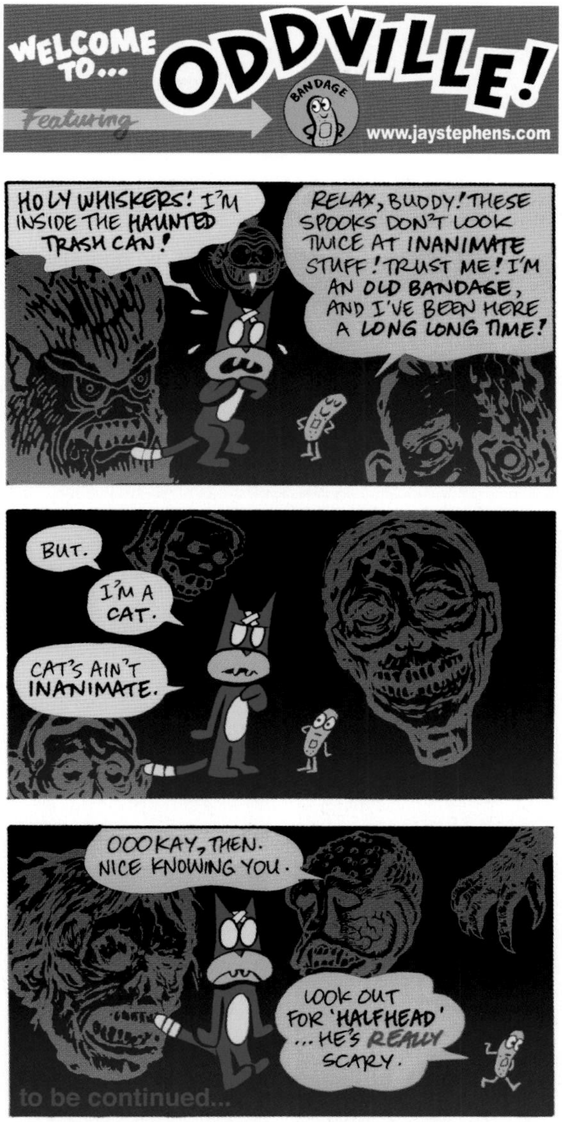
WELCOME TO... ODDVILLE!
Featuring BANDAGE
www.jaystephens.com
HOLY WHISKERS! I'M INSIDE THE HAUNTED TRASH CAN!
RELAX, BUDDY! THESE SPOOKS DON'T LOOK TWICE AT INANIMATE STUFF! TRUST ME! I'M AN OLD BANDAGE, AND I'VE BEEN HERE A LONG LONG TIME!
BUT.
I'M A CAT.
CAT'S AIN'T INANIMATE.
OOOKAY, THEN. NICE KNOWING YOU.
LOOK OUT FOR 'HALFHEAD' ...HE'S REALLY SCARY.
to be continued...

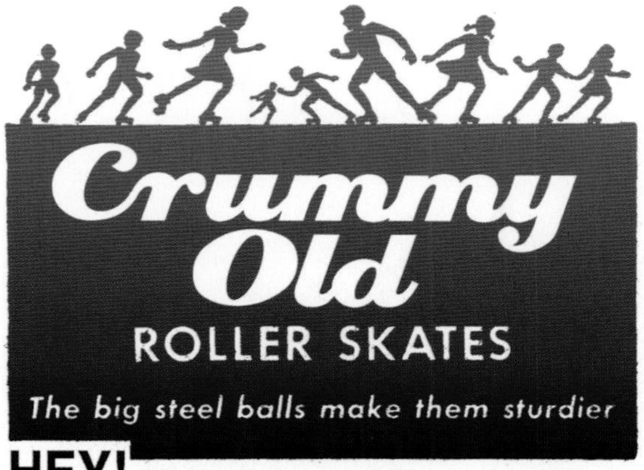
Crummy Old
ROLLER SKATES
The big steel balls make them sturdier
HEY! CAN'T GET YOUR FOLKS TO BUY YOU SOME ROLLERBLADES? GET THESE CRUMMY THINGS INSTEAD!

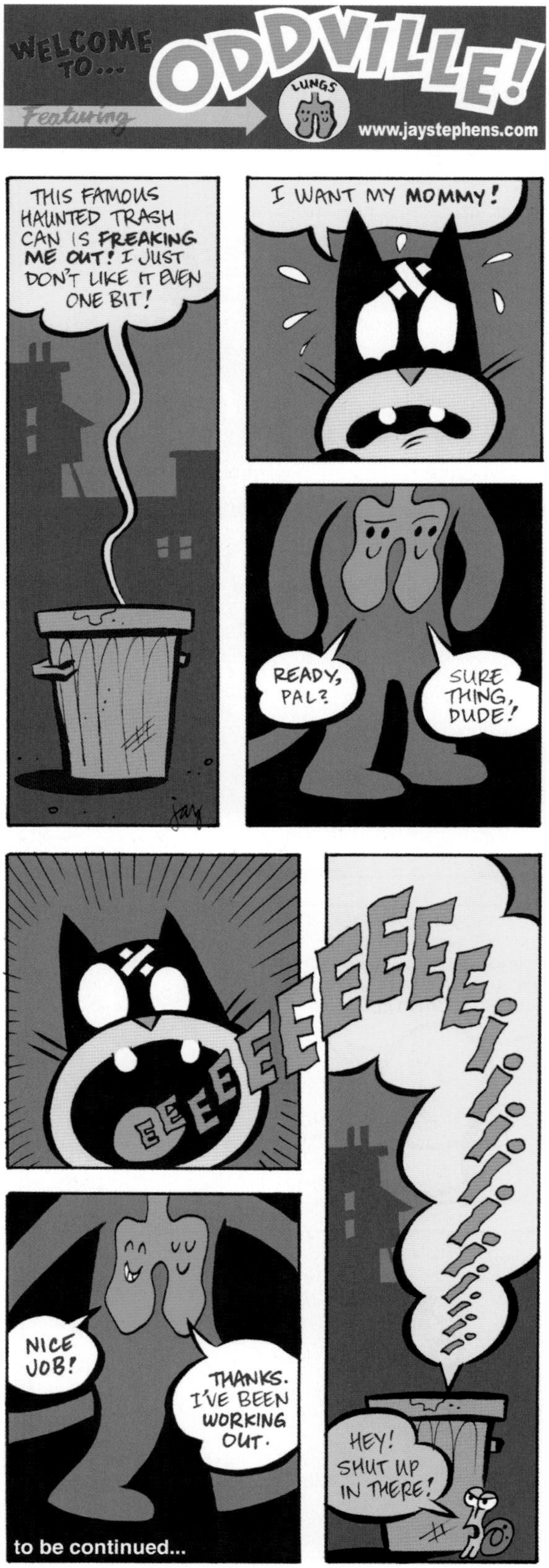
WELCOME TO... ODDVILLE!
Featuring LUNGS
www.jaystephens.com
THIS FAMOUS HAUNTED TRASH CAN IS FREAKING ME OUT! I JUST DON'T LIKE IT EVEN ONE BIT!
I WANT MY MOMMY!
READY, PAL?
SURE THING, DUDE!
NICE JOB!
THANKS. I'VE BEEN WORKING OUT.
HEY! SHUT UP IN THERE!
to be continued...

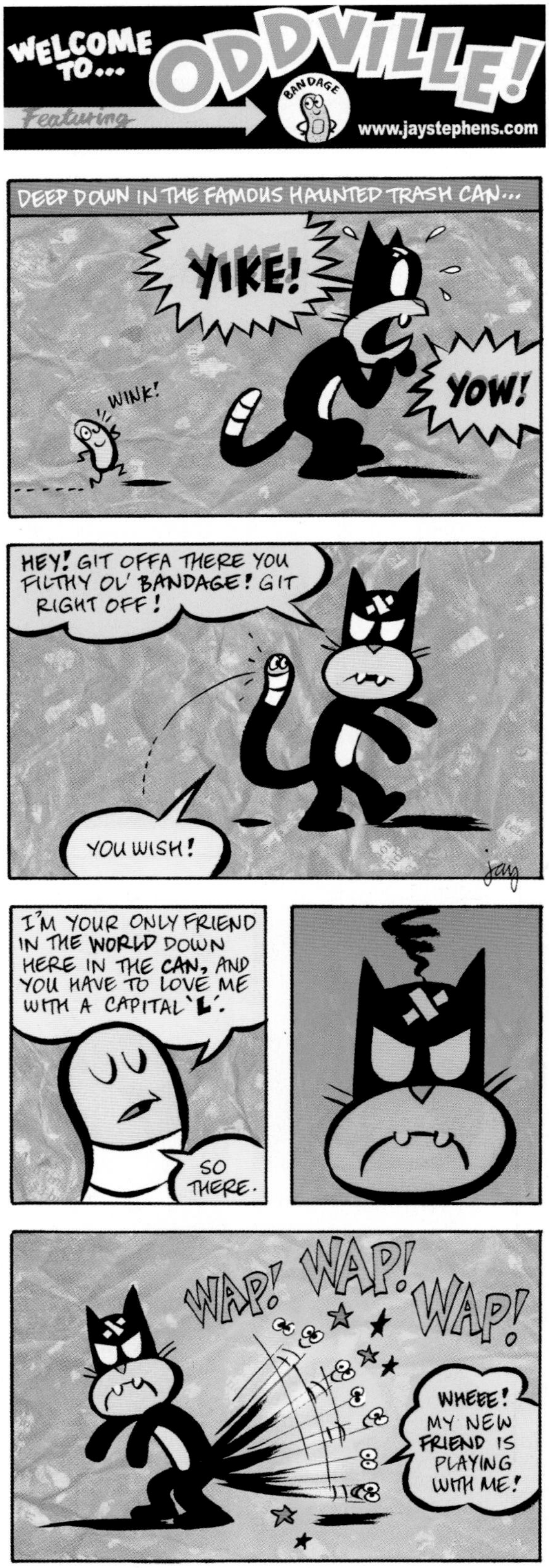
WELCOME TO... ODDVILLE!
Featuring
BANDAGE
www.jaystephens.com
DEEP DOWN IN THE FAMOUS HAUNTED TRASH CAN...
YIKE!
YOW!
WINK!
HEY! GIT OFFA THERE YOU FILTHY OL' BANDAGE! GIT RIGHT OFF!
YOU WISH!
jay
I'M YOUR ONLY FRIEND IN THE WORLD DOWN HERE IN THE CAN, AND YOU HAVE TO LOVE ME WITH A CAPITAL 'L'.
SO THERE.
WAP! WAP! WAP!
WHEEE! MY NEW FRIEND IS PLAYING WITH ME!

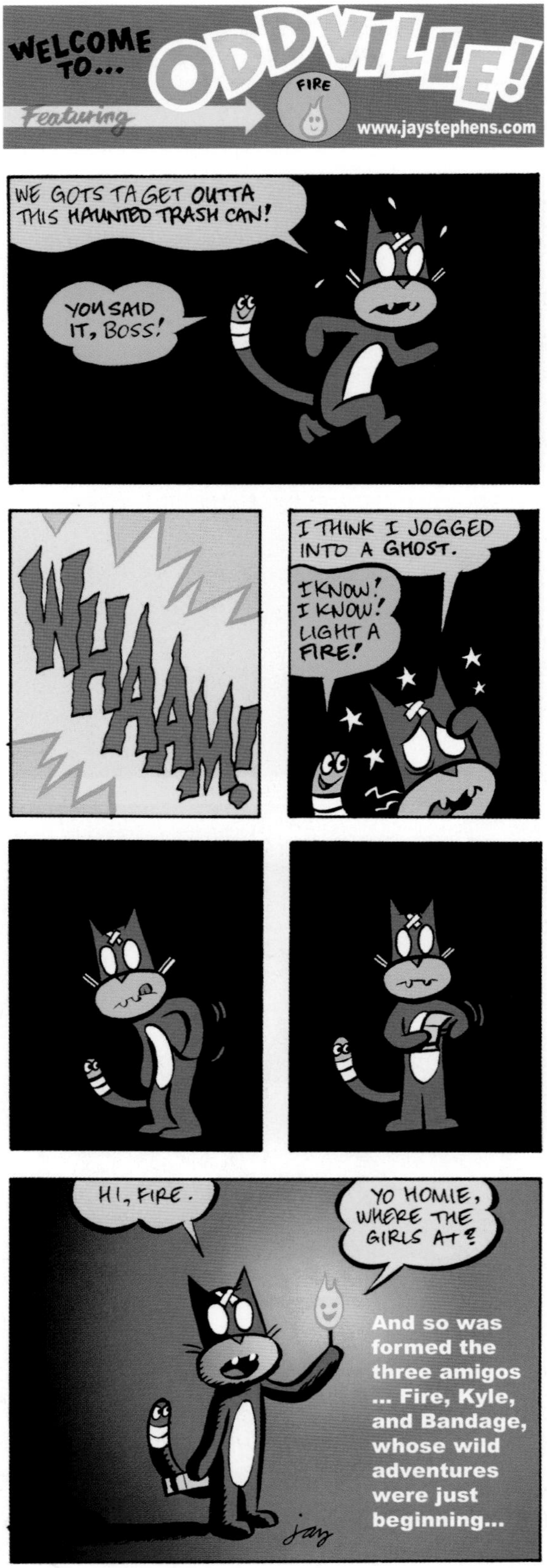
WELCOME TO... ODDVILLE!
Featuring
FIRE
www.jaystephens.com
WE GOTS TA GET OUTTA THIS HAUNTED TRASH CAN!
YOU SAID IT, BOSS!
WHAAM!
I THINK I JOGGED INTO A GHOST.
I KNOW! I KNOW! LIGHT A FIRE!
HI, FIRE.
YO HOMIE, WHERE THE GIRLS AT?
And so was formed the three amigos ... Fire, Kyle, and Bandage, whose wild adventures were just beginning...
jay

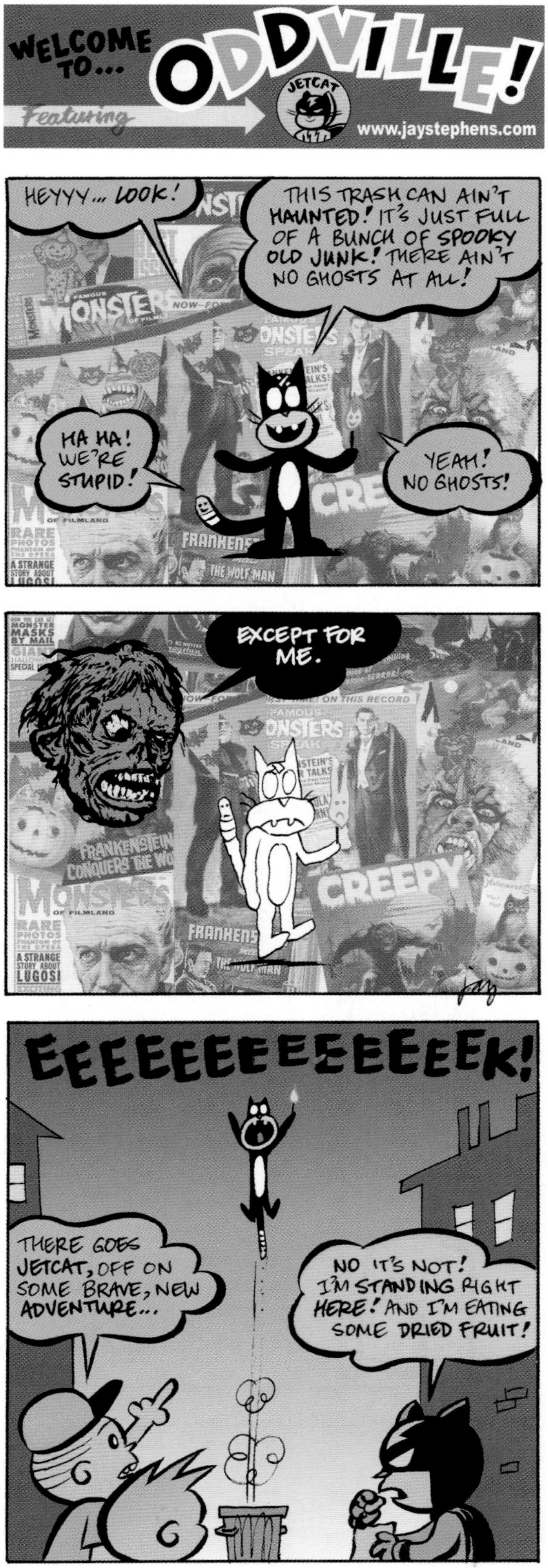
WELCOME TO... ODDVILLE!
Featuring
JETCAT
www.jaystephens.com
HEYYY... LOOK!
THIS TRASH CAN AIN'T HAUNTED! IT'S JUST FULL OF A BUNCH OF SPOOKY OLD JUNK! THERE AIN'T NO GHOSTS AT ALL!
HA HA! WE'RE STUPID!
YEAH! NO GHOSTS!
EXCEPT FOR ME.
EEEEEEEEEEEEEK!
THERE GOES JETCAT, OFF ON SOME BRAVE, NEW ADVENTURE...
NO IT'S NOT! I'M STANDING RIGHT HERE! AND I'M EATING SOME DRIED FRUIT!

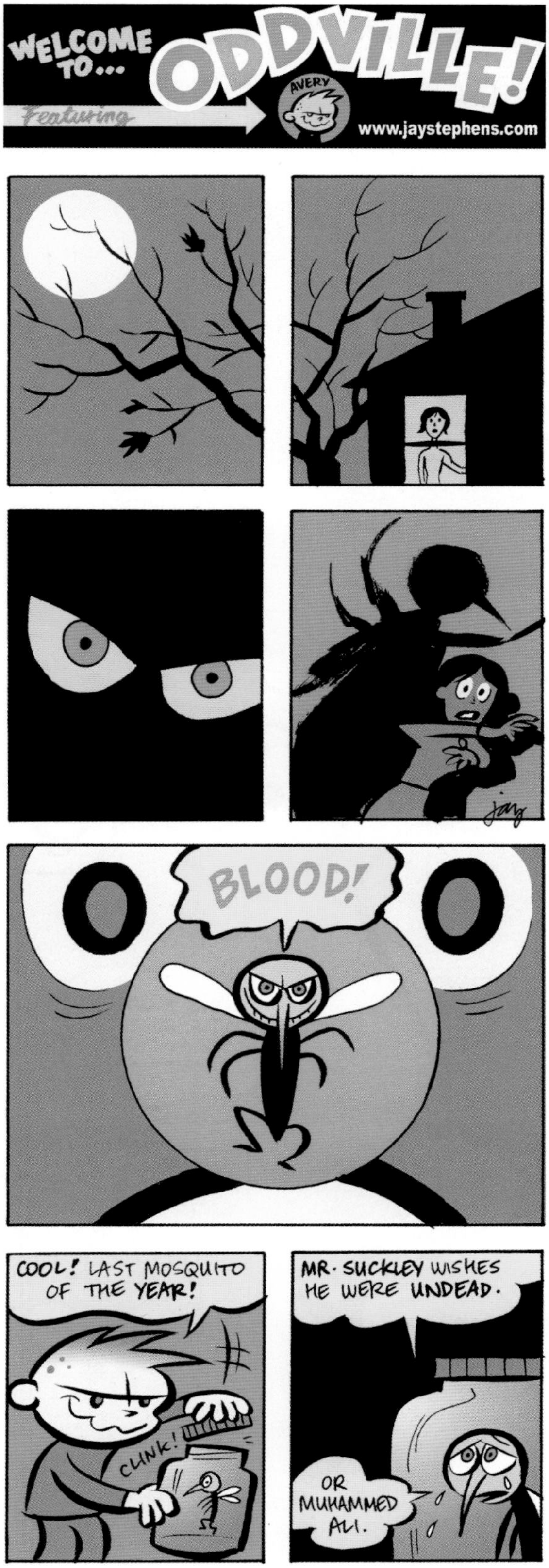
WELCOME TO... ODDVILLE!
Featuring
AVERY
www.jaystephens.com
BLOOD!
COOL! LAST MOSQUITO OF THE YEAR!
CLINK!
MR. SUCKLEY WISHES HE WERE UNDEAD.
OR MUHAMMED ALI.

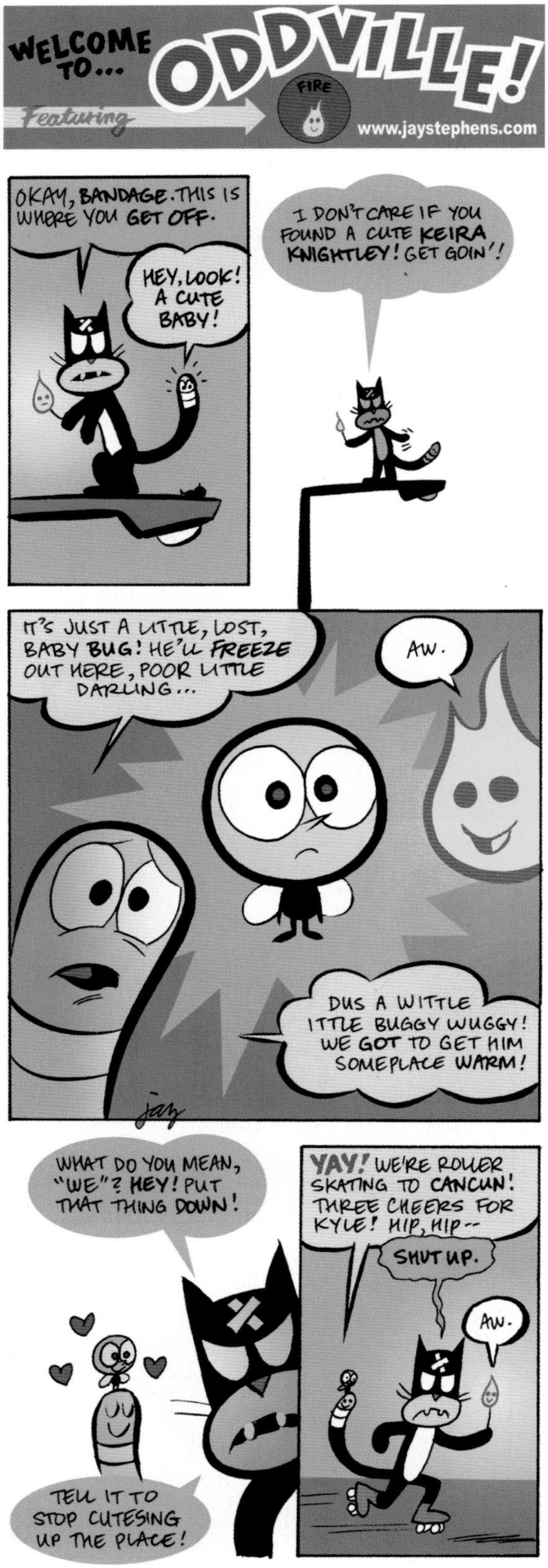
WELCOME TO... ODDVILLE!
Featuring FIRE
www.jaystephens.com
OKAY, BANDAGE. THIS IS WHERE YOU GET OFF.
HEY, LOOK! A CUTE BABY!
I DON'T CARE IF YOU FOUND A CUTE KEIRA KNIGHTLEY! GET GOIN'!
IT'S JUST A LITTLE, LOST, BABY BUG! HE'LL FREEZE OUT HERE, POOR LITTLE DARLING...
AW.
DUS A WITTLE ITTLE BUGGY WUGGY! WE GOT TO GET HIM SOMEPLACE WARM!
WHAT DO YOU MEAN, "WE"? HEY! PUT THAT THING DOWN!
TELL IT TO STOP CUTESING UP THE PLACE!
YAY! WE'RE ROLLER SKATING TO CANCUN! THREE CHEERS FOR KYLE! HIP, HIP--
SHUT UP.
AW.

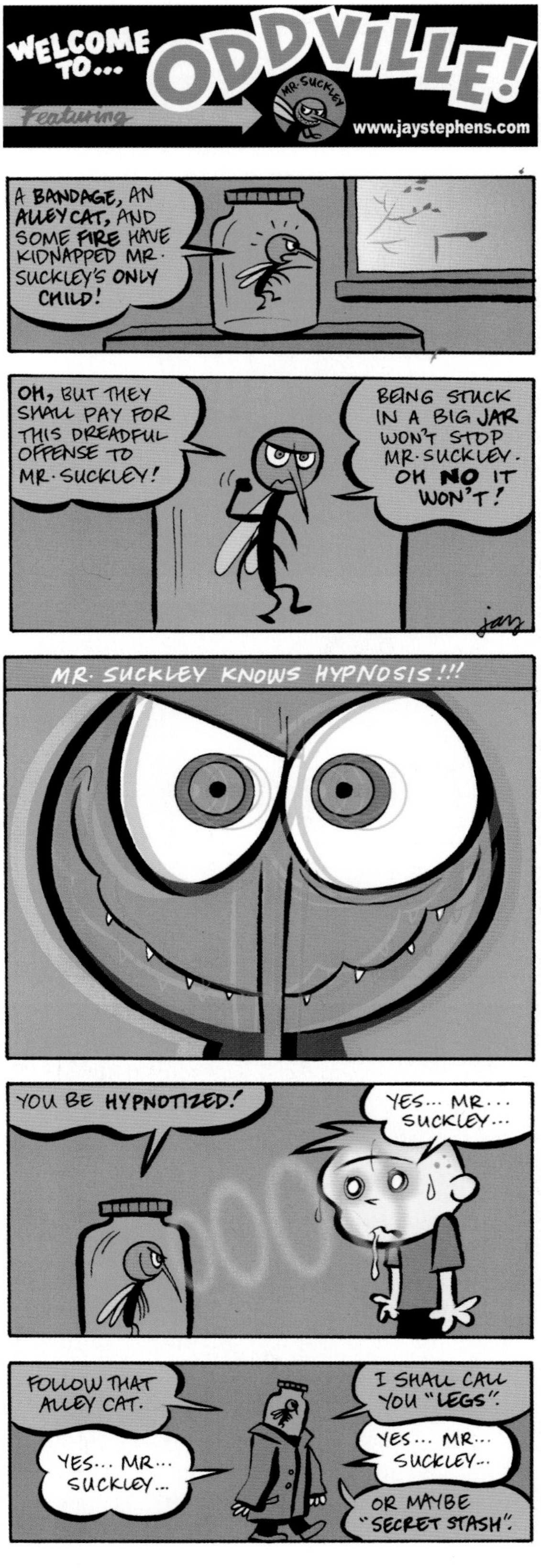
WELCOME TO... ODDVILLE!
Featuring MR. SUCKLEY
www.jaystephens.com
A BANDAGE, AN ALLEY CAT, AND SOME FIRE HAVE KIDNAPPED MR. SUCKLEY'S ONLY CHILD!
OH, BUT THEY SHALL PAY FOR THIS DREADFUL OFFENSE TO MR. SUCKLEY!
BEING STUCK IN A BIG JAR WON'T STOP MR. SUCKLEY. OH NO IT WON'T!
MR. SUCKLEY KNOWS HYPNOSIS!!!
YOU BE HYPNOTIZED!
YES... MR... SUCKLEY...
FOLLOW THAT ALLEY CAT.
YES... MR... SUCKLEY...
I SHALL CALL YOU "LEGS".
YES... MR... SUCKLEY...
OR MAYBE "SECRET STASH".

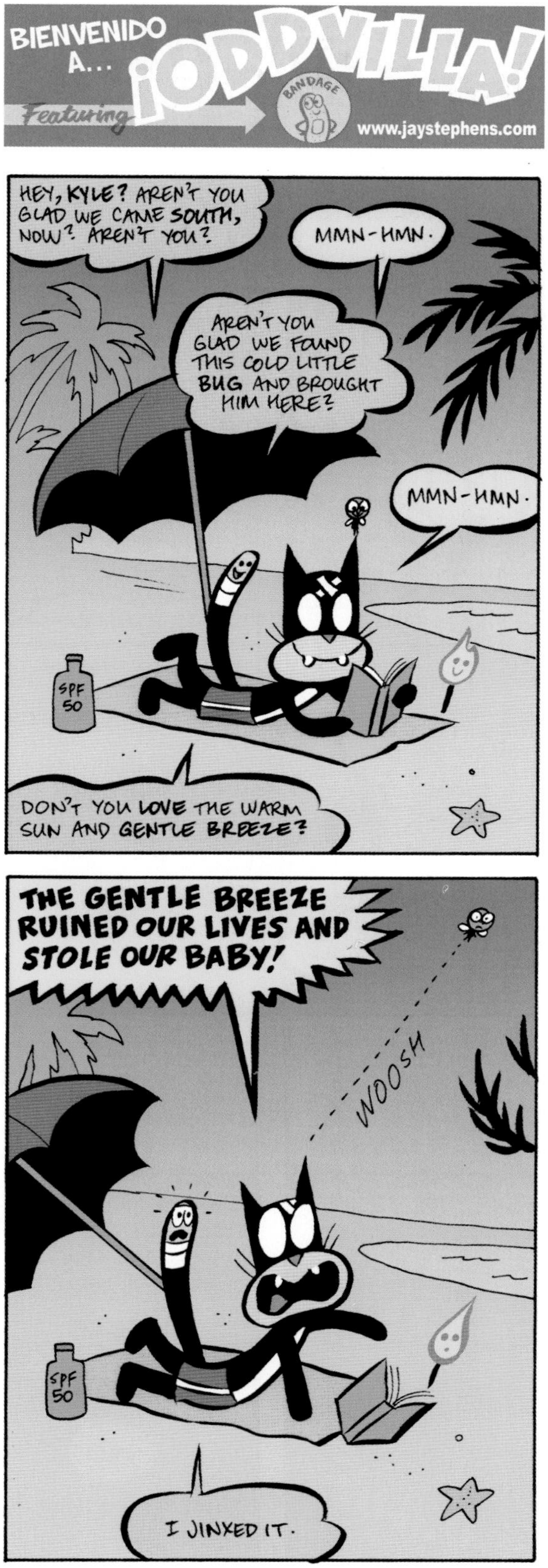
BIENVENIDO A... ¡ODDVILLA!
Featuring BANDAGE
www.jaystephens.com
HEY, KYLE? AREN'T YOU GLAD WE CAME SOUTH, NOW? AREN'T YOU?
MMN-HMN.
AREN'T YOU GLAD WE FOUND THIS COLD LITTLE BUG AND BROUGHT HIM HERE?
MMN-HMN.
SPF 50
DON'T YOU LOVE THE WARM SUN AND GENTLE BREEZE?
THE GENTLE BREEZE RUINED OUR LIVES AND STOLE OUR BABY!
WOOSH
SPF 50
I JINXED IT.

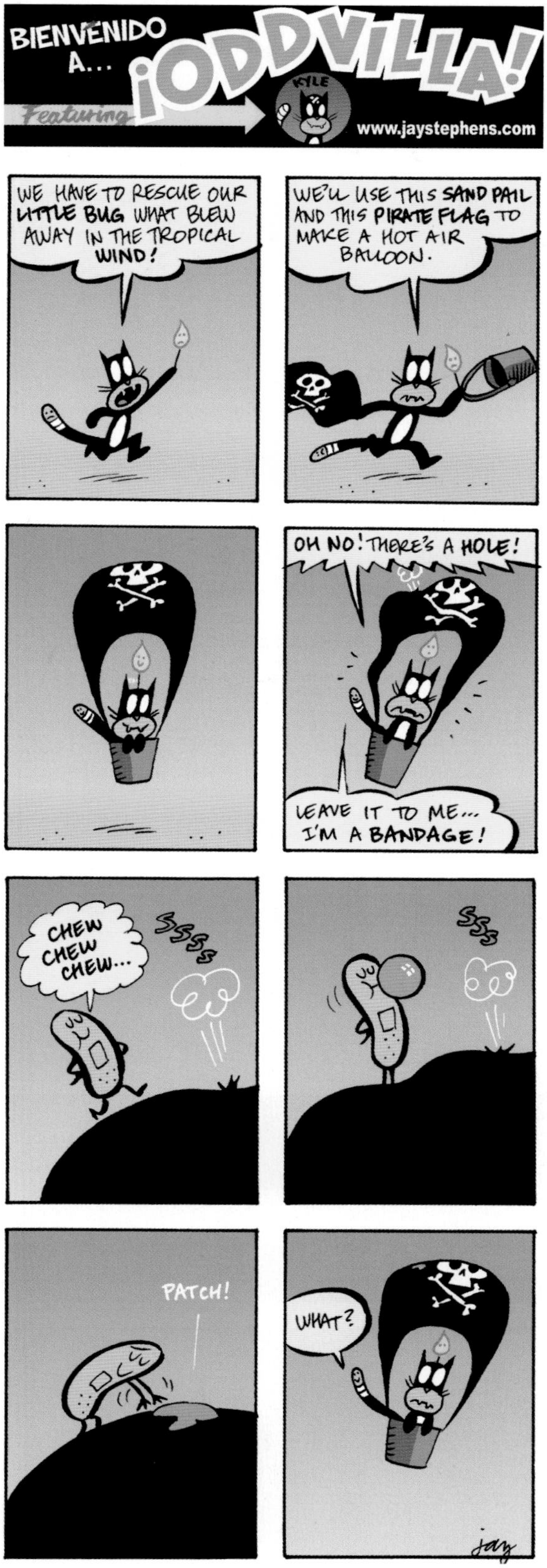
BIENVENIDO A... ¡ODDVILLA!
Featuring KYLE
www.jaystephens.com
WE HAVE TO RESCUE OUR LITTLE BUG WHAT BLEW AWAY IN THE TROPICAL WIND!
WE'LL USE THIS SAND PAIL AND THIS PIRATE FLAG TO MAKE A HOT AIR BALLOON.
OH NO! THERE'S A HOLE!
LEAVE IT TO ME... I'M A BANDAGE!
CHEW CHEW CHEW...
SSSS
SSS
PATCH!
WHAT?
jay

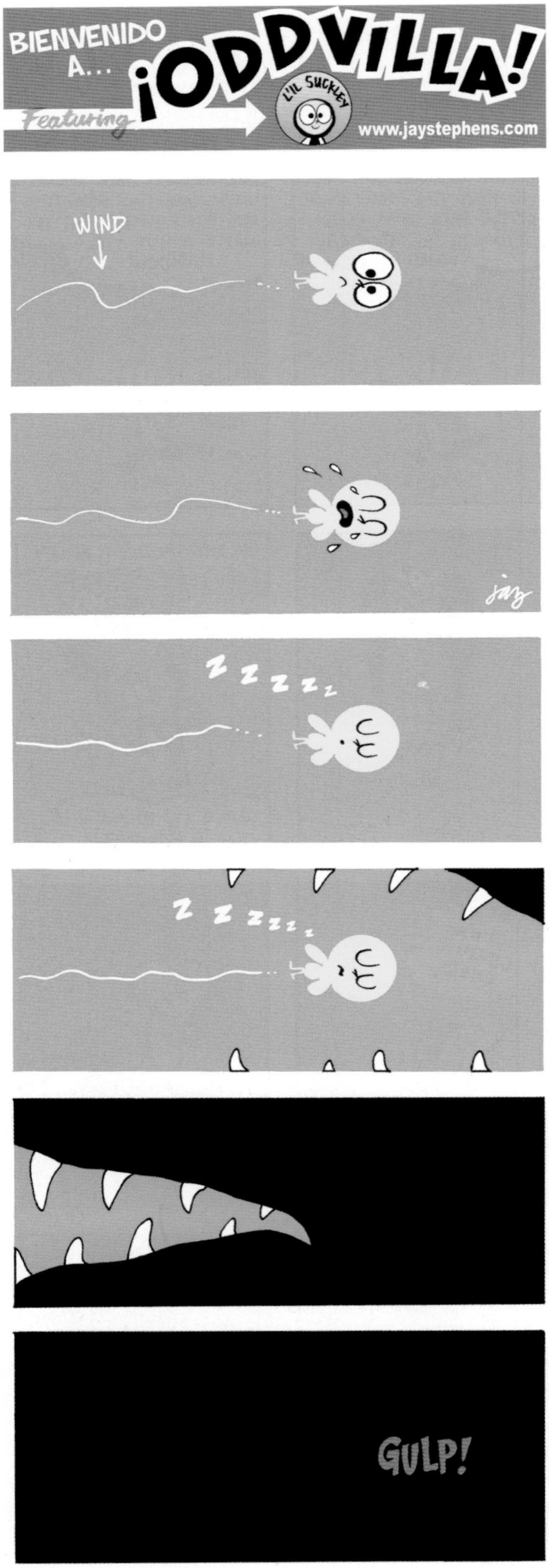
BIENVENIDO A... ¡ODDVILLA!
Featuring L'IL SUCKLEY
www.jaystephens.com
WIND
Z Z Z Z Z
Z Z Z Z Z Z
GULP!

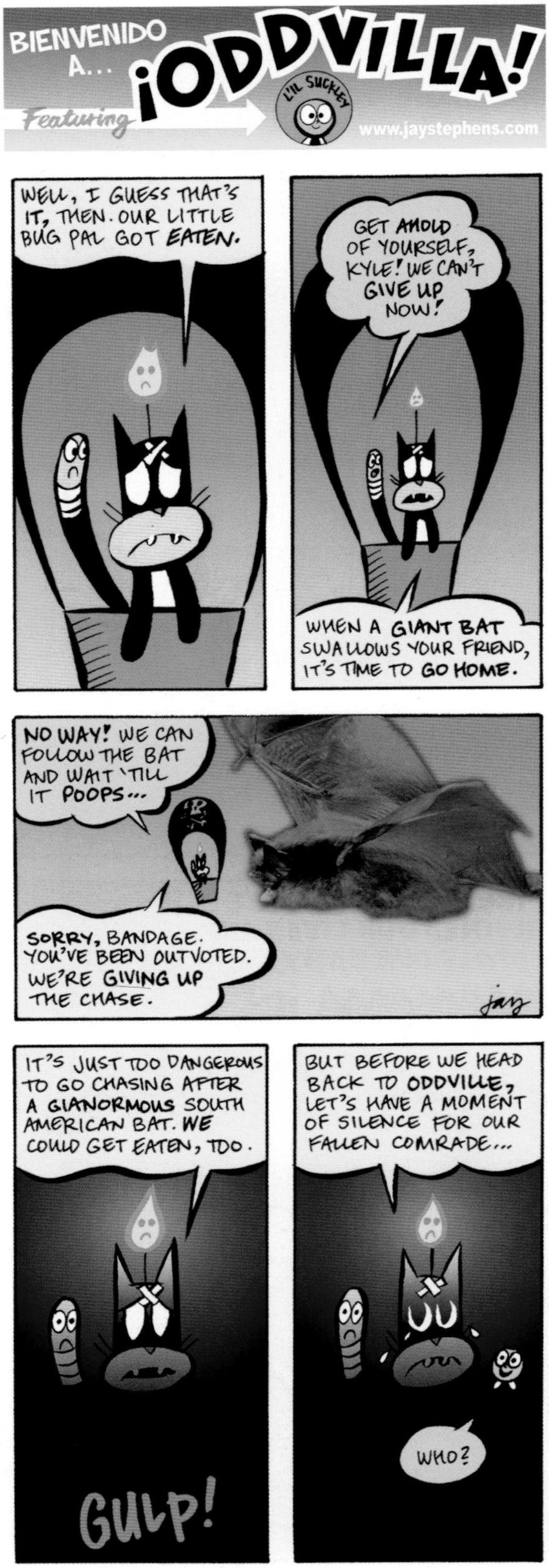
BIENVENIDO A... ¡ODDVILLA!
Featuring L'IL SUCKLEY
www.jaystephens.com
WELL, I GUESS THAT'S IT, THEN. OUR LITTLE BUG PAL GOT EATEN.
GET AHOLD OF YOURSELF, KYLE! WE CAN'T GIVE UP NOW!
WHEN A GIANT BAT SWALLOWS YOUR FRIEND, IT'S TIME TO GO HOME.
NO WAY! WE CAN FOLLOW THE BAT AND WAIT 'TILL IT POOPS...
SORRY, BANDAGE. YOU'VE BEEN OUTVOTED. WE'RE GIVING UP THE CHASE.
IT'S JUST TOO DANGEROUS TO GO CHASING AFTER A GIANORMOUS SOUTH AMERICAN BAT. WE COULD GET EATEN, TOO.
GULP!
BUT BEFORE WE HEAD BACK TO ODDVILLE, LET'S HAVE A MOMENT OF SILENCE FOR OUR FALLEN COMRADE...
WHO?

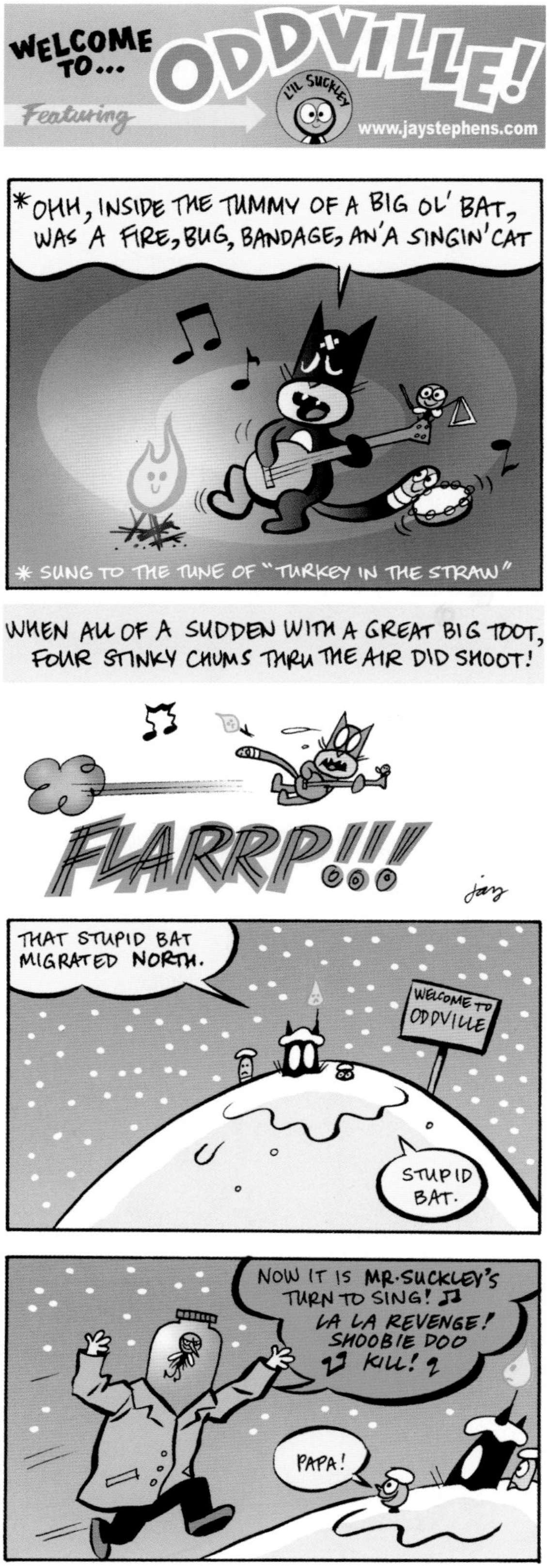
WELCOME TO... ODDVILLE!
Featuring L'IL SUCKLEY
www.jaystephens.com
*OHH, INSIDE THE TUMMY OF A BIG OL' BAT, WAS A FIRE, BUG, BANDAGE, AN'A SINGIN' CAT
* SUNG TO THE TUNE OF "TURKEY IN THE STRAW"
WHEN ALL OF A SUDDEN WITH A GREAT BIG TOOT, FOUR STINKY CHUMS THRU THE AIR DID SHOOT!
FLARRP!!!
jay
THAT STUPID BAT MIGRATED NORTH.
WELCOME TO ODDVILLE
STUPID BAT.
NOW IT IS MR. SUCKLEY'S TURN TO SING! LA LA REVENGE! SHOOBIE DOO KILL!
PAPA!

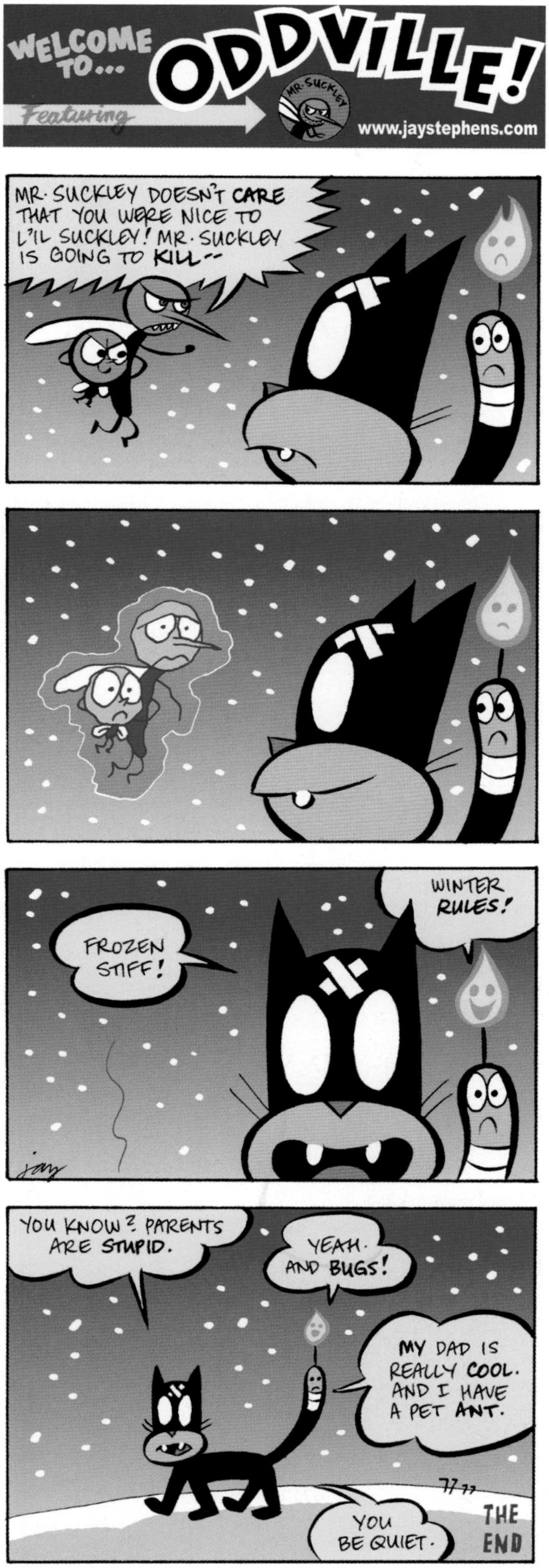
WELCOME TO... ODDVILLE!
Featuring MR. SUCKLEY
www.jaystephens.com
MR. SUCKLEY DOESN'T CARE THAT YOU WERE NICE TO L'IL SUCKLEY! MR. SUCKLEY IS GOING TO KILL--
FROZEN STIFF!
WINTER RULES!
jay
YOU KNOW? PARENTS ARE STUPID.
YEAH. AND BUGS!
MY DAD IS REALLY COOL. AND I HAVE A PET ANT.
YOU BE QUIET.
THE END

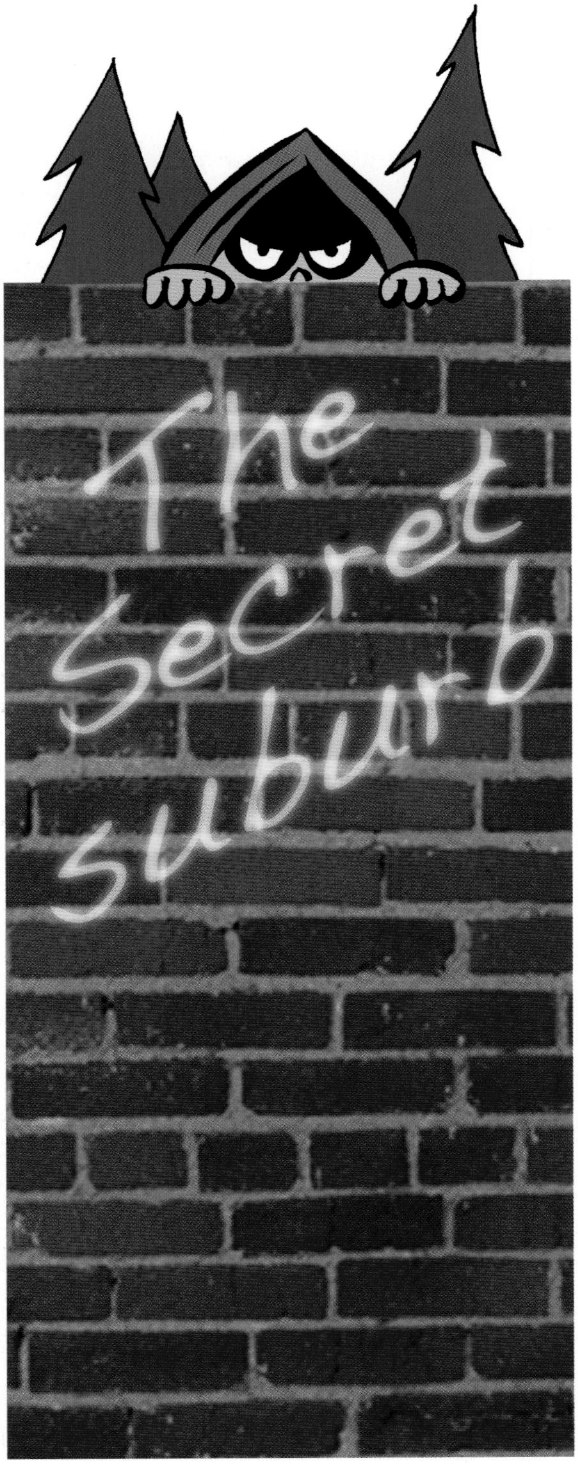
The Secret Suburb

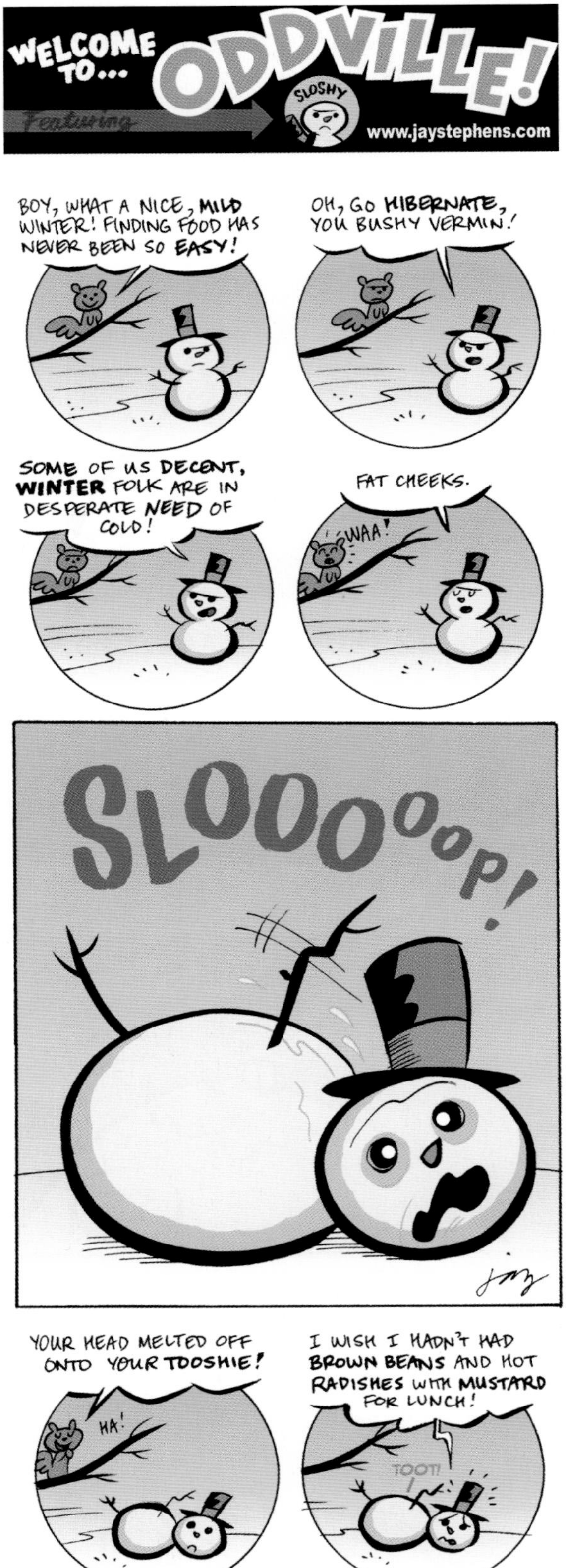
WELCOME TO... ODDVILLE!
Featuring
SLOSHY
www.jaystephens.com
BOY, WHAT A NICE, MILD WINTER! FINDING FOOD HAS NEVER BEEN SO EASY!
OH, GO HIBERNATE, YOU BUSHY VERMIN!
SOME OF US DECENT, WINTER FOLK ARE IN DESPERATE NEED OF COLD!
FAT CHEEKS.
WAA!
SLOOOOoop!
YOUR HEAD MELTED OFF ONTO YOUR TOOSHIE!
HA!
I WISH I HADN'T HAD BROWN BEANS AND HOT RADISHES WITH MUSTARD FOR LUNCH!
TOOT!

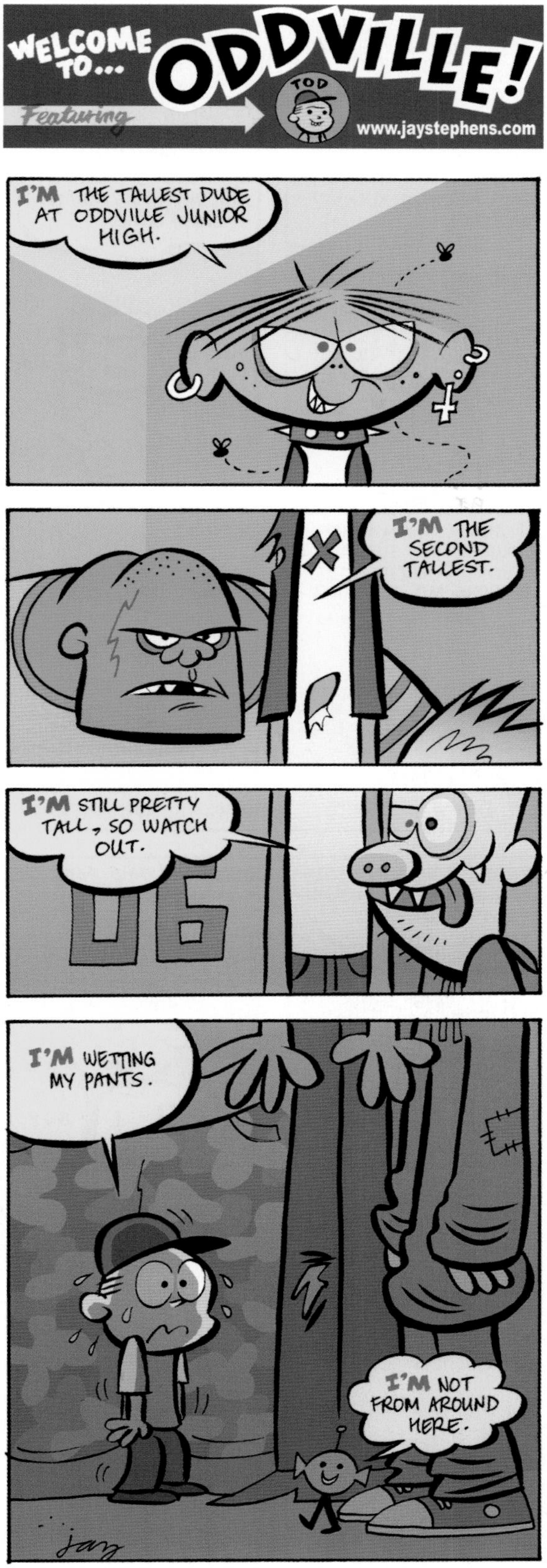
WELCOME TO... ODDVILLE!
Featuring
TOD
www.jaystephens.com
I'M THE TALLEST DUDE AT ODDVILLE JUNIOR HIGH.
I'M THE SECOND TALLEST.
I'M STILL PRETTY TALL, SO WATCH OUT.
06
I'M WETTING MY PANTS.
I'M NOT FROM AROUND HERE.
jay

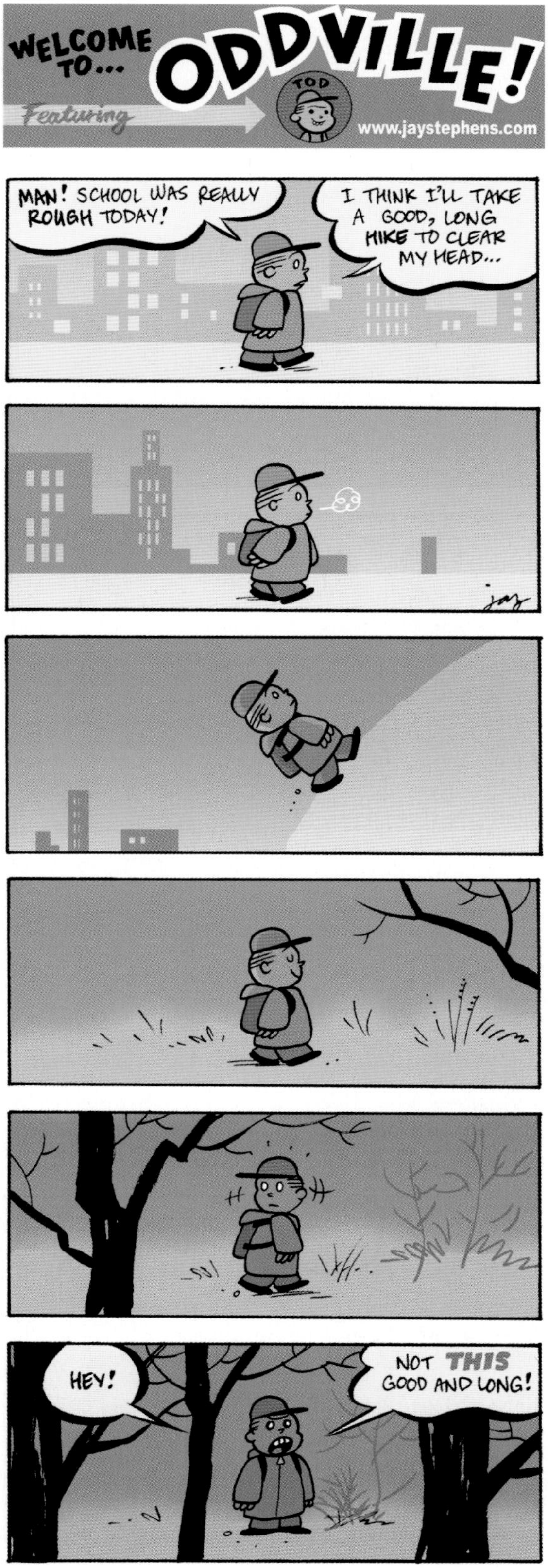
WELCOME TO... ODDVILLE!
Featuring
TOD
www.jaystephens.com
MAN! SCHOOL WAS REALLY ROUGH TODAY!
I THINK I'LL TAKE A GOOD, LONG HIKE TO CLEAR MY HEAD...
jay
HEY!
NOT THIS GOOD AND LONG!

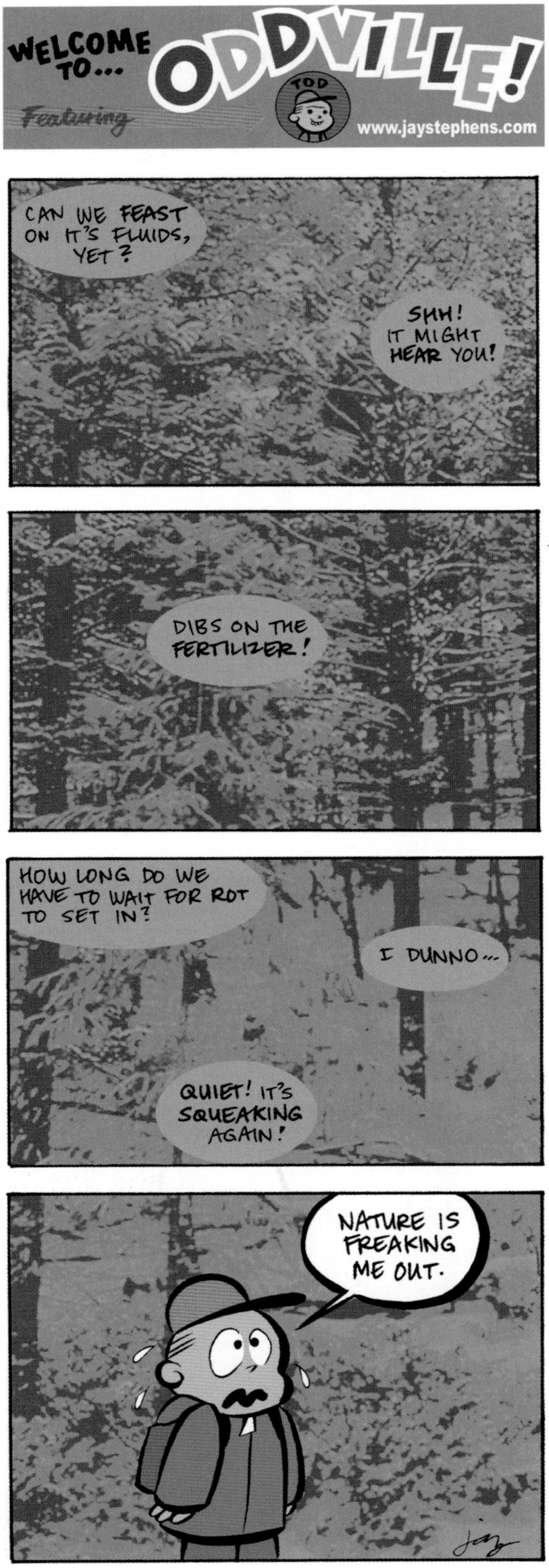
WELCOME TO... ODDVILLE!
Featuring TOD
www.jaystephens.com
CAN WE FEAST ON IT'S FLUIDS, YET?
SHH! IT MIGHT HEAR YOU!
DIBS ON THE FERTILIZER!
HOW LONG DO WE HAVE TO WAIT FOR ROT TO SET IN?
I DUNNO...
QUIET! IT'S SQUEAKING AGAIN!
NATURE IS FREAKING ME OUT.

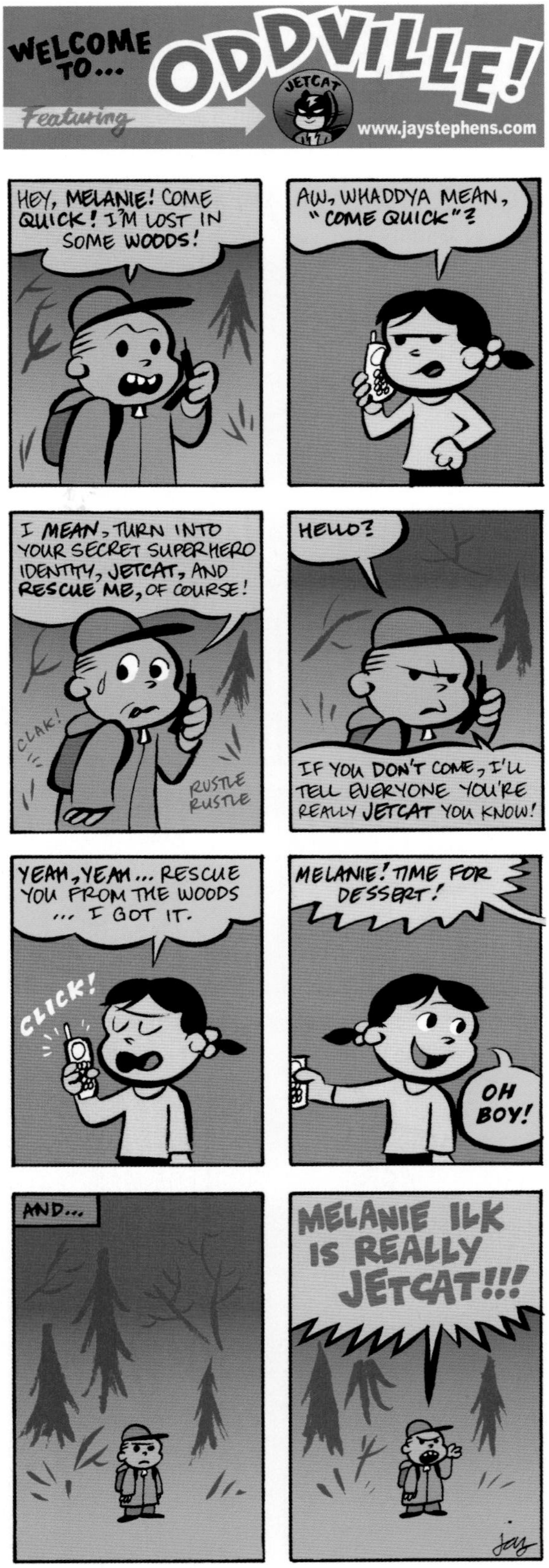
WELCOME TO... ODDVILLE!
Featuring JETCAT
www.jaystephens.com
HEY, MELANIE! COME QUICK! I'M LOST IN SOME WOODS!
AW, WHADDYA MEAN, "COME QUICK"?
I MEAN, TURN INTO YOUR SECRET SUPERHERO IDENTITY, JETCAT, AND RESCUE ME, OF COURSE!
CLAK!
RUSTLE RUSTLE
HELLO?
IF YOU DON'T COME, I'LL TELL EVERYONE YOU'RE REALLY JETCAT YOU KNOW!
YEAH, YEAH... RESCUE YOU FROM THE WOODS ... I GOT IT.
CLICK!
MELANIE! TIME FOR DESSERT!
OH BOY!
AND...
MELANIE ILK IS REALLY JETCAT!!!

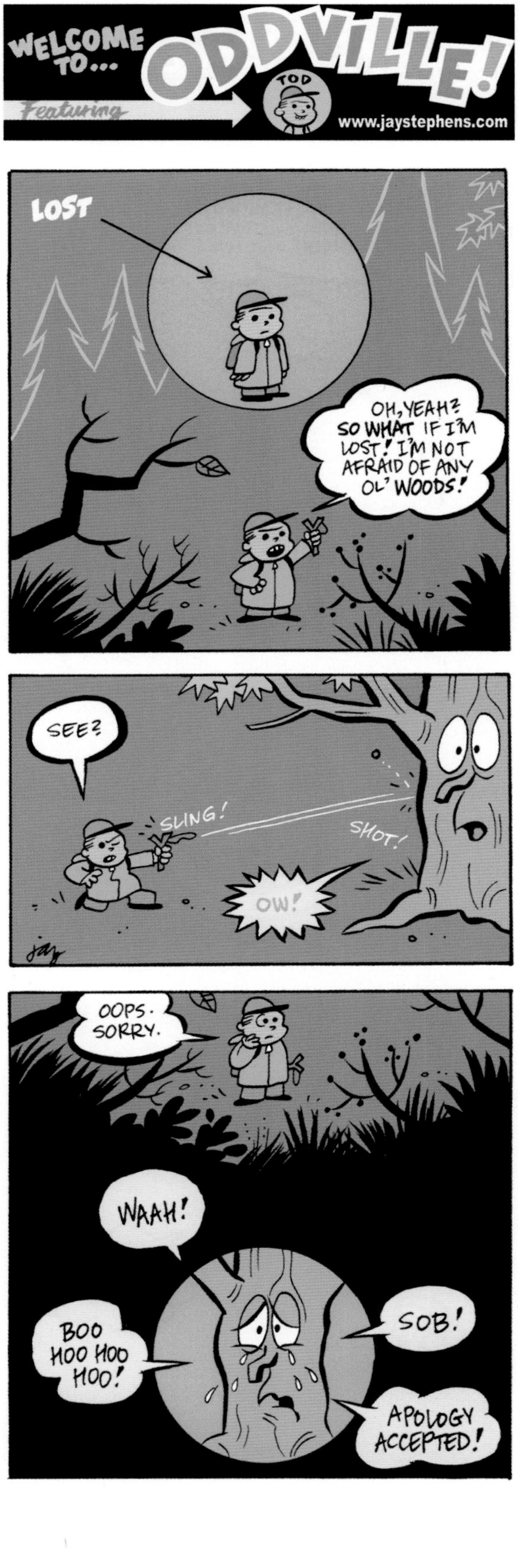
WELCOME TO... ODDVILLE!
Featuring TOD
www.jaystephens.com
LOST
OH, YEAH? SO WHAT IF I'M LOST! I'M NOT AFRAID OF ANY OL' WOODS!
SEE?
SLING!
SHOT!
OW!
jay
OOPS. SORRY.
WAAH!
BOO HOO HOO HOO!
SOB!
APOLOGY ACCEPTED!

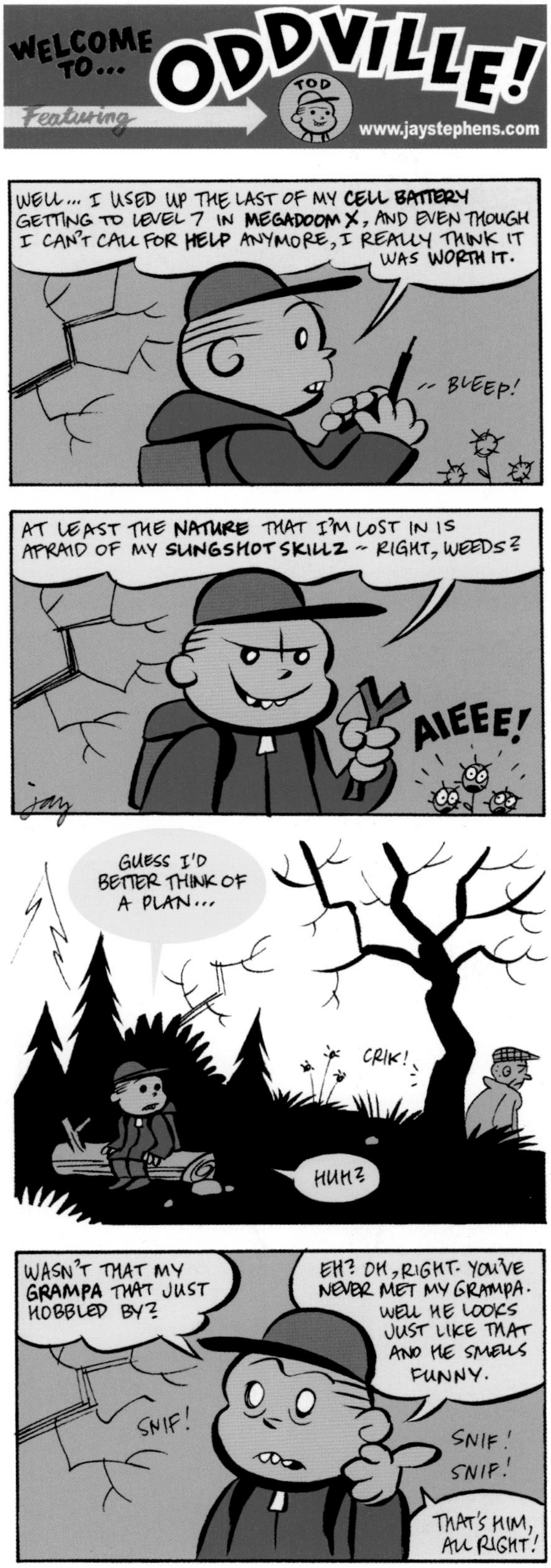
WELCOME TO... ODDVILLE!
Featuring TOD
www.jaystephens.com
WELL... I USED UP THE LAST OF MY CELL BATTERY GETTING TO LEVEL 7 IN MEGADOOM X, AND EVEN THOUGH I CAN'T CALL FOR HELP ANYMORE, I REALLY THINK IT WAS WORTH IT.
BLEEP!
AT LEAST THE NATURE THAT I'M LOST IN IS AFRAID OF MY SLINGSHOT SKILLZ ~ RIGHT, WEEDS?
AIEEE!
jay
GUESS I'D BETTER THINK OF A PLAN...
CRIK!
HUH?
WASN'T THAT MY GRAMPA THAT JUST HOBBLED BY?
EH? OH, RIGHT. YOU'VE NEVER MET MY GRAMPA. WELL HE LOOKS JUST LIKE THAT AND HE SMELLS FUNNY.
SNIF!
SNIF! SNIF!
THAT'S HIM, ALL RIGHT!

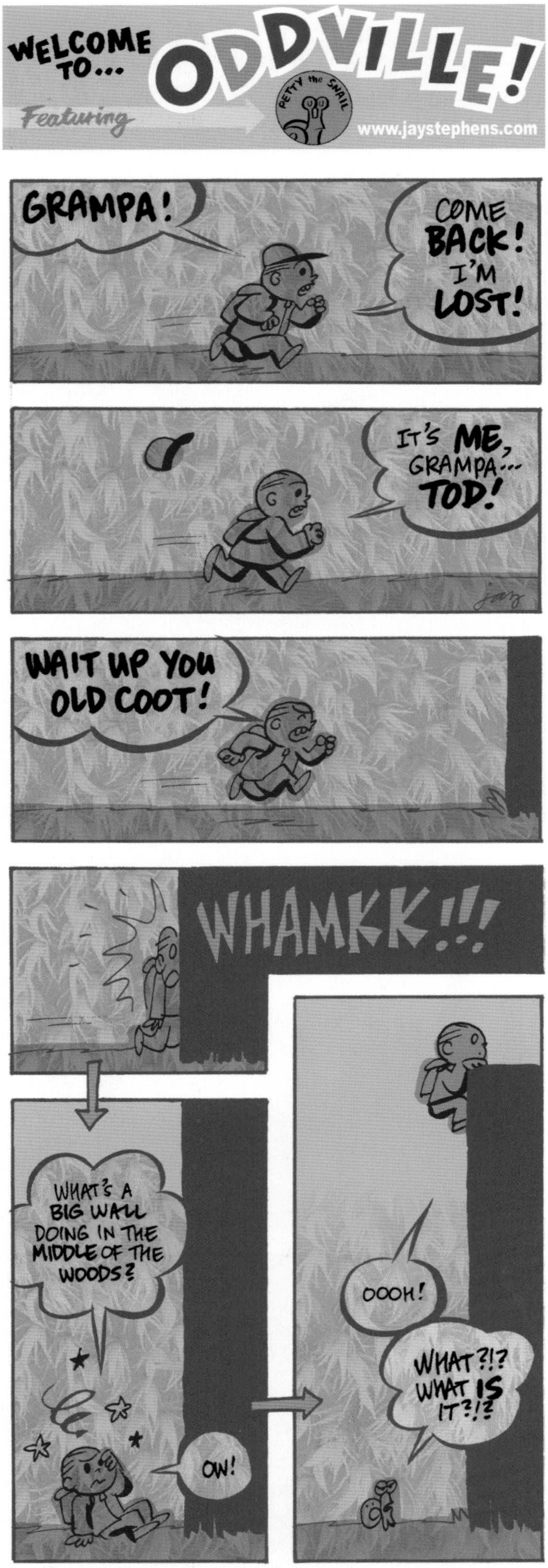
WELCOME TO... ODDVILLE!
Featuring
PETTY the SNAIL
www.jaystephens.com
GRAMPA!
COME BACK! I'M LOST!
IT'S ME, GRAMPA... TOD!
WAIT UP YOU OLD COOT!
WHAMKK!!!
WHAT'S A BIG WALL DOING IN THE MIDDLE OF THE WOODS?
OW!
OOOH!
WHAT?!? WHAT IS IT?!?

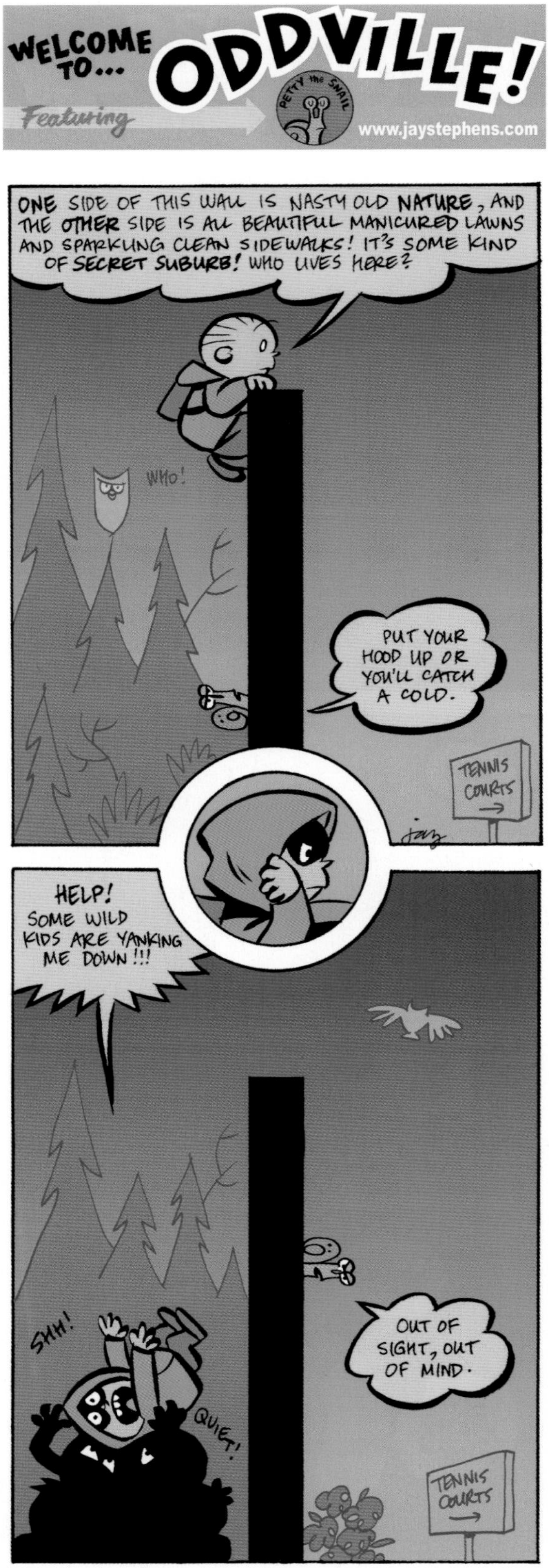
WELCOME TO... ODDVILLE!
Featuring
PETTY the SNAIL
www.jaystephens.com
ONE SIDE OF THIS WALL IS NASTY OLD NATURE, AND THE OTHER SIDE IS ALL BEAUTIFUL MANICURED LAWNS AND SPARKLING CLEAN SIDEWALKS! IT'S SOME KIND OF SECRET SUBURB! WHO LIVES HERE?
WHO!
PUT YOUR HOOD UP OR YOU'LL CATCH A COLD.
TENNIS COURTS →
HELP! SOME WILD KIDS ARE YANKING ME DOWN!!!
SHH!
QUIET!
OUT OF SIGHT, OUT OF MIND.
TENNIS COURTS →

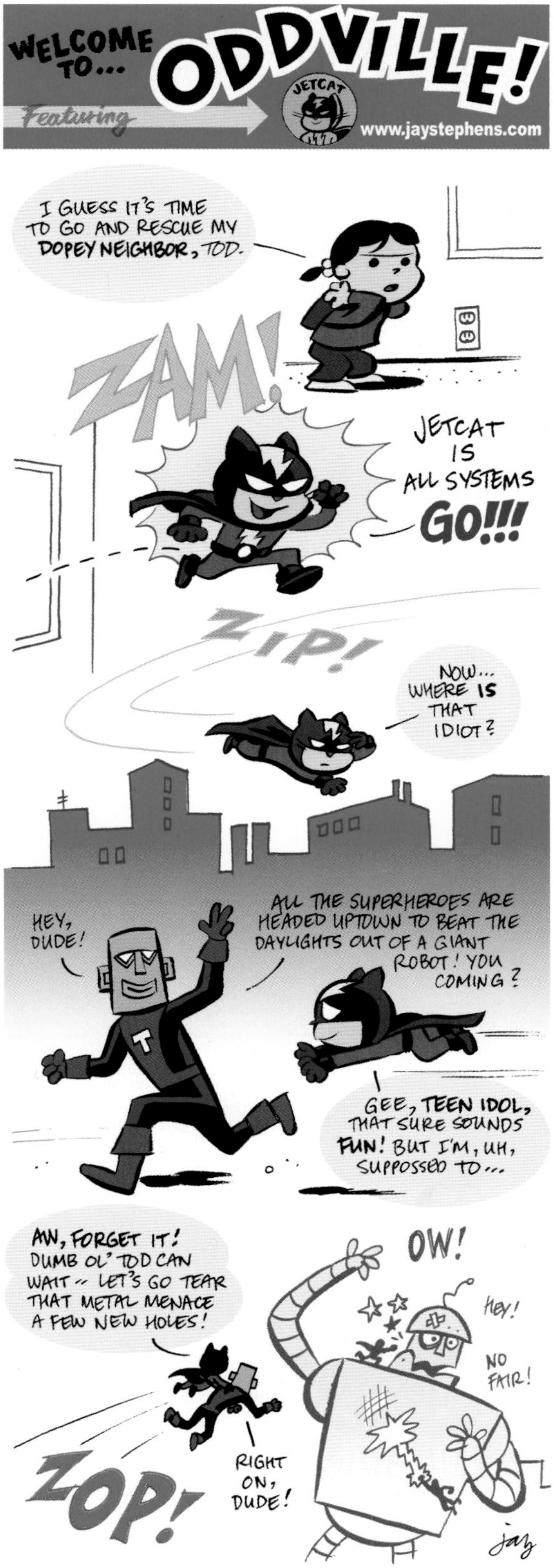
WELCOME TO... ODDVILLE!
Featuring
JETCAT
www.jaystephens.com
I GUESS IT'S TIME TO GO AND RESCUE MY DOPEY NEIGHBOR, TOD.
ZAM!
JETCAT IS ALL SYSTEMS GO!!!
ZIP!
NOW... WHERE IS THAT IDIOT?
HEY, DUDE!
ALL THE SUPERHEROES ARE HEADED UPTOWN TO BEAT THE DAYLIGHTS OUT OF A GIANT ROBOT! YOU COMING?
GEE, TEEN IDOL, THAT SURE SOUNDS FUN! BUT I'M, UH, SUPPOSED TO...
AW, FORGET IT! DUMB OL' TOD CAN WAIT -- LET'S GO TEAR THAT METAL MENACE A FEW NEW HOLES!
OW!
HEY!
NO FAIR!
ZOP!
RIGHT ON, DUDE!
jay

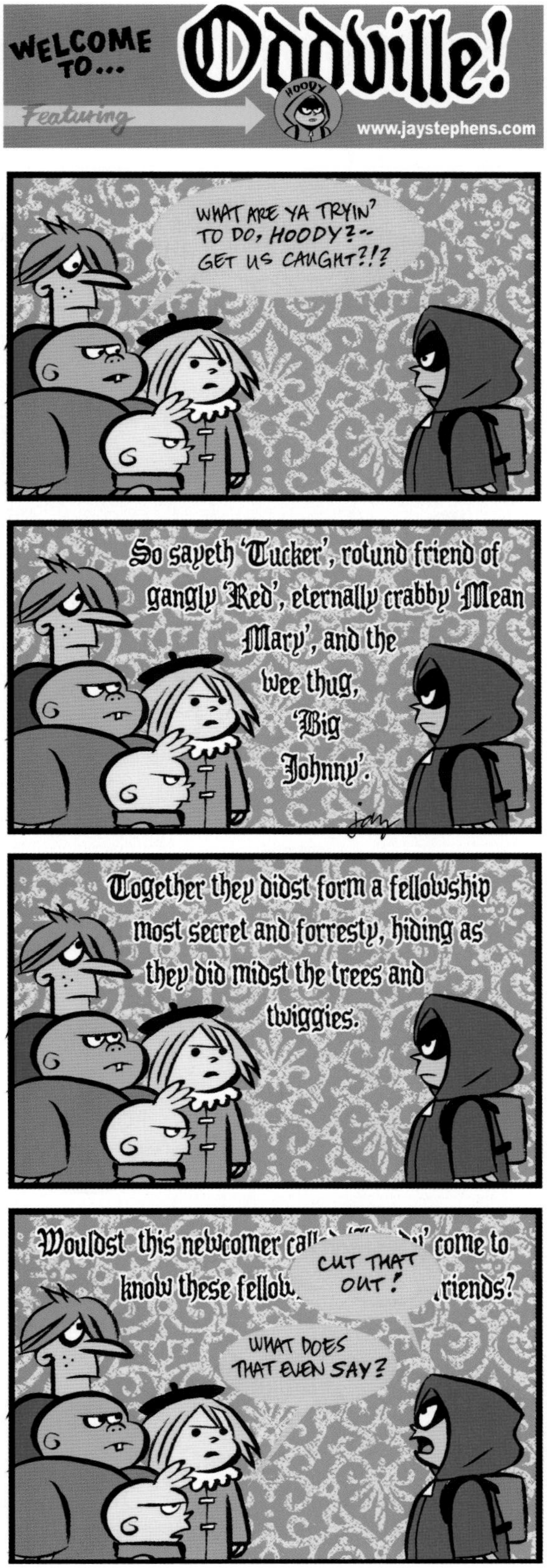
WELCOME TO... Oddville!
Featuring
HOODY
www.jaystephens.com
WHAT ARE YA TRYIN' TO DO, HOODY?-- GET US CAUGHT?!?
So sayeth 'Tucker', rotund friend of gangly 'Red', eternally crabby 'Mean Mary', and the wee thug, 'Big Johnny'.
jay
Together they didst form a fellowship most secret and forresty, hiding as they did midst the trees and twiggies.
Wouldst this newcomer cal ' come to know these fellow riends?
CUT THAT OUT!
WHAT DOES THAT EVEN SAY?

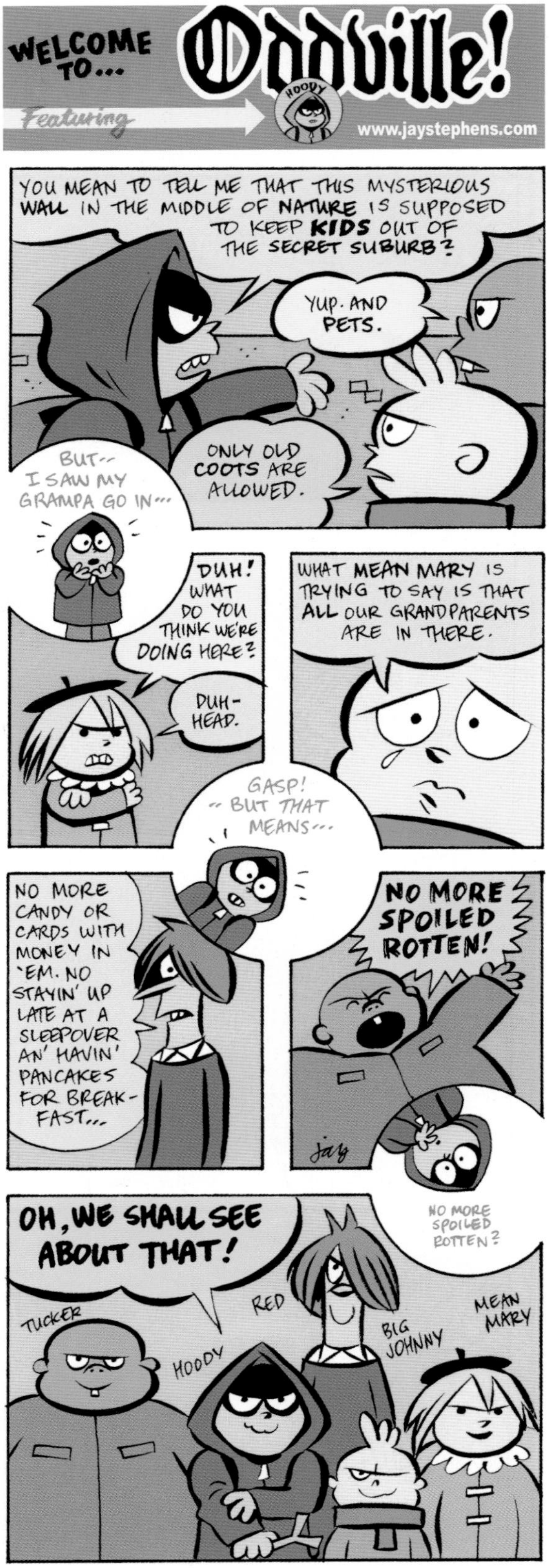
WELCOME TO...
Oddville!
Featuring
HOODY
www.jaystephens.com
YOU MEAN TO TELL ME THAT THIS MYSTERIOUS WALL IN THE MIDDLE OF NATURE IS SUPPOSED TO KEEP KIDS OUT OF THE SECRET SUBURB?
YUP. AND PETS.
ONLY OLD COOTS ARE ALLOWED.
BUT-- I SAW MY GRAMPA GO IN...
DUH! WHAT DO YOU THINK WE'RE DOING HERE?
DUH-HEAD.
WHAT MEAN MARY IS TRYING TO SAY IS THAT ALL OUR GRANDPARENTS ARE IN THERE.
GASP! -- BUT THAT MEANS...
NO MORE CANDY OR CARDS WITH MONEY IN 'EM. NO STAYIN' UP LATE AT A SLEEPOVER AN' HAVIN' PANCAKES FOR BREAK-FAST...
NO MORE SPOILED ROTTEN!
OH, WE SHALL SEE ABOUT THAT!
NO MORE SPOILED ROTTEN?
TUCKER
HOODY
RED
BIG JOHNNY
MEAN MARY

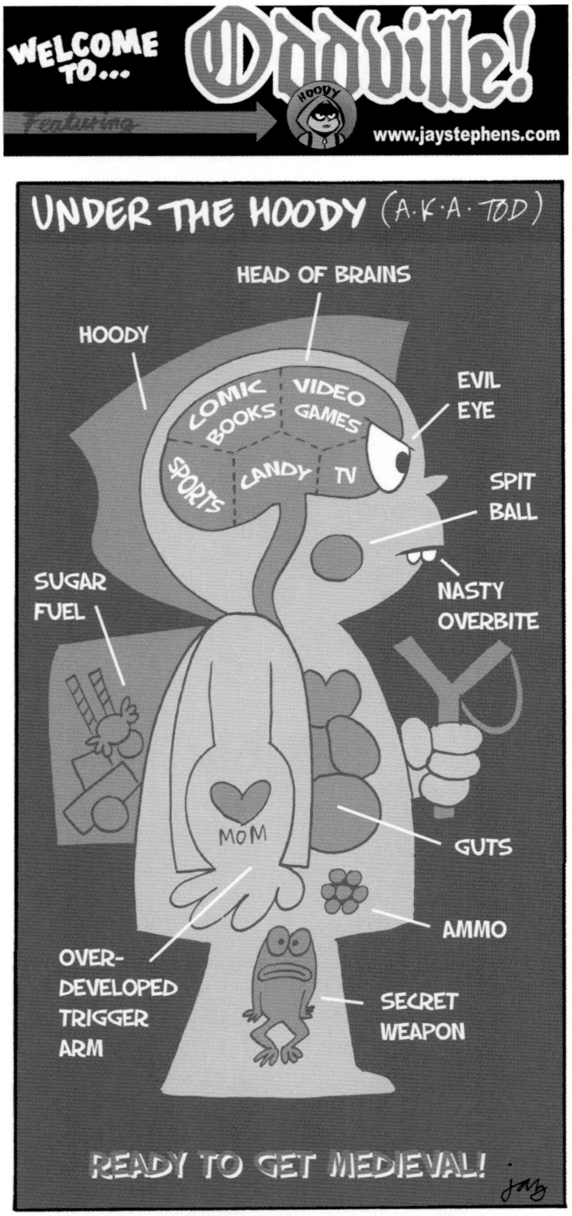
WELCOME TO...
Oddville!
Featuring
HOODY
www.jaystephens.com
UNDER THE HOODY (A.K.A. TOD)
HEAD OF BRAINS
HOODY
COMIC BOOKS
VIDEO GAMES
SPORTS
CANDY
TV
EVIL EYE
SPIT BALL
NASTY OVERBITE
SUGAR FUEL
MOM
GUTS
AMMO
OVER-DEVELOPED TRIGGER ARM
SECRET WEAPON
READY TO GET MEDIEVAL!

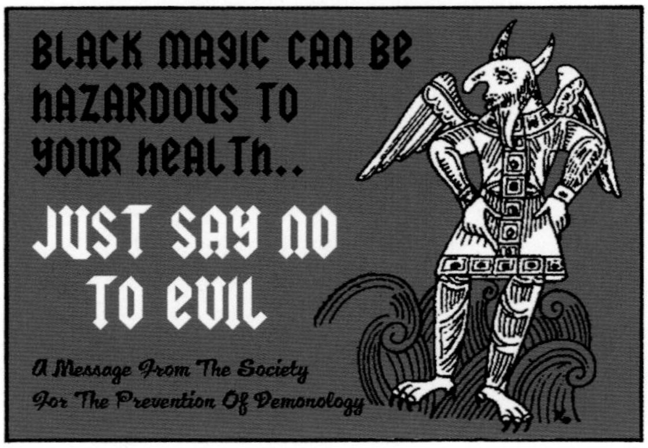
BLACK MAGIC CAN BE HAZARDOUS TO YOUR HEALTH..
JUST SAY NO TO EVIL
A Message From The Society For The Prevention Of Demonology

WELCOME TO... ODDVILLE!
Featuring
JETCAT
www.jaystephens.com
HMN.
TOD'S HAT.
TOD'S DIRTY OLD FOOTPRINTS...
MORE KID FOOTPRINTS! AND A STRUGGLE! WHAT A HIDEOUS MYSTERY!
... AND OVER THIS WALL IS A SECRET SUBURB! OOOOH!
jay
THAT'S RIGHT! AND NO CHILDREN ARE ALLOWED ON THE PREMISES... NOT EVEN SUPER CHILDREN! DON'T MAKE ME PUT YOU IN JAIL LIKE THOSE OTHER KIDS!
SHERI NOTINGHAM
GOSH! MY SUPERHERO CODE PREVENTS ME FROM BREAKING RULES! I'M STYMIED!!!

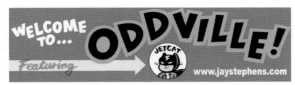

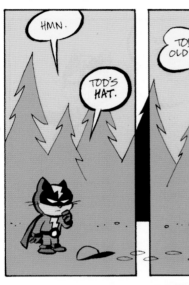

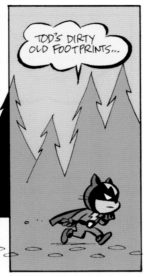

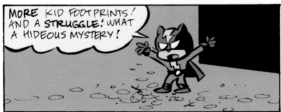

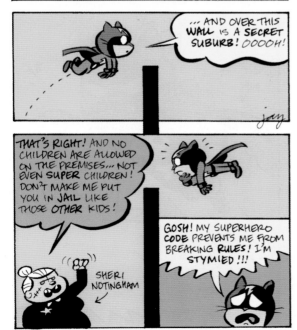

How in heck will **Jetcat** be able to get around this super-problem ????????

Stay tuned for the ultra-dramatic super-duper solution!!!!!!

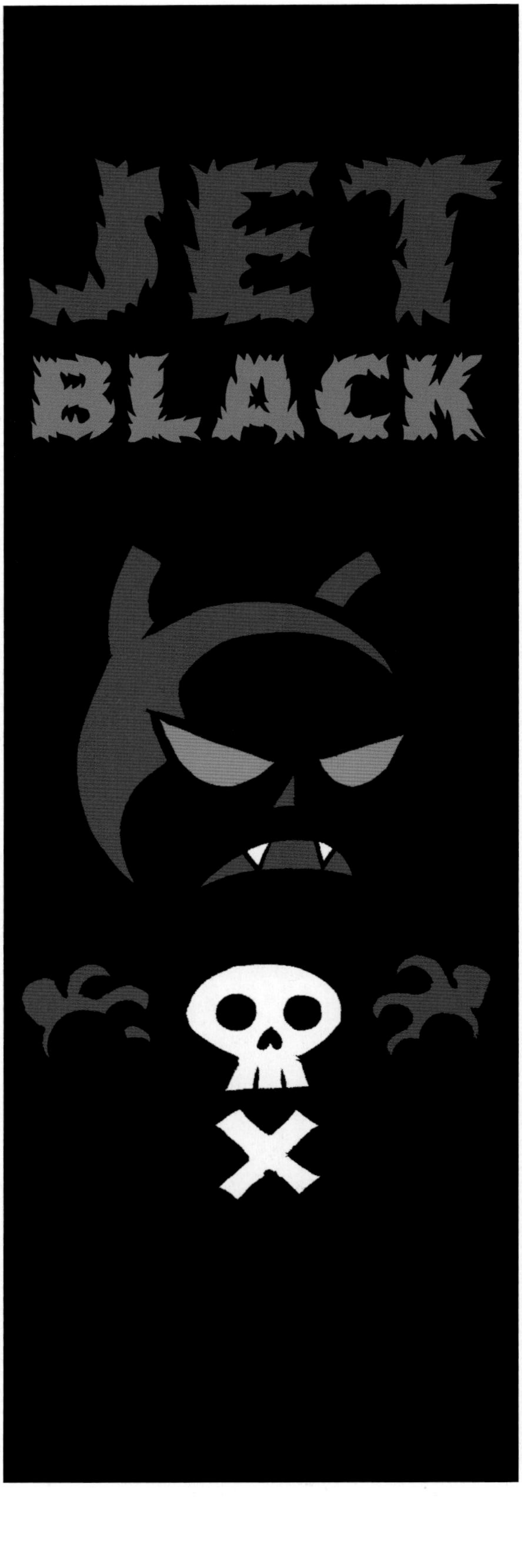
JET BLACK

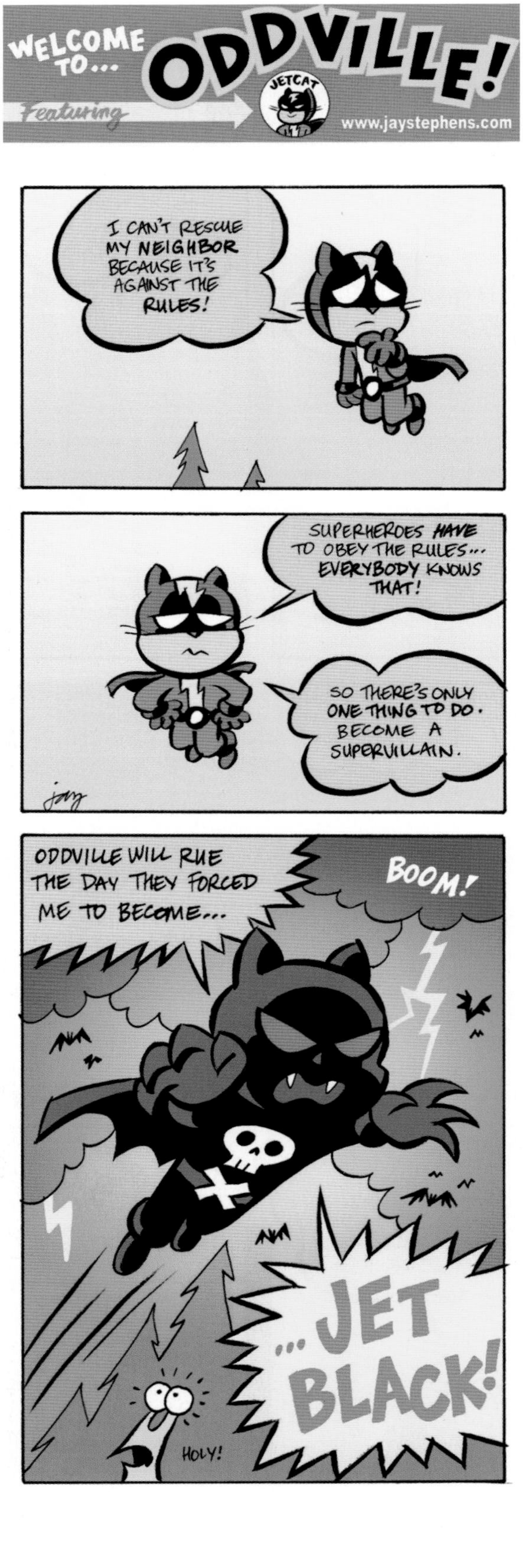
WELCOME TO...
ODDVILLE!
Featuring
JETCAT
www.jaystephens.com
I CAN'T RESCUE MY NEIGHBOR BECAUSE IT'S AGAINST THE RULES!
SUPERHEROES HAVE TO OBEY THE RULES... EVERYBODY KNOWS THAT!
SO THERE'S ONLY ONE THING TO DO. BECOME A SUPERVILLAIN.
jay
ODDVILLE WILL RUE THE DAY THEY FORCED ME TO BECOME...
BOOM!
...JET BLACK!
HOLY!

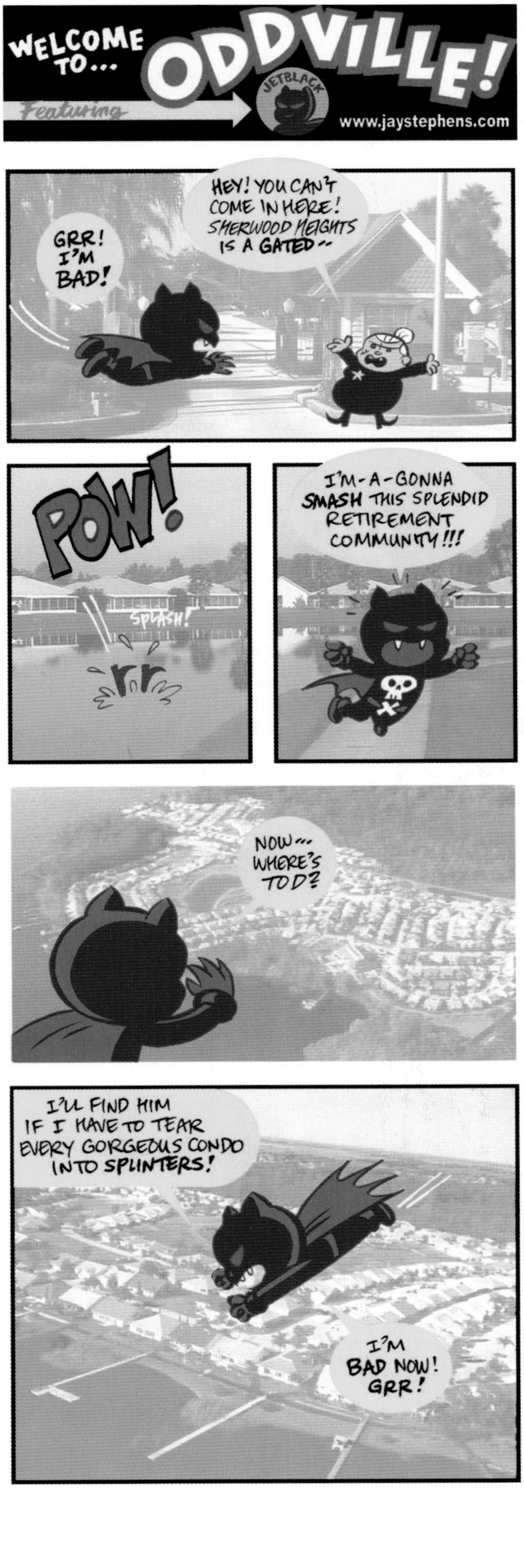
WELCOME TO... ODDVILLE!
Featuring JETBLACK
www.jaystephens.com
GRR! I'M BAD!
HEY! YOU CAN'T COME IN HERE! SHERWOOD HEIGHTS IS A GATED --
POW!
SPLASH!
I'M-A-GONNA SMASH THIS SPLENDID RETIREMENT COMMUNITY!!!
NOW... WHERE'S TOD?
I'LL FIND HIM IF I HAVE TO TEAR EVERY GORGEOUS CONDO INTO SPLINTERS!
I'M BAD NOW! GRR!

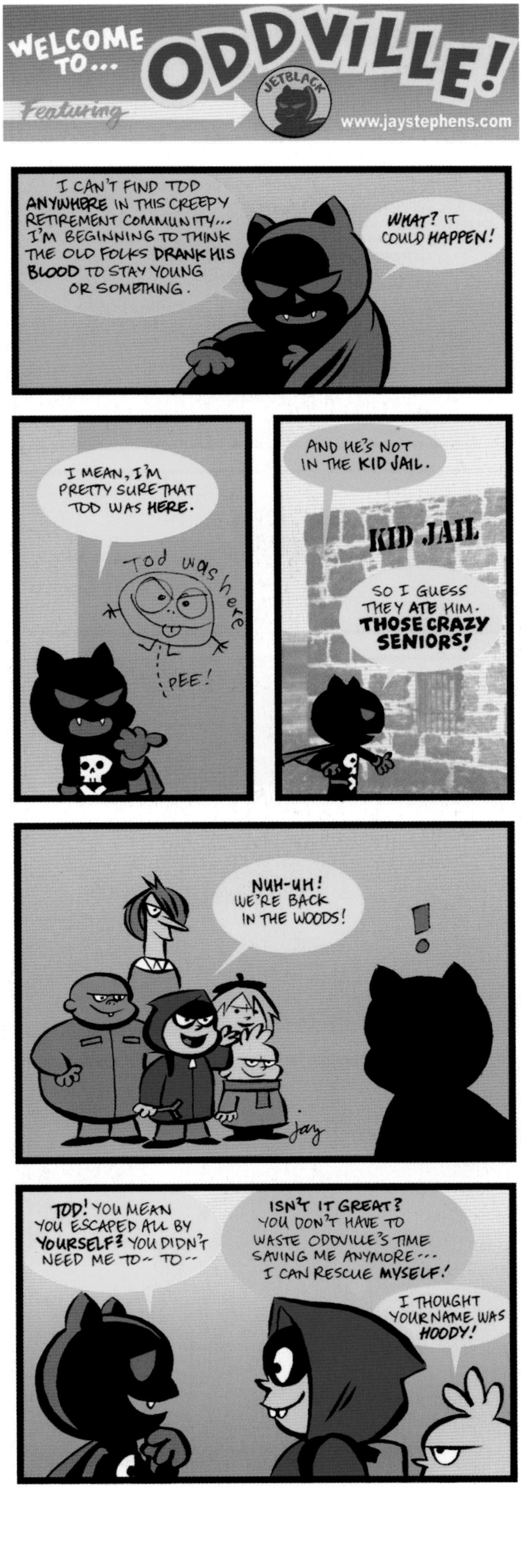
WELCOME TO... ODDVILLE!
Featuring JETBLACK
www.jaystephens.com
I CAN'T FIND TOD ANYWHERE IN THIS CREEPY RETIREMENT COMMUNITY... I'M BEGINNING TO THINK THE OLD FOLKS DRANK HIS BLOOD TO STAY YOUNG OR SOMETHING.
WHAT? IT COULD HAPPEN!
I MEAN, I'M PRETTY SURE THAT TOD WAS HERE.
Tod was here
PEE!
AND HE'S NOT IN THE KID JAIL.
KID JAIL
SO I GUESS THEY ATE HIM. THOSE CRAZY SENIORS!
NUH-UH! WE'RE BACK IN THE WOODS!
!
Jay
TOD! YOU MEAN YOU ESCAPED ALL BY YOURSELF? YOU DIDN'T NEED ME TO-- TO--
ISN'T IT GREAT? YOU DON'T HAVE TO WASTE ODDVILLE'S TIME SAVING ME ANYMORE... I CAN RESCUE MYSELF!
I THOUGHT YOUR NAME WAS HOODY!

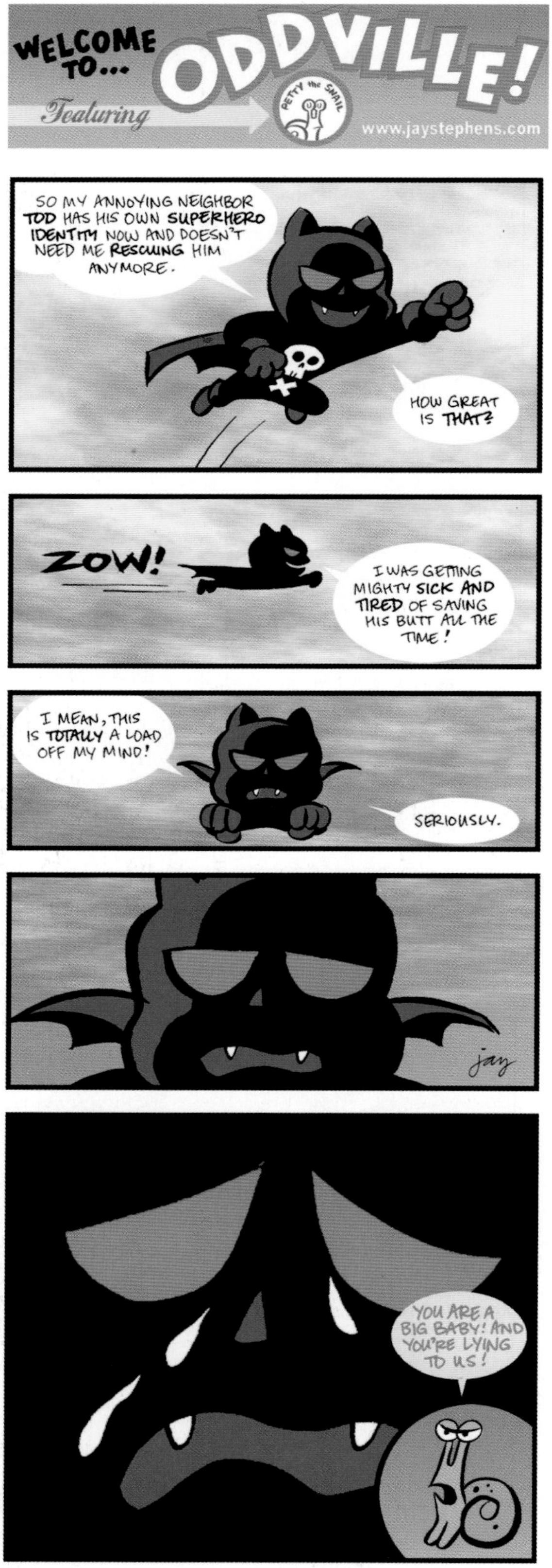
WELCOME TO... ODDVILLE!
Featuring
PETTY the SNAIL
www.jaystephens.com
SO MY ANNOYING NEIGHBOR TOD HAS HIS OWN SUPERHERO IDENTITY NOW AND DOESN'T NEED ME RESCUING HIM ANYMORE.
HOW GREAT IS THAT?
ZOW!
I WAS GETTING MIGHTY SICK AND TIRED OF SAVING HIS BUTT ALL THE TIME!
I MEAN, THIS IS TOTALLY A LOAD OFF MY MIND!
SERIOUSLY.
jay
YOU ARE A BIG BABY! AND YOU'RE LYING TO US!

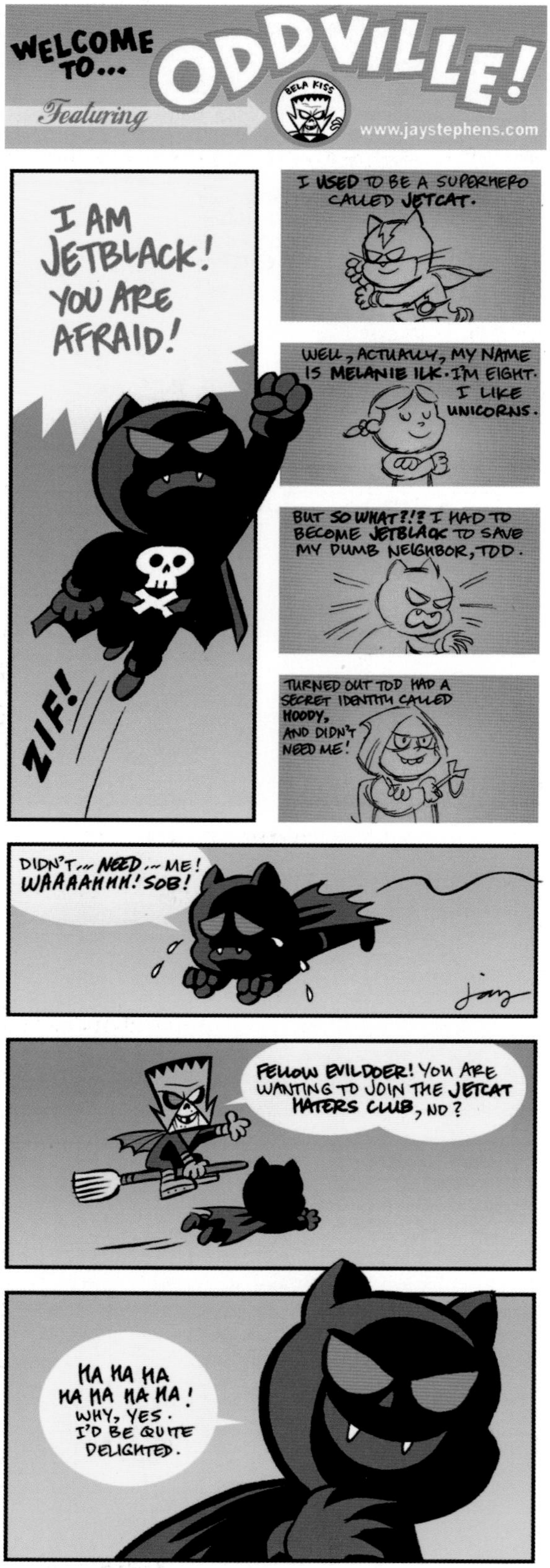
WELCOME TO... ODDVILLE!
Featuring
BELA KISS
www.jaystephens.com
I AM JETBLACK! YOU ARE AFRAID!
ZIF!
I USED TO BE A SUPERHERO CALLED JETCAT.
WELL, ACTUALLY, MY NAME IS MELANIE ILK. I'M EIGHT. I LIKE UNICORNS.
BUT SO WHAT?!? I HAD TO BECOME JETBLACK TO SAVE MY DUMB NEIGHBOR, TOD.
TURNED OUT TOD HAD A SECRET IDENTITY CALLED HOODY, AND DIDN'T NEED ME!
DIDN'T... NEED... ME! WAAAAHHH! SOB!
jay
FELLOW EVILDOER! YOU ARE WANTING TO JOIN THE JETCAT HATERS CLUB, NO?
HA HA HA HA HA HA HA! WHY, YES. I'D BE QUITE DELIGHTED.

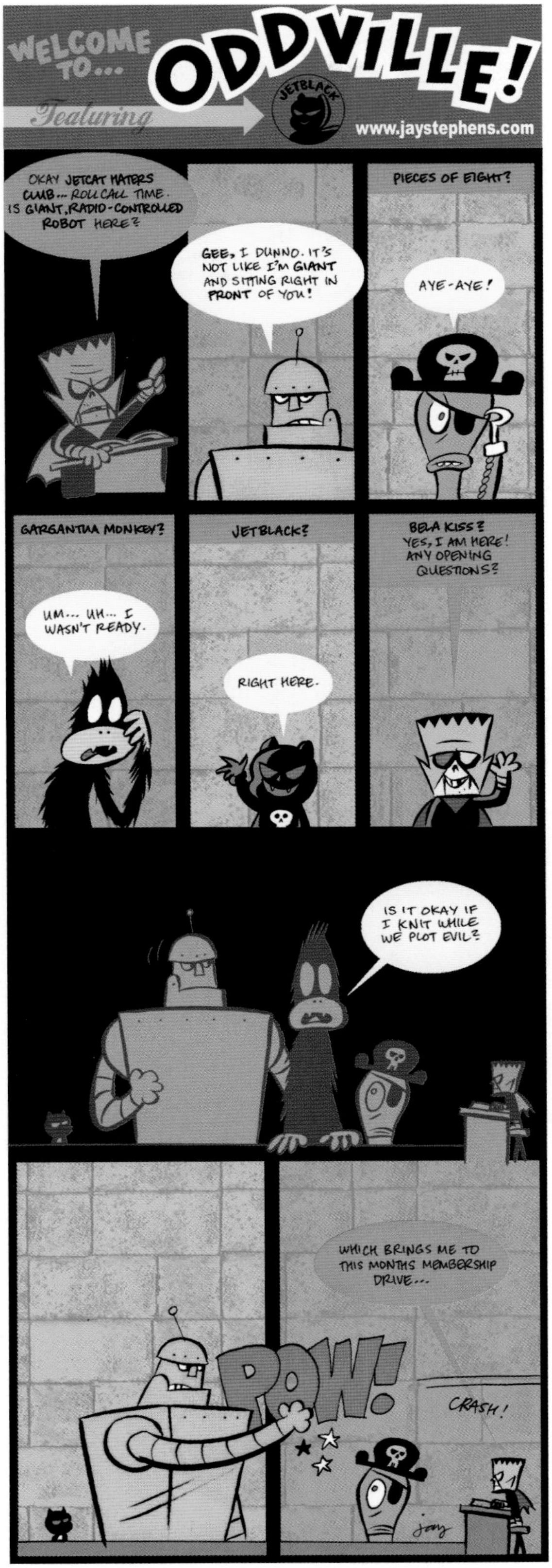

WELCOME TO... ODDVILLE!
Featuring JETBLACK
www.jaystephens.com
OKAY JETCAT HATERS CLUB... ROLL CALL TIME. IS GIANT, RADIO-CONTROLLED ROBOT HERE?
GEE, I DUNNO. IT'S NOT LIKE I'M GIANT AND SITTING RIGHT IN FRONT OF YOU!
PIECES OF EIGHT?
AYE-AYE!
GARGANTUA MONKEY?
UM... UH... I WASN'T READY.
JETBLACK?
RIGHT HERE.
BELA KISS? YES, I AM HERE! ANY OPENING QUESTIONS?
IS IT OKAY IF I KNIT WHILE WE PLOT EVIL?
POW!
WHICH BRINGS ME TO THIS MONTHS MEMBERSHIP DRIVE...
CRASH!
Jay

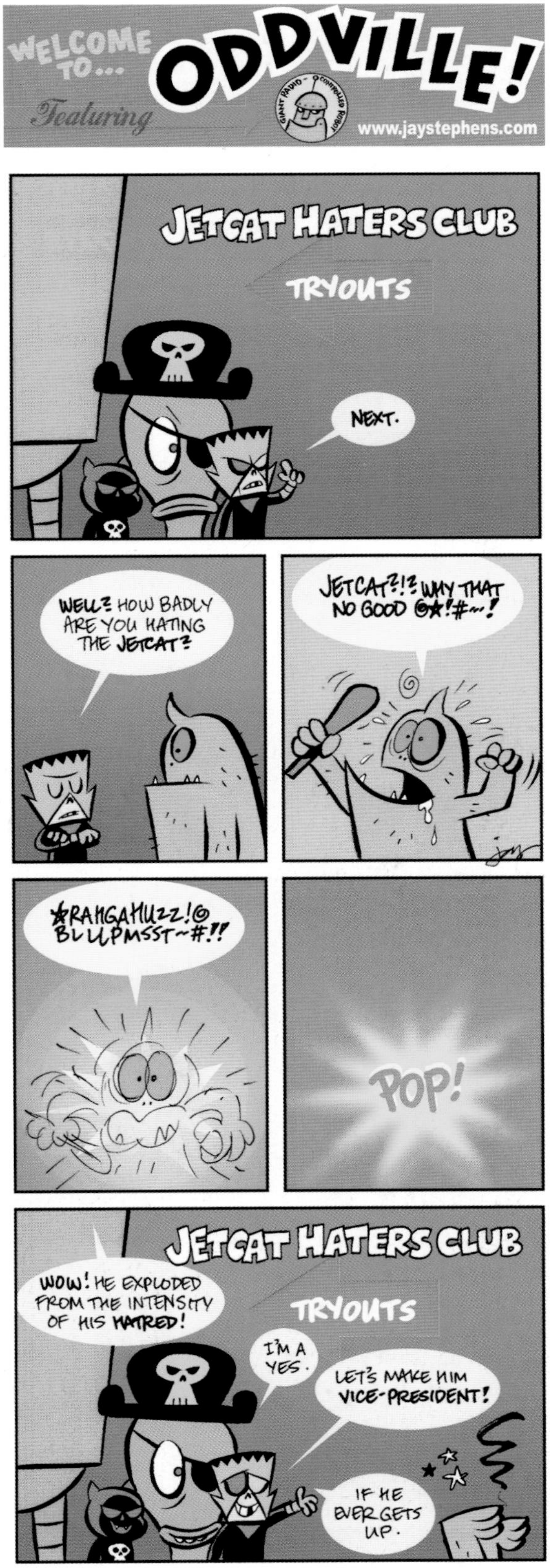

WELCOME TO... ODDVILLE!
Featuring GIANT RADIO-CONTROLLED ROBOT
www.jaystephens.com
JETCAT HATERS CLUB
TRYOUTS
NEXT.
WELL? HOW BADLY ARE YOU HATING THE JETCAT?
JETCAT?!? WHY THAT NO GOOD @*!#~!
Jay
*RAMGAHUZZ!@ BLLLPMSST~#!!
POP!
JETCAT HATERS CLUB
TRYOUTS
WOW! HE EXPLODED FROM THE INTENSITY OF HIS HATRED!
I'M A YES.
LET'S MAKE HIM VICE-PRESIDENT!
IF HE EVER GETS UP.

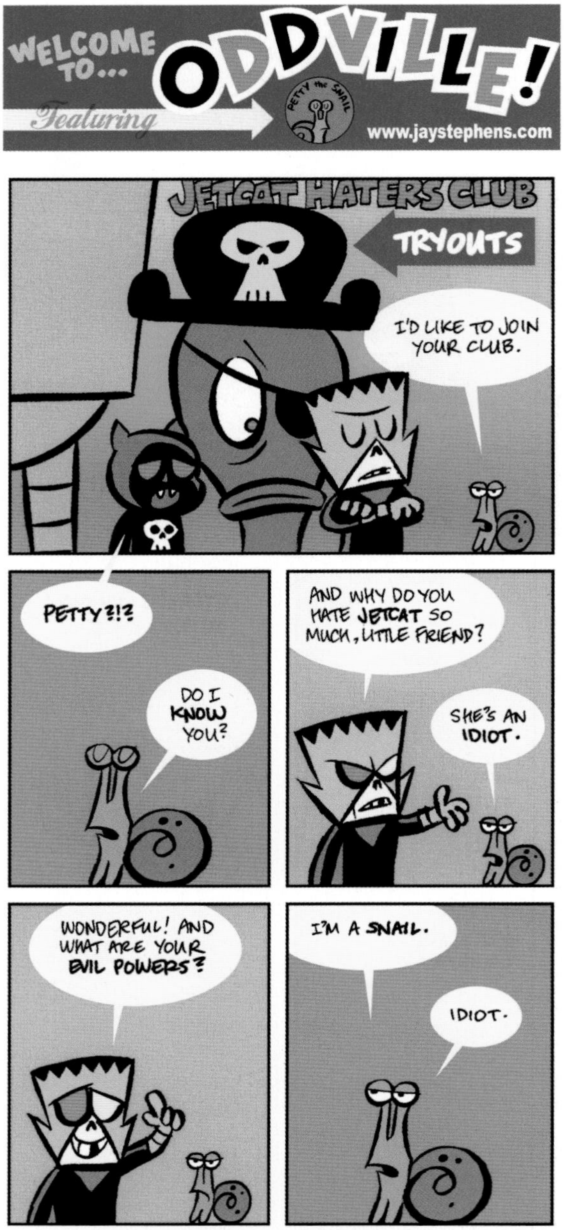
WELCOME TO... ODDVILLE!
Featuring
PETTY the SNAIL
www.jaystephens.com
JETCAT HATERS CLUB
TRYOUTS
I'D LIKE TO JOIN YOUR CLUB.
PETTY ?!?
DO I KNOW YOU?
AND WHY DO YOU HATE JETCAT SO MUCH, LITTLE FRIEND?
SHE'S AN IDIOT.
WONDERFUL! AND WHAT ARE YOUR EVIL POWERS?
I'M A SNAIL.
IDIOT.

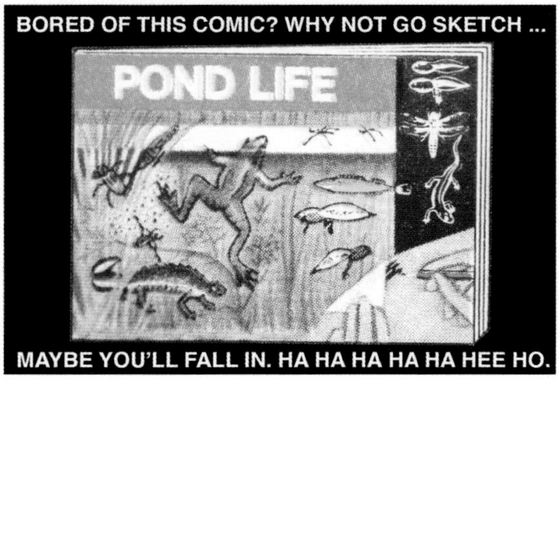
BORED OF THIS COMIC? WHY NOT GO SKETCH ...
POND LIFE
MAYBE YOU'LL FALL IN. HA HA HA HA HA HEE HO.

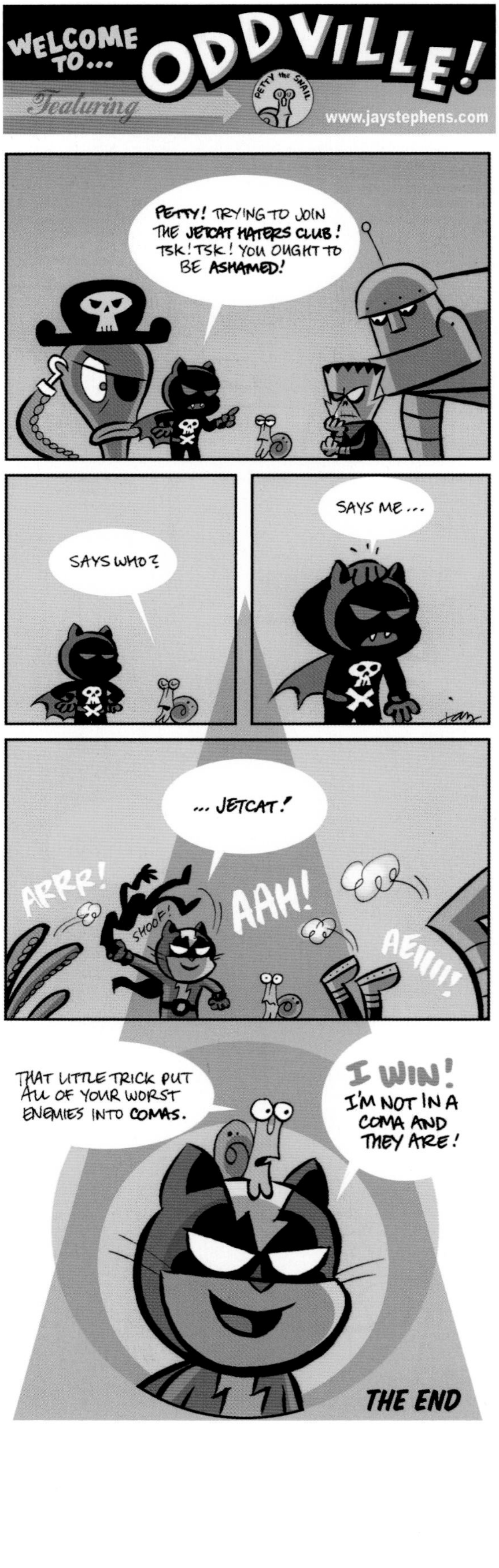
WELCOME TO... ODDVILLE!
Featuring
PETTY the SNAIL
www.jaystephens.com
PETTY! TRYING TO JOIN THE JETCAT HATERS CLUB! TSK! TSK! YOU OUGHT TO BE ASHAMED!
SAYS WHO?
SAYS ME...
... JETCAT!
ARRR!
SHOOF
AAH!
AE!!!!
THAT LITTLE TRICK PUT ALL OF YOUR WORST ENEMIES INTO COMAS.
I WIN! I'M NOT IN A COMA AND THEY ARE!
THE END

ЛЕНИНГРАД 16188
SOUTH POLE 1253 km
МОСКВА 15575
МАК МЕРДО 1307 км
МИРНЫЙ 1410 km
МОЛОДЕЖНАЯ 2140 км
ЖЕЛТЫЕ ВОДЫ 14876
ЗЕЛЕНОГРАД 15634
TOGLIATTI
CANBERRA 7326
ДУШАНБЕ 13353 KM
RIGA
БУДЕННОВСК 14304
МИНСК 16260 KM
ТОКМАК

ODDVILLE!
LOST MONSTERS
THIS COOL STORY IS CALLED 'LOST MONSTERS'!
KNOW ABOUT IT.
WHAT DO YOU HAVE TO DO WITH THIS STORY, KYLE?
NUTHIN.
SO, AH... YOU'RE KIND OF JUST WASTING OUR TIME, THEN?
SIGH...
HEY, LOOK! IT SAYS 'THE END'!
THE END

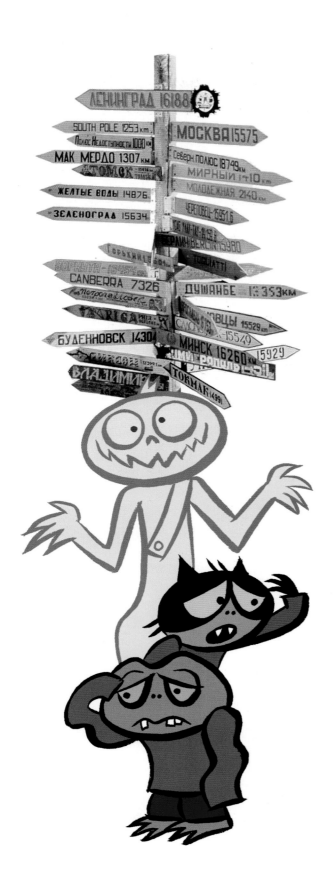

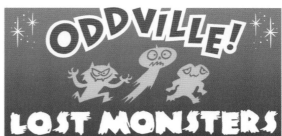

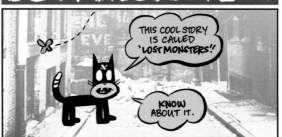

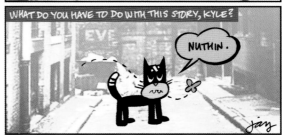

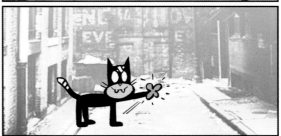

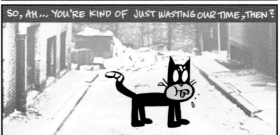

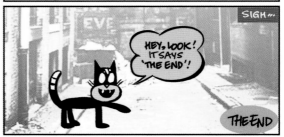

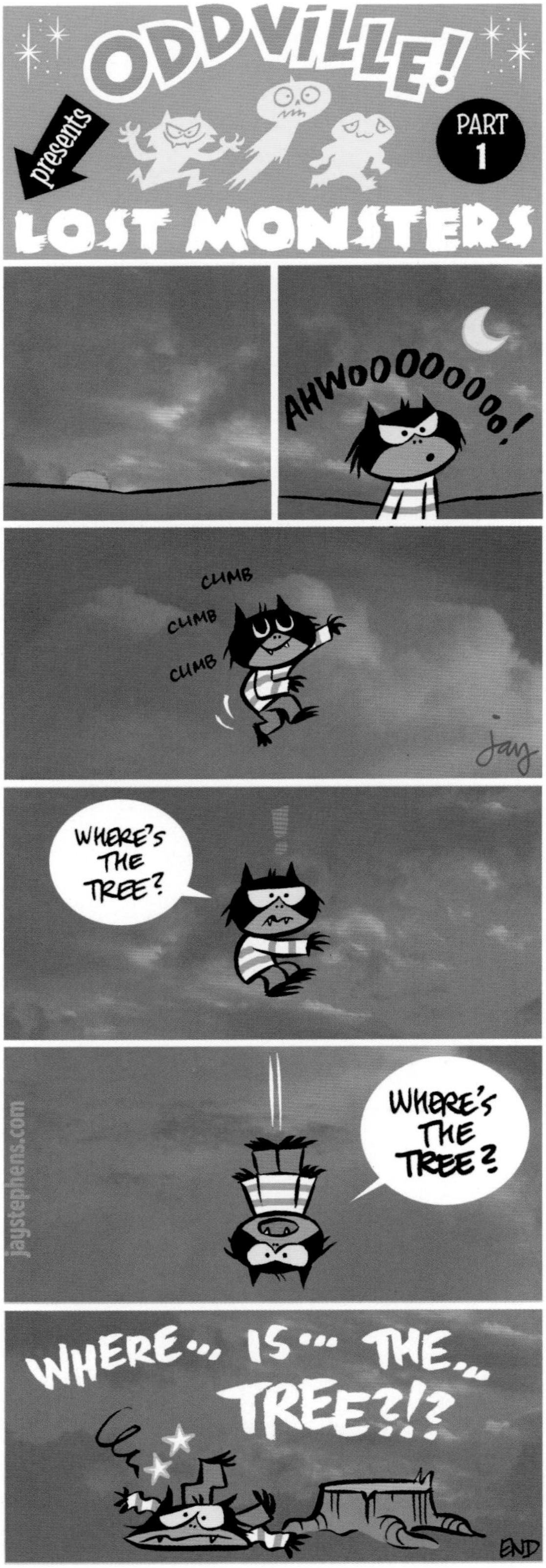
ODDVILLE!
presents
PART 1
LOST MONSTERS
AHWOOOOOOOOO!
CLIMB
CLIMB
CLIMB
jay
WHERE'S THE TREE?
WHERE'S THE TREE?
jaystephens.com
WHERE... IS... THE... TREE?!?
END

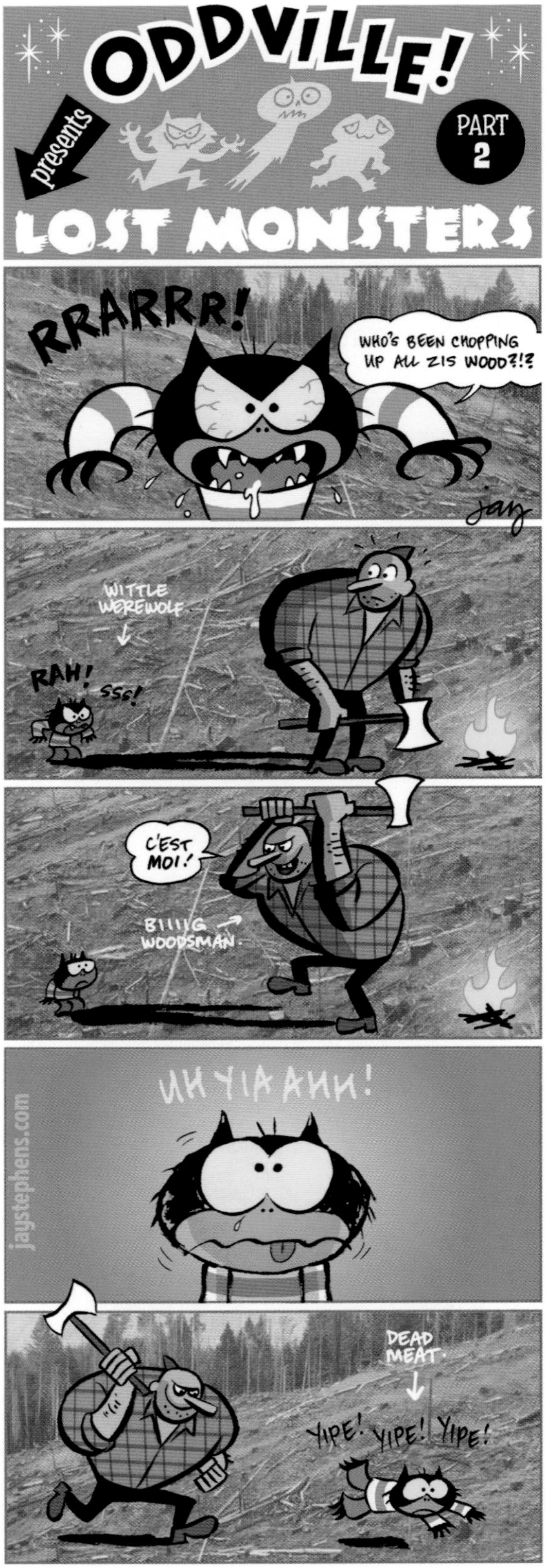
ODDVILLE!
presents
PART 2
LOST MONSTERS
RRARRRR!
WHO'S BEEN CHOPPING UP ALL ZIS WOOD?!?
jay
WITTLE WEREWOLF
RAH!
SSS!
C'EST MOI!
BIIIIG WOODSMAN.
UH YIA AHH!
jaystephens.com
DEAD MEAT.
YIPE! YIPE! YIPE!

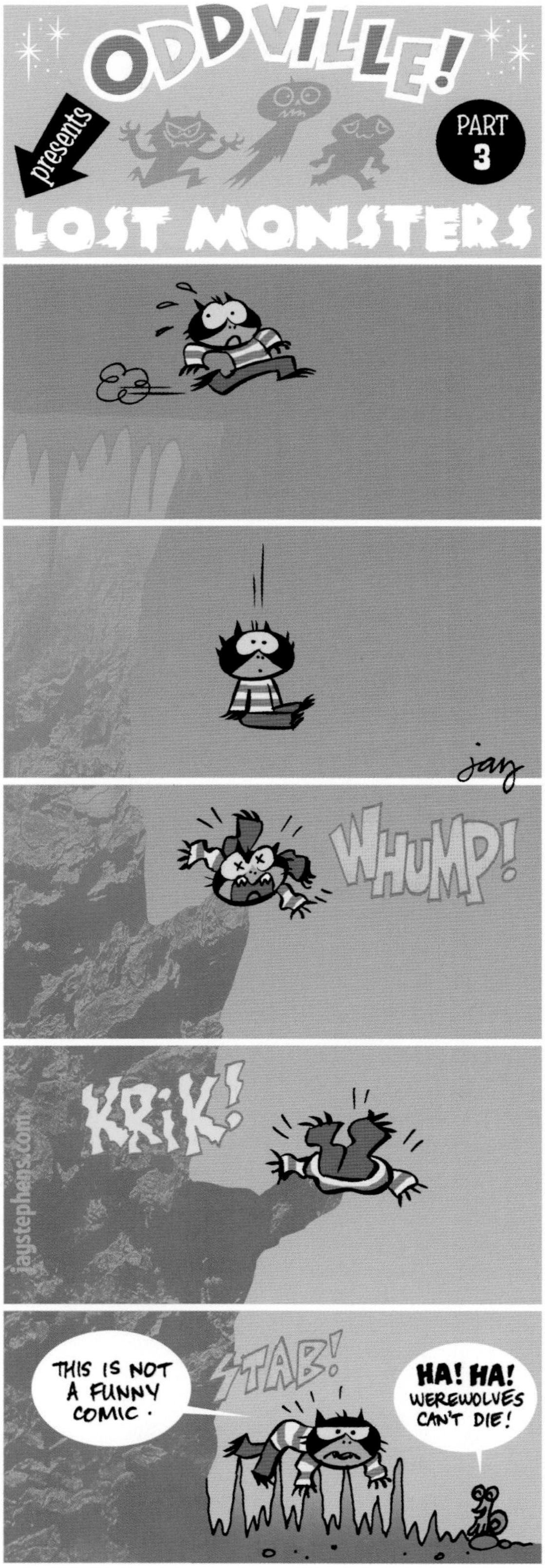
ODDVILLE!
presents
PART 3
LOST MONSTERS
jay
WHUMP!
KRIK!
jaystephens.com
THIS IS NOT A FUNNY COMIC.
STAB!
HA! HA! WEREWOLVES CAN'T DIE!

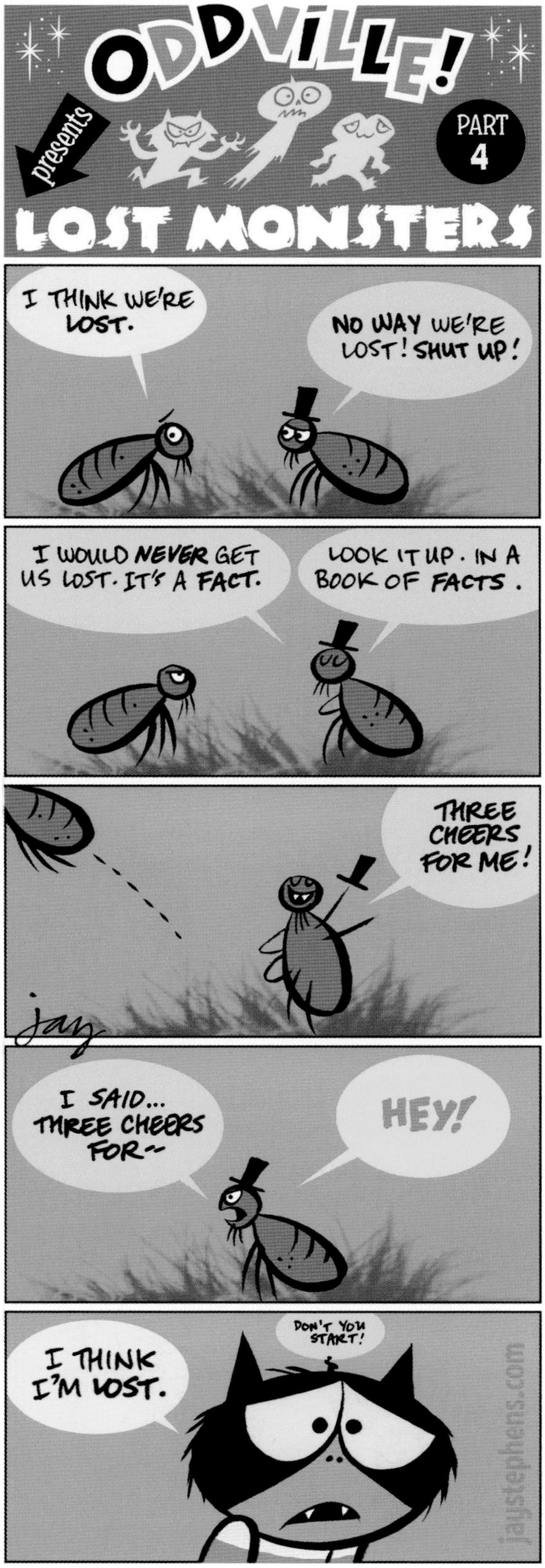
ODDVILLE!
presents
PART 4
LOST MONSTERS
I THINK WE'RE LOST.
NO WAY WE'RE LOST! SHUT UP!
I WOULD NEVER GET US LOST. IT'S A FACT.
LOOK IT UP. IN A BOOK OF FACTS.
THREE CHEERS FOR ME!
jay
I SAID... THREE CHEERS FOR--
HEY!
I THINK I'M LOST.
DON'T YOU START!
jaystephens.com

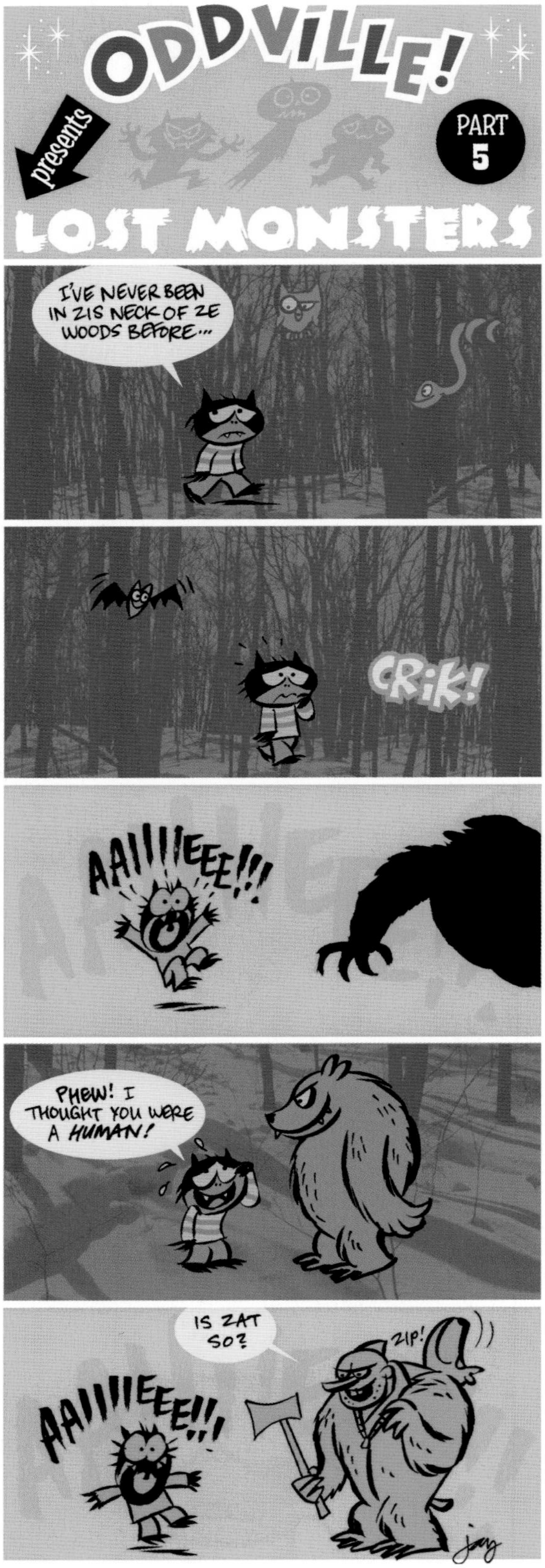
ODDVILLE!
presents
PART 5
LOST MONSTERS
I'VE NEVER BEEN IN ZIS NECK OF ZE WOODS BEFORE...
CRIK!
AAIIIIEEE!!!
PHEW! I THOUGHT YOU WERE A HUMAN!
IS ZAT SO?
ZIP!
AAIIIIEEE!!!
jay

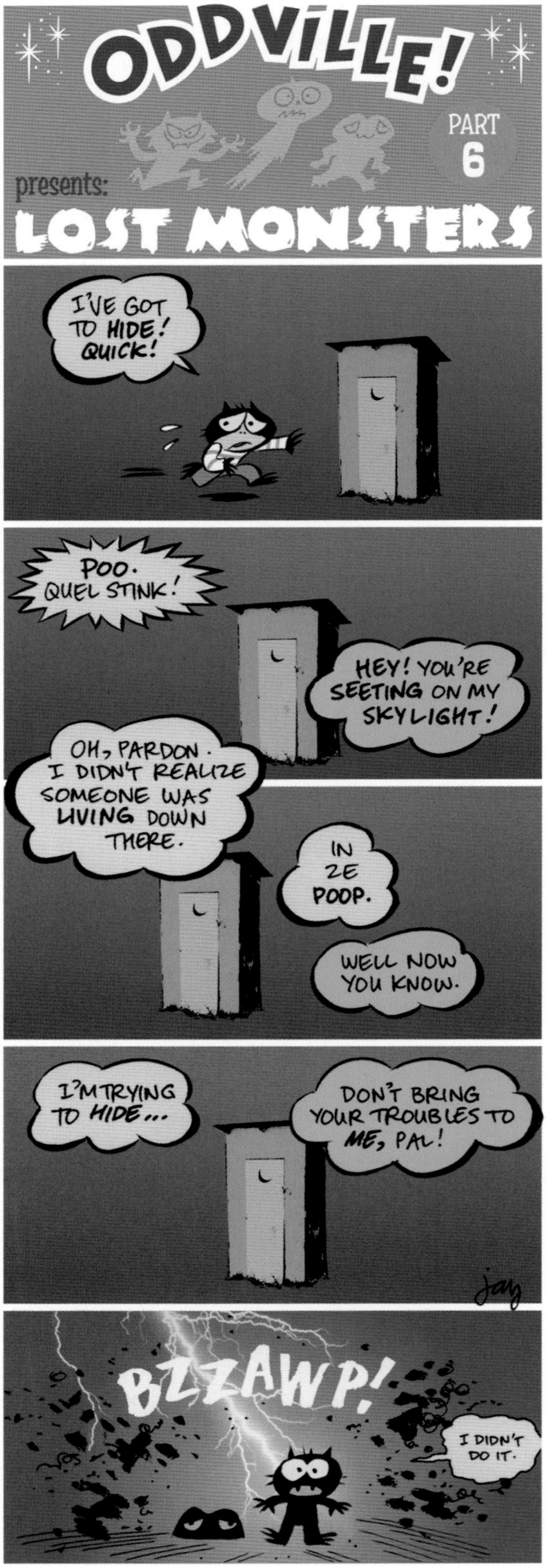
ODDVILLE!
presents:
PART 6
LOST MONSTERS
I'VE GOT TO HIDE! QUICK!
POO. QUEL STINK!
HEY! YOU'RE SEETING ON MY SKYLIGHT!
OH, PARDON. I DIDN'T REALIZE SOMEONE WAS LIVING DOWN THERE.
IN ZE POOP.
WELL NOW YOU KNOW.
I'M TRYING TO HIDE...
DON'T BRING YOUR TROUBLES TO ME, PAL!
jay
BZZZAWP!
I DIDN'T DO IT.

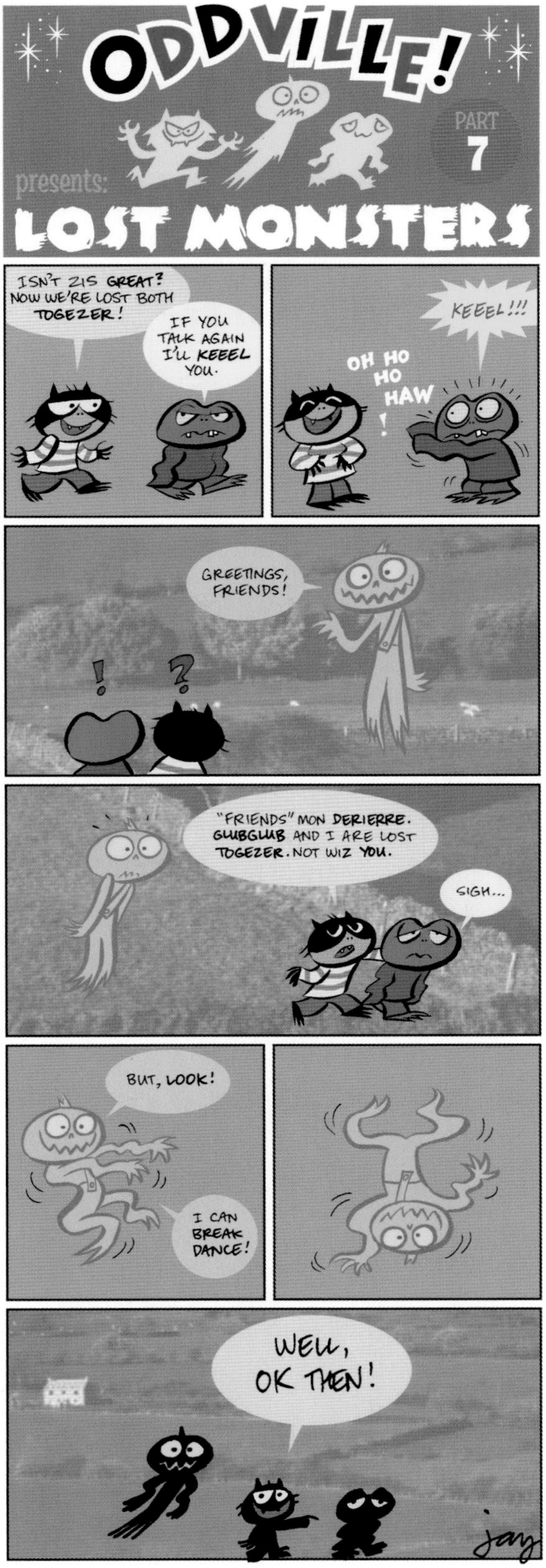
ODDVILLE!
presents:
LOST MONSTERS
PART 7
ISN'T ZIS GREAT? NOW WE'RE LOST BOTH TOGEZER!
IF YOU TALK AGAIN I'LL KEEEL YOU.
KEEEL!!!
OH HO HO HAW
GREETINGS, FRIENDS!
"FRIENDS" MON DERIERRE. GLUBGLUB AND I ARE LOST TOGEZER. NOT WIZ YOU.
SIGH...
BUT, LOOK!
I CAN BREAK DANCE!
WELL, OK THEN!
jay

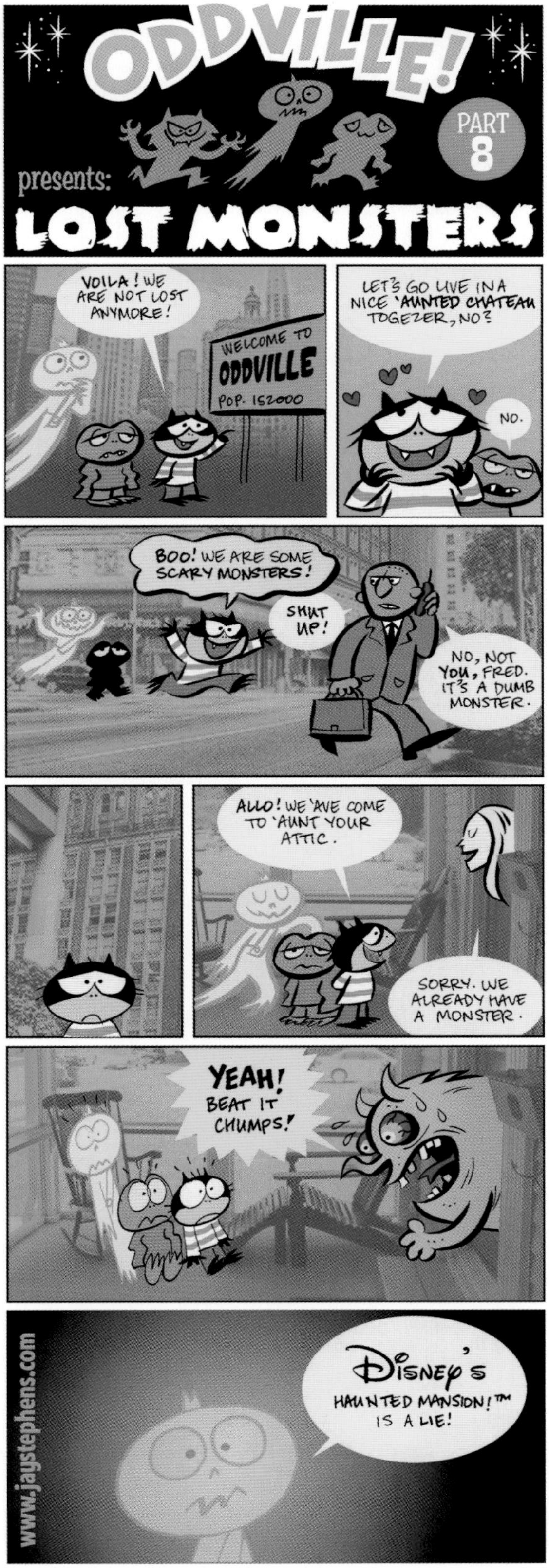
ODDVILLE!
presents:
LOST MONSTERS
PART 8
VOILA! WE ARE NOT LOST ANYMORE!
WELCOME TO ODDVILLE POP. 152000
LET'S GO LIVE IN A NICE 'AUNTED CHATEAU TOGEZER, NO?
NO.
BOO! WE ARE SOME SCARY MONSTERS!
SHUT UP!
NO, NOT YOU, FRED. IT'S A DUMB MONSTER.
ALLO! WE 'AVE COME TO 'AUNT YOUR ATTIC.
SORRY. WE ALREADY HAVE A MONSTER.
YEAH! BEAT IT CHUMPS!
www.jaystephens.com
DISNEY'S HAUNTED MANSION!™ IS A LIE!

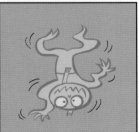

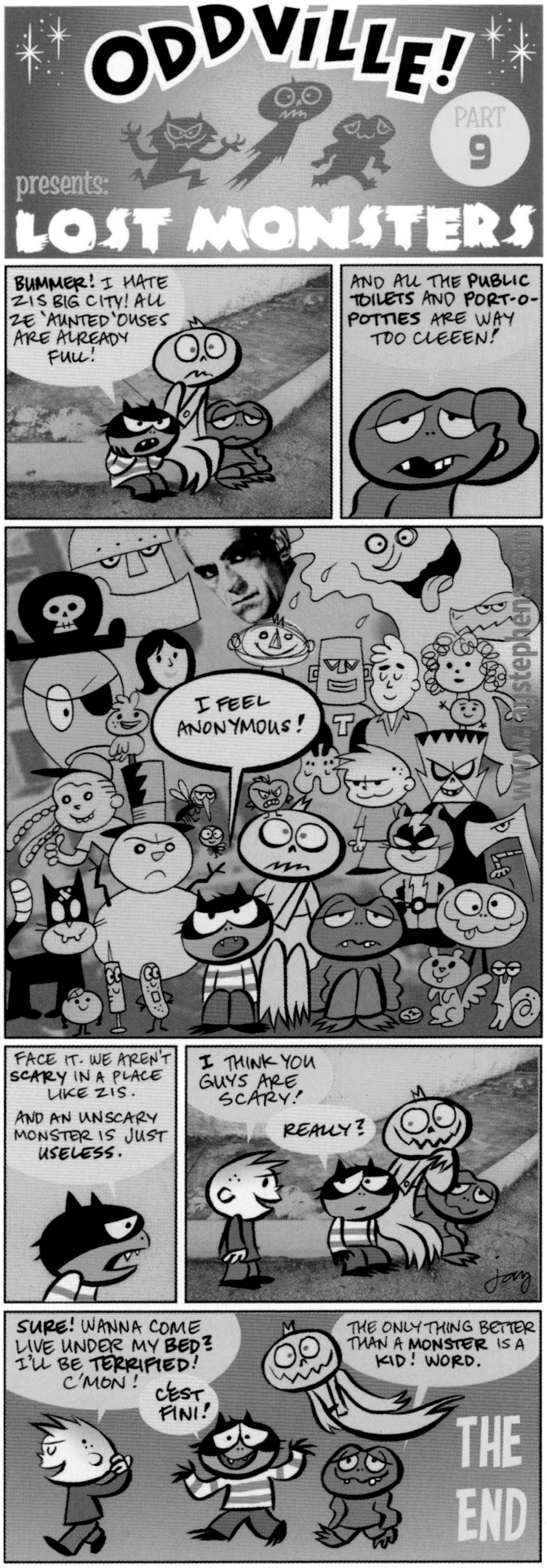
ODDVILLE!
PART 9
presents:
LOST MONSTERS
BUMMER! I HATE ZIS BIG CITY! ALL ZE 'AUNTED 'OUSES ARE ALREADY FULL!
AND ALL THE PUBLIC TOILETS AND PORT-O-POTTIES ARE WAY TOO CLEEEN!
I FEEL ANONYMOUS!
FACE IT. WE AREN'T SCARY IN A PLACE LIKE ZIS.
AND AN UNSCARY MONSTER IS JUST USELESS.
I THINK YOU GUYS ARE SCARY!
REALLY?
jay
SURE! WANNA COME LIVE UNDER MY BED? I'LL BE TERRIFIED! C'MON!
C'EST FINI!
THE ONLY THING BETTER THAN A MONSTER IS A KID! WORD.
THE END

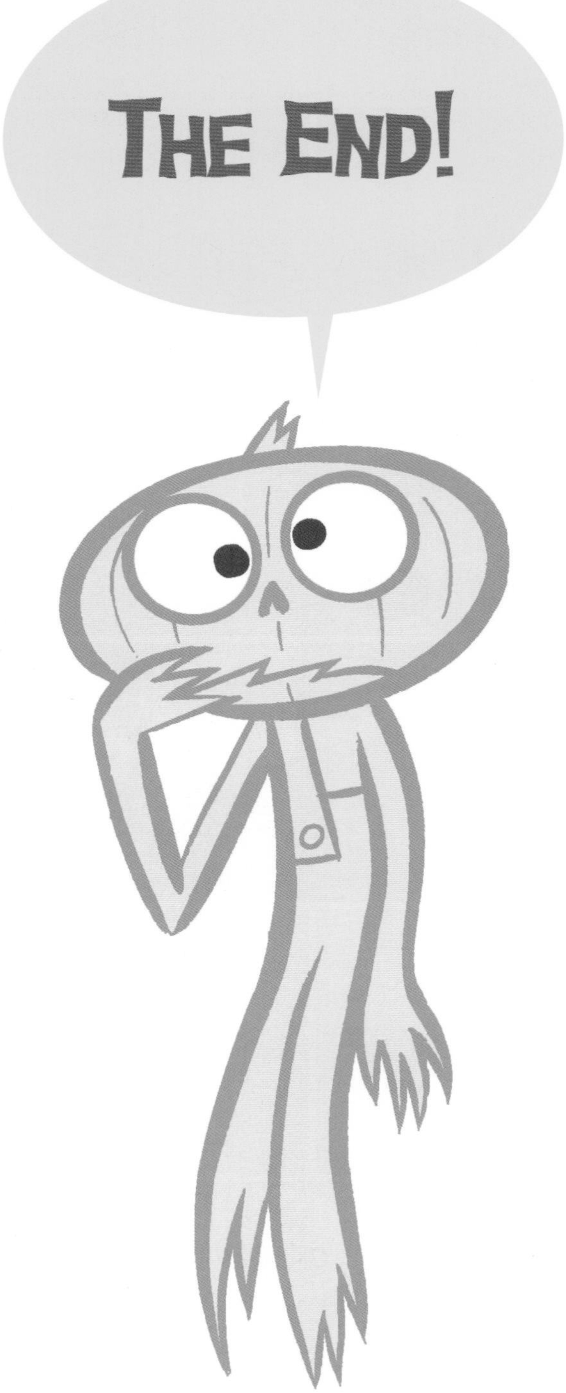
THE END!

SCRAPBOOK

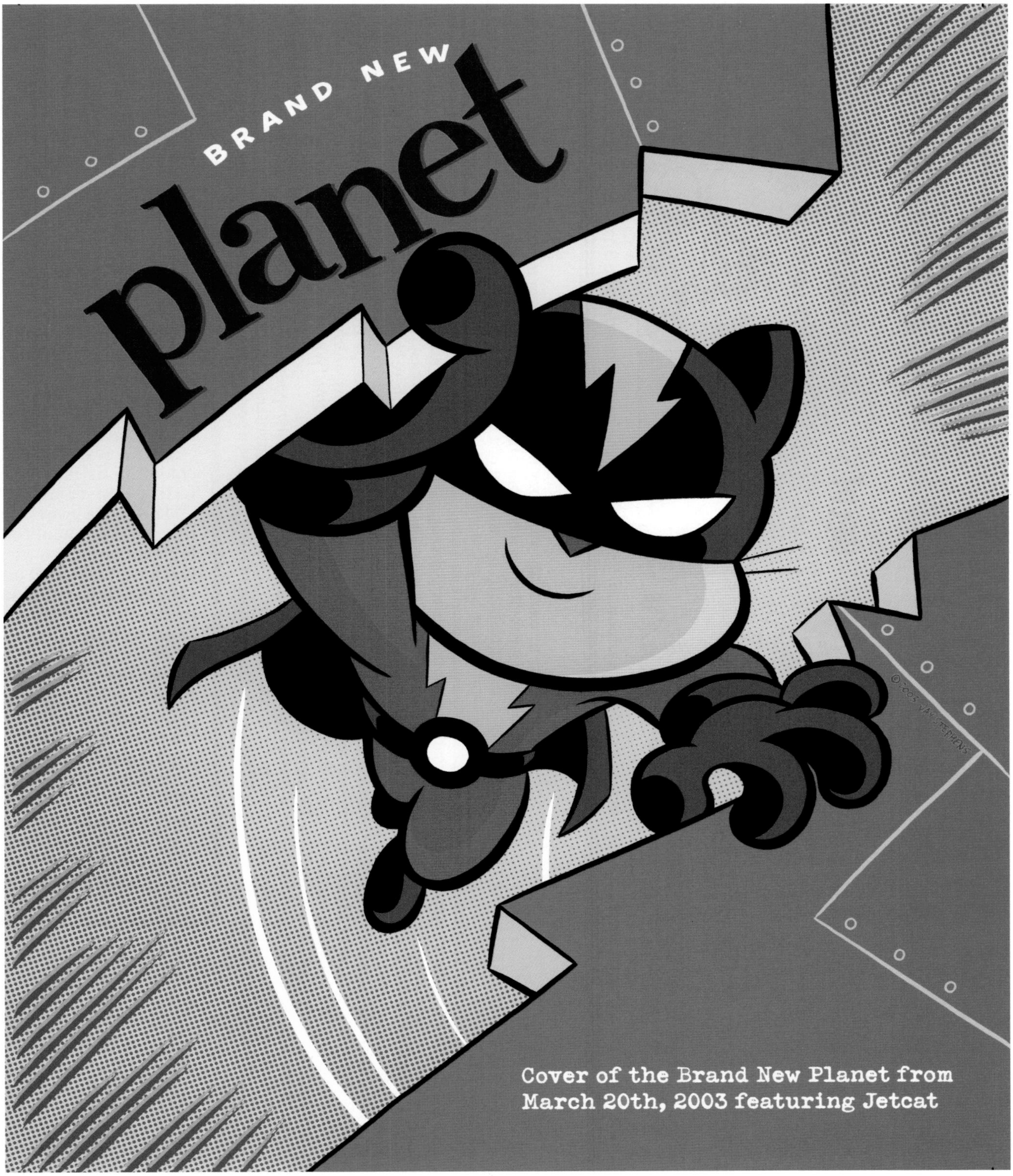
BRAND NEW
planet

Cover of the Brand New Planet from March 20th, 2003 featuring Jetcat

So you want to be in the funny papers

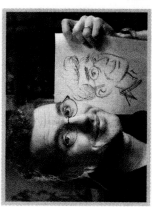

JIM ROSS/TORONTO STAR

Jay Stephens: Cartoonist debuts 'Jetcat' (right) in Welcome To Oddville!

1
HELP!
OH, CHILL OUT.
ZIP!
2
HELP!
OH, CHILL OUT.
ZIP!
3
HELP!
OH, CHILL OUT.
ZIP!
4
HELP!
OH, CHILL OUT.
ZIP!

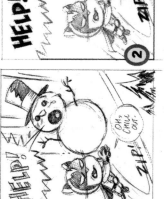

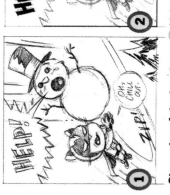

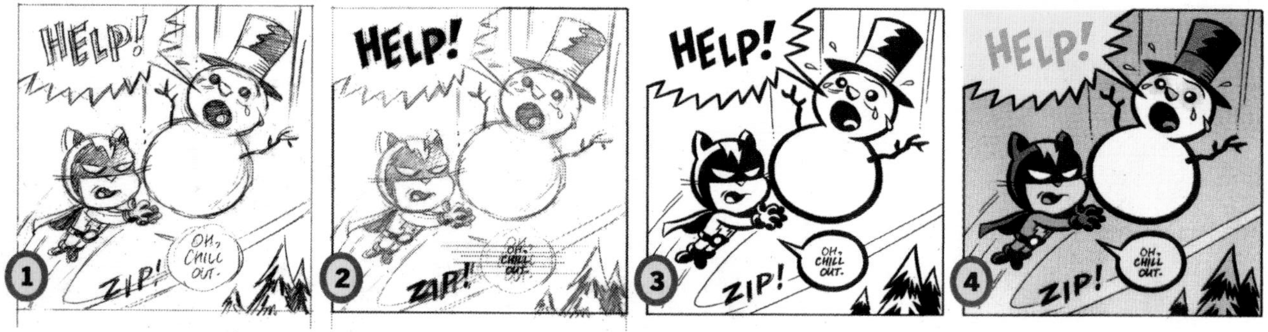

Stages to a Jetcat cartoon: 1 Using a 2H pencil, Jay sketches the onto Bristol board 2 He then hand-letters the comic 3 India ink is used over the pencil to enhance the drawing 4 Finally, he scans it and colours it in Photoshop. **Presto!**

JAY STEPHENS
SPECIAL TO BRAND NEW PLANET

I write and draw funny stories for a living. Think, think . . . stupid, stupid . . . doodle, doodle . . . and I'm done for the day. I get to use onomatopoeia like "ZZZzzz — BLAAM!!!," "YaarrrOOOOOOO!!!" and "Fla-SWOINK!" on a regular basis, and more exclamation marks on one page than you'd normally find in an entire novel. Plus, I can actually claim that watching cartoons and reading comic books is "research." I'm pretty sure my high-school teachers are rolling in their graves. Oh, wait. They're still alive? My apologies.

Sure the pressure to come up with wacky new material week after week is tough, my eyes are permanently bloodshot, and the hand cramps can get so it feels like I'm squeezing dew from a fistful of marbles, but it's a pretty decent way to make a living, and I'm not complaining. At least not to you.

The best part about having my own cartoon studio is that there's nobody around to boss me. I mean, besides all the editors, accountants, art directors, TV network executives, publishers, focus groups, lawyers, agents and fans I have to be accountable too . . . where was I? Oh, right. The freedom of being my own boss. I could draw in nothing but a big felt hat with a feather sticking out of it if I wanted to, or eat beans and onions all the livelong day. There's nobody to report me to the authorities. Nobody at all . . . just me . . .

God, it gets lonely. Sometimes it's so quiet around here that I start to hear little voices, and imagine I can see colourful little twerps frolicking around the baseboards, which answers that oft-asked question, "Where do you get your ideas?"

The other question I get a lot is, "How do you make a comic?" Well, I'll show you, you nosy quizzers!

First off, I get a dumb idea. That's easy because I'm dumb. Then I use a 2H pencil to sketch out the idea on to bristol. This, unfortunately, requires some math in order to ensure the art will fit the printed space. And since I usually work twice as large as printed size, I am forced to use algebra to convert measurements. Sometimes I cry.

The next step is to hand-letter the thing. Some folks these days just drop in computer fonts at the end. Some folks are cheaters. This is the stage to draw in the borders, too.

➤ Please see **Oddville, P15**

Funny papers

➤ Oddville, p. 5

Now the ink. This is my favourite part, using a brush to glide india ink over the skeletal pencils, bringing out the real drawing. I use Staedler waterproof pigment liners for the fine details (and lettering). When it's dry, my least favourite part arrives . . . erasing the underdrawing.

Then I scan it in and colour it in Photoshop, using old-fashioned CMYK. I use layers to do this, but I'm out of room for explaining, so you'll just have to figure it out.

It's fun, it's easy, it pays better than investing in "new technologies." But don't you dare try it, because, honestly, I don't need the competition. No, really. Don't make me come down there.

Jay Stephens is known for his creations CHICK AND DEE, TUTENSTEIN (coming to NBC Sat. mornings), and JETCAT, from Nickelodeon's *KaBlam!* and in Jetcat Clubhouse.

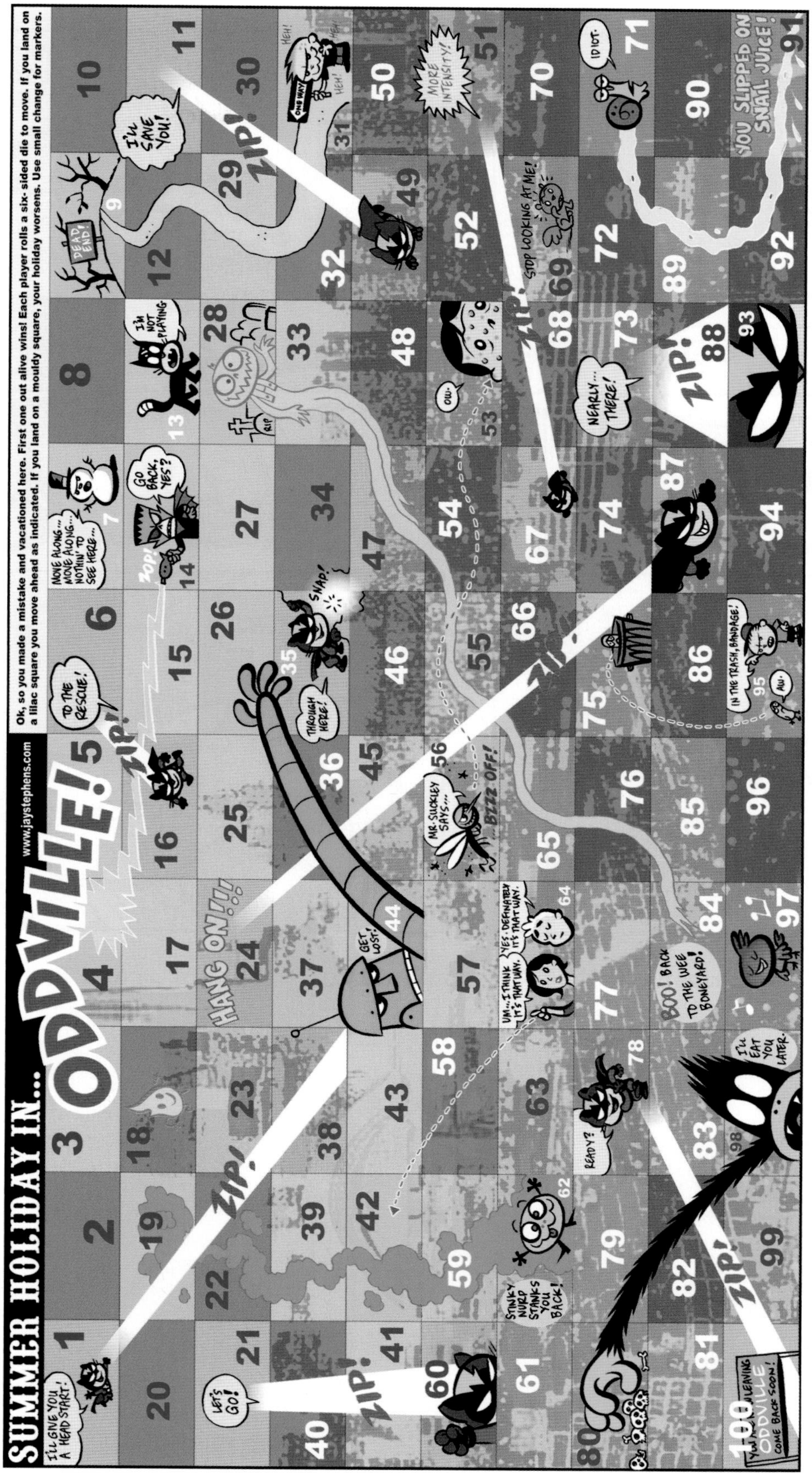
SUMMER HOLIDAY IN...
ODDVILLE!
www.jaystephens.com
Ok, so you made a mistake and vacationed here. First one out alive wins! Each player rolls a six- sided die to move. If you land on a lilac square you move ahead as indicated. If you land on a mouldy square, your holiday worsens. Use small change for markers.
I'LL GIVE YOU A HEAD START.
TO THE RESCUE!
MOVE ALONG... MOVE ALONG... NOTHIN' TO SEE HERE...
I'M NOT PLAYING.
DEAD END!
I'LL SAVE YOU!
ONE WAY
HANG ON!!!
GO BACK, YES?
THROUGH HERE!
SNAP!
GET LOST.
MR. SUCKLEY SAYS...
...BZZZ OFF!
MORE INTENSITY!
STOP LOOKING AT ME!
NEARLY... THERE!
IDIOT.
YOU SLIPPED ON SNAIL JUICE!
IN THE TRASH, BANDAGE!
UM... I THINK IT'S THAT WAY.
YES. DEFINATELY IT'S THAT WAY.
STINKY NURP STANKS YOU BACK!
READY?
BOO! BACK TO THE WEE BONEYARD!
I'LL EAT YOU LATER.
LET'S GO!
ZIP!
YOU'RE NOW LEAVING ODDVILLE COME BACK SOON!

Oddville! Game board from the summer 2004 issue of Brand New Planet

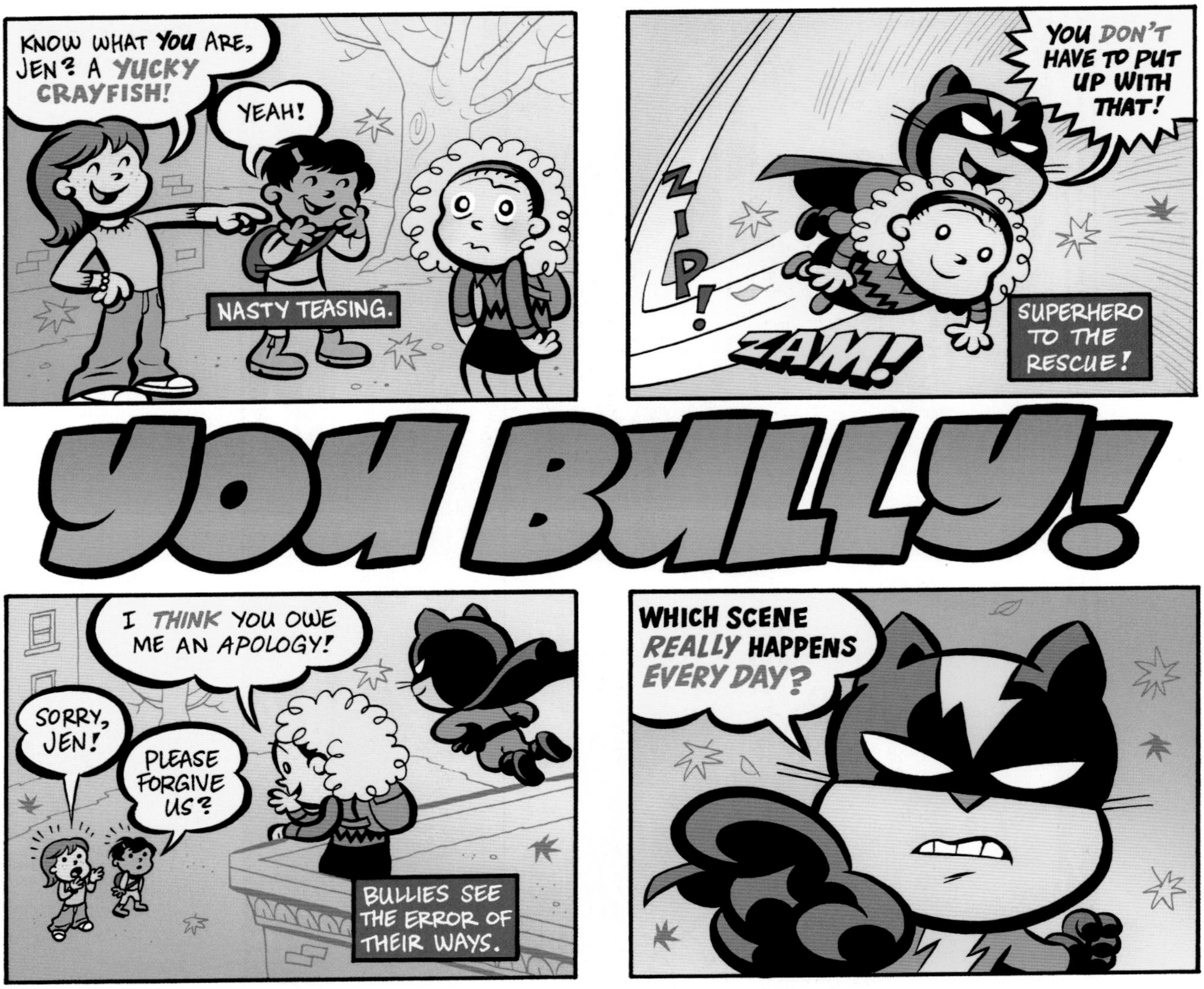
KNOW WHAT YOU ARE, JEN? A YUCKY CRAYFISH!
YEAH!
NASTY TEASING.
YOU DON'T HAVE TO PUT UP WITH THAT!
ZIP!
ZAM!
SUPERHERO TO THE RESCUE!
YOU BULLY!
I THINK YOU OWE ME AN APOLOGY!
SORRY, JEN!
PLEASE FORGIVE US?
BULLIES SEE THE ERROR OF THEIR WAYS.
WHICH SCENE REALLY HAPPENS EVERY DAY?

Cover for the September 25th, 2003 "Anti-Bullying" issue of Brand New Planet

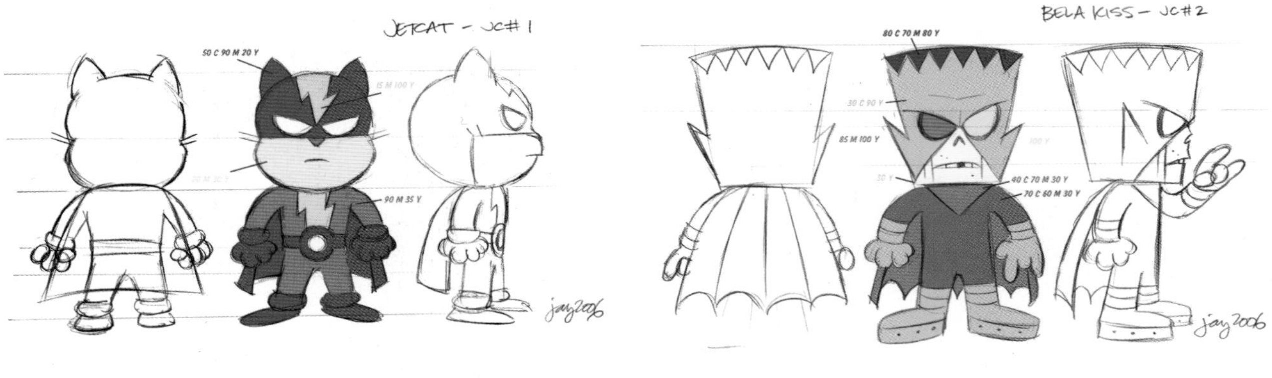
JETCAT - JC#1
BELA KISS - JC#2
jay2006
jay2006

Rough designs for Oddville! action figures

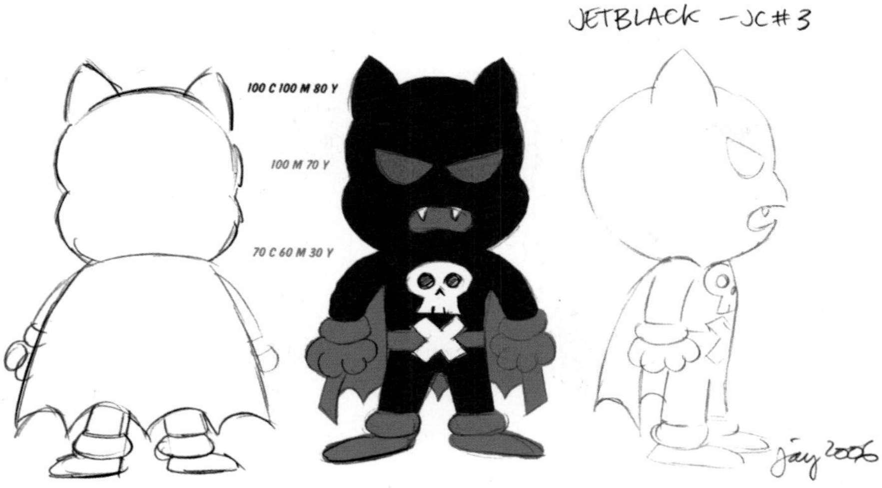
JETBLACK - JC#3
100 C 100 M 80 Y
100 M 70 Y
70 C 60 M 30 Y
jay2006

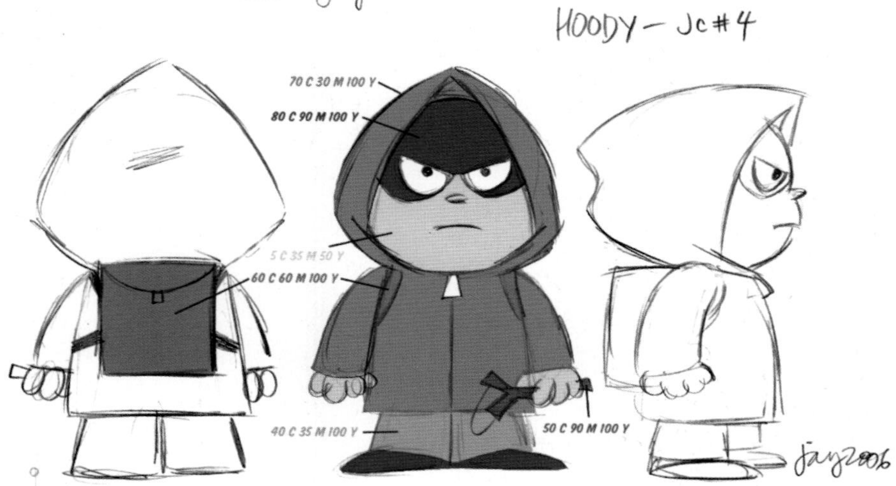
HOODY - JC#4
70 C 30 M 100 Y
80 C 90 M 100 Y
5 C 35 M 50 Y
60 C 60 M 100 Y
40 C 35 M 100 Y
50 C 90 M 100 Y
jay2006

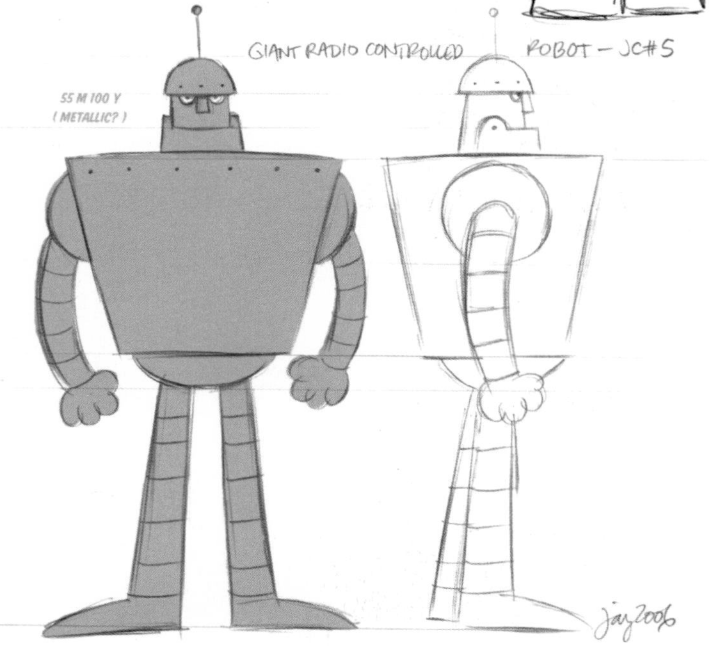
GIANT RADIO CONTROLLED ROBOT - JC#5
55 M 100 Y
(METALLIC?)
jay2006

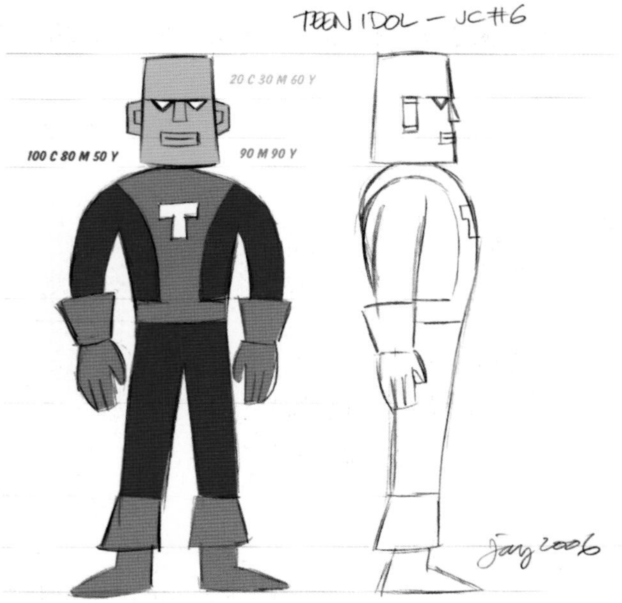
TEEN IDOL - JC#6
20 C 30 M 60 Y
100 C 80 M 50 Y
90 M 90 Y
jay2006

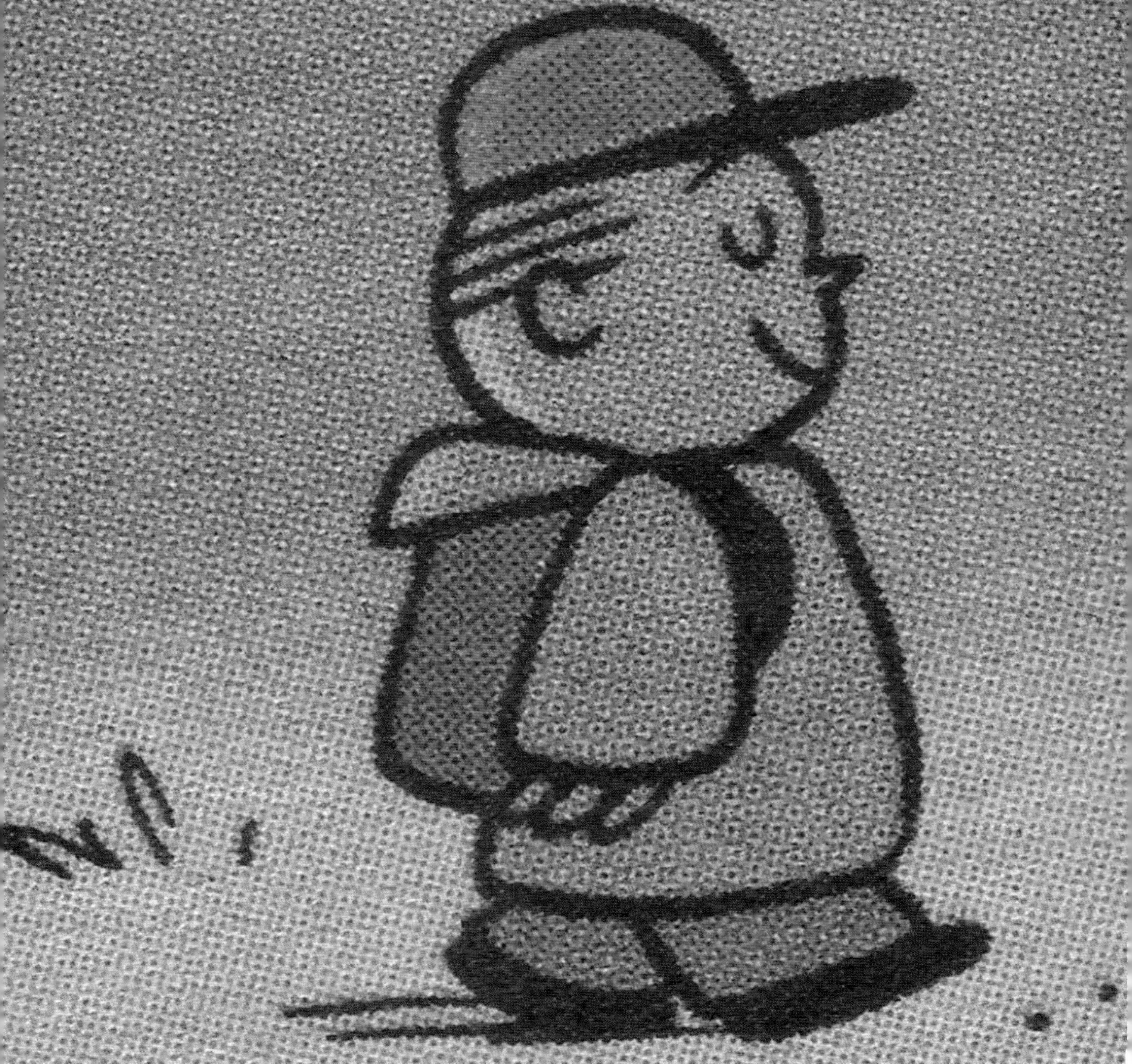